VEGETARIAN IND

This book is a valuable asset—both to a novice and an experienced cook. Besides recipes for dishes, it provides basic information about the kitchen, vernacular names of ingredients, cookery vocabulary, handy hints and a balanced diet.

Variety being the spice of life, the author brings you a wide range of fascinating recipes: soups, salads, chutneys, desserts, rice, jams and marmalades, *parathas*, snacks, syrups and squashes, numerous vegetable dishes. The author also tells you how to make use of odds and ends with a view to avoiding wastage, a must in these hard days. As a bonus, a few Chinese dishes are also included. The style, language and methods employed are so simple and interesting that you are bound to develop a liking for cooking.

Kaushi N. Bhatia *has written many articles on the culinary art in newspapers and journals. She holds a B.A. (Hons.) degree in Psychology and a diploma in Journalism. Married, she lives in Mumbai. She had the privilege of being a judge in a cookery contest in Mumbai. She has also given cookery demonstrations. In writing cookbooks her main aim is to initiate even the most reluctant persons (both sexes) into the great art of cooking. She believes that home-cooked food is the mainstay of life. Other popular books by the same author are* Vegetarian Chinese Cooking *and* Ice Creams & Desserts.

Books on COOKERY

COOKERY

Punjabi Cooking
ISBN 81 207 0179 8, Rs. 60

A Cook's Tour of South India
ISBN 81 207 0947 0, Rs. 60

Non-Veg. Indian Cookery
ISBN 81 207 1408 3, Rs. 60

Indian Cooking Overseas
ISBN 81 207 1613 2, Rs. 65

Chinese Cookery
ISBN 81 207 0938 1, Rs. 90

Party Cuisine
ISBN 81 207 1534 9, Rs. 55

Indian Cookery
ISBN 81 207 0018 x, Rs. 50

Delights of Indian Appetizers
ISBN 81 207 1353 2, Rs. 45

Indian & Mughlai Rice Treats
ISBN 81 207 1070 3, Rs. 55

Cooking the Healthy Way
ISBN 81 207 1354 0, Rs. 45

GOURMET'S CHOICE

(In Colour)

Cakes
ISBN 81 207 1749 x, Rs. 35

Salads
ISBN 81 207 1750 3, Rs. 35

Seafood
ISBN 81 207 1751 1, Rs. 35

Soups
ISBN 81 207 1752 x, Rs. 35

COOKING IS FUN

Potato Delights
ISBN 81 207 1734 1, Rs. 30

Soups
ISBN 81 207 1732 5, Rs. 30

Meat Delights
ISBN 81 207 1741 4, Rs. 30

Chocolate Delights
ISBN 81 207 1736 8, Rs. 30

Chinese Cuisine
ISBN 81 207 1733 3, Rs. 30

Desserts
ISBN 81 207 1739 2, Rs. 30

Pasta Delights
ISBN 81 207 1738 4, Rs. 30

Barbecue
ISBN 81 207 1735 x, Rs. 30

Cakes
ISBN 81 207 1693 0, Rs. 30

Cocktails
ISBN 81 207 1694 9, Rs. 30

Mughlai
ISBN 81 207 1692 2, Rs. 30

Salads
ISBN 81 207 1695 7, Rs. 30

Egg Delights
ISBN 81 207 1786 4, Rs. 30

Vegetable Delights
ISBN 81 207 1730 9, Rs. 30

Breakfast Delights
ISBN 81 207 1789 9, Rs. 30

Seafood
ISBN 81 207 1854 2, Rs. 30

Published by
Sterling Publishers Private Limited

VEGETARIAN INDIAN COOKBOOK

KAUSHI N. BHATIA

A Sterling Paperback

STERLING PAPERBACKS
An imprint of
Sterling Publishers (P) Ltd.
L-10, Green Park Extension, New Delhi-110016
Ph.: 6191784, 6191785, 6191023 Fax: 91-11-6190028
E-mail: sterlin.gpvb@axcess.net.in

Vegetarian Indian Cookbook
© 1998, Kaushi N. Bhatia
ISBN 81 207 1947 6
First Edition 1986
Reprint 1989, 1991, 1992, 1994, 1995
Revised Edition 1998

All rights are reserved. No part of this publication may be reproduced, stored in a retrieval system or transmitted, in any form or by any means, mechanical, photocopying, recording or otherwise, without prior written permission of the publisher.

Published by Sterling Publishers Pvt. Ltd., New Delhi-110016.
Lasertypeset by Vikas Compographics, New Delhi.
Printed at Saurabh Print-O-Pack, Noida
Cover design by Sterling Studio
Colour Transparencies: Sterling Studio

To
Naveen, my husband

INTRODUCTION

Cooking is a subject every housewife should be interested in. After all, the way to a man's heart is through his stomach! Besides, who does not relish good food? Cooking is neither difficult nor boring, if done systematically. Some people have the wrong notion that culinary art cannot be acquired through books. As a matter of fact, many housewives owe their expertise in cooking to good cookery books. A book written in simple language and with detailed instructions is indeed a boon to every housewife and especially to the newly-weds.

This book is a comprehensive, yet concise, guide to cookery focussing on vegetables, with eggs included in a few recipes. It would be relevant to mention that no one can dispute the merits of vegetarian food. In fact, vegetarianism is the in thing these days, as vegetarian food is akin to good health. Handy hints are also included.

This book is intended to be useful on all occasions. It is written in simple language and all the recipes are tried and tested.

It has been my experience that most Indians are so used to talking about cookery in regional languages that it is little wonder to find recipes in English not always clear. Many women do not know English names for various fruits, vegetables, spices, pulses, etc. Further, they do not know the exact meanings of words like saute, steep, bake, blanche, mince, etc. There are others who are confused between two different words like garnish and season, deep and shallow fry, batter and dough, etc. I have, therefore, devoted one chapter to Vernacular Names and another to Cookery Vocabulary. I personally feel that one must study these chapters before proceeding to other chapters.

For some people, cooking is a tedious job. In most cases, aversion to cooking is due to a haphazardly organised kitchen. The basic thing in any job is organisation and system. The kitchen should essentially be a place of comfort and convenience. There should be proper utensils, labelled containers and shelves to store the various items. There should be a specific place for everything. It is not uncommon to find many housewives frantically searching for things in the kitchen. This sort of working will sap half the energy of a person. Keeping this in mind, I have devoted the very first chapter to the 'Kitchen'. Another way of making cooking a pleasure is to inculcate the habit of using the improved cooking gadgets like pressure cooker, oven, mixer-grinder, etc., which are a boon.

My book covers mainly Indian cooking. Specialities like Gujarati Undhia, South Indian Masala Dosa, Sindhi Curry, Punjabi Chhole and many more mouth-watering preparations are all there for you to try out.

I take this opportunity to thank my husband, Shri Naveen L. Bhatia, who not only encouraged me but also helped me in getting this book published.

Kaushi N. Bhatia

CONTENTS

	Introduction	vii
1.	The Kitchen	1
2.	Vernacular Names	7
3.	Cookery Vocabulary	12
4.	Prelude to a Meal (Salads)	14
5.	Soups	24
6.	Parathas	31
7.	Rice Preparations	39
8.	Curries	49
9.	Koftas	55
10.	Vegetable Treats	62
11.	Miscellaneous Vegetables	107
12.	Stuffed Surprises	113
13.	From Odds and Ends (Leftovers)	119
14.	Snacks	131
15.	Chutneys	155
16.	Desserts	159
17.	Jams and Marmalades	166
18.	Squashes and Syrups	170
19.	Handy Hints	175
20.	A Balanced Diet	178

1

THE KITCHEN

Major Items
Storing Arrangements
Cooking Equipment
Crockery and Cutlery
Miscellaneous Items

THE KITCHEN should be a place designed for convenience. It should be so planned that everything has a specific place so that you can easily find whatever you need. Since equipping the kitchen is not an everyday affair, one should use enough forethought while planning it. There are many people who do something in haste and later realise that it is not suited to their requirements. It is, therefore, essential to plan the kitchen set-up as well as the things that go into it carefully.

It is a good idea to invest in stainless steel utensils because they are durable, easy to wash and give a neat appearance. There is a wide selection of beautiful kitchenware available. The factors that should be taken into consideration are one's budget, size of the family, number and frequency of guests, type of cooking and the items suitable for the purpose. A well planned kitchen can be a pleasure to work in, apart from minimising the cooking time.

Major Items

Every housewife must invest in the following items. However, if her budget does not permit, they can be acquired gradually.

1. Cooking range or gas stove with 2, 3 or 4 burners and two gas cylinders placed on trolleys.
2. Pressure cooker (preferably 2)
3. Pressure Pan
4. Refrigerator (preferably frost-free)
5. Mixer-Grinder
6. Electric toaster } or Electric Toaster-Oven-Grill
7. Electric Oven
8. Food processor
9. Microwave
10. Electric Rice cooker
11. Milk cooker (preferably 2)
12. Water filter
13. Exhaust fan
14. Instant water heater
15. Gas lighter

Storing Arrangements

Suitable cupboards with shelves should be provided to store various items. However, items required of and on, like spices, tea, sugar, coffee, etc., should be kept close by. If the storing

The Kitchen

arrangement is haphazard, you will be fagged out at the end of the day. Therefore, this aspect is important. The list of storing items is as under:

1. One round plastic, aluminium or stainless steel box with 7 or 8 small containers to store spices for daily use.
2. Bottles for storing larger quantities of spices.
3. Plastic, aluminium or stainless steel containers for storing sugar, tea and coffee.
4. Bread box.
5. Plastic, aluminium or stainless steel boxes for keeping chapaties and storing sweets and other miscellaneous items.
6. Large aluminium or stainless steel tins for preserving wheat, flours of different types, rice, etc.
7. Medium size containers of plastic, aluminium or stainless steel for storing pulses, papads and other miscellaneous items.
8. Large china jars with airtight lids (preferably screw type) for preserving pickles, murabbas, etc.
9. Empty syrup or liquor bottles for preserving squashes and syrups.
10. Butter dish.
11. Egg rack.
12. Empty syrup or liquor bottles for storing water in the refrigerator.
13. Spare square or oblong containers with fitting covers (plastic, aluminium or stainless steel) for storing various items.
14. Polythene bags for wrapping raw vegetables.
15. Aluminium foil for multi-purpose wrapping.
16. Fruit baskets.
17. Vegetable baskets.
18. Earthen pot with tap attached and lid for storing drinking water.

Cooking Equipment

Utensils should be in various sizes and to save space fit into one another. They should be easily accessible and kept spick and span. Handle them carefully and they will last you a lifetime. The following is the list of items:

1. *Dekchis* or pots in various sizes to fit into one another with fitting lids. They should be heavy bottomed and made of iron, stainless steel, aluminium, copper or brass. However, copper and brass pots should be tinned from time to time. Iron, aluminium, copper and brass pots are good for slow cooking and can stand rough use.
2. *Karahi* or frying pans should also be of various sizes so that they enable space saving by fitting into one another. They should be made of stainless steel, aluminium, copper, brass or iron. Pans made of brass and copper require tinning occasionally. The most important thing to remember while buying pans is that they should have a thick bottom.
3. Stainless steel pots and pans with copper bottom.
4. Non-stick pots and pans and tawa with wooden spatulas.
5. A wooden board with a firm grip for rolling and a rolling pin *(belan)* made of wood. The rolling pin should neither be very thin nor very thick.
6. An iron plate or griddle called *tawa* which should not be very thin. This can be stored under your gas stove or if you have one with a ring, it can be hung from a nail.
7. Racks with slots for holding plates, thalis, cups and saucers, glasses, spoons, etc.
8. Flat spatulas made of stainless steel. Aluminium spatulas are not advisable as they become hot quickly.
9. Perforated spatulas for frying.
10. Ladles of different sizes.
11. A butter spreader.
12. Small and big knives for chopping.
13. A paring knife or a peeler with scallops on one side. This is very useful for peeling potatoes, cucumber, etc. The scalloped side is useful for cutting vegetables for salads attractively.
14. A chopping board for chopping vegetables.
15. A wafer chopper attached to a piece of wood.
16. A bread knife.
17. A long-handled colander for straining rice and other items. A colander without a handle is also quite convenient.

The Kitchen

18. Strainers for tea, juices, soups, etc.
19. A grater, preferably made of stainless steel.
20. A funnel.
21. A lemon squeezer.
22. A coconut grater—a circular piece of iron with teeth fixed to a piece of wood. This can also serve as a chopper.
23. Citrus fruit extractor.
24. Juicer.
25. Salt and pepper sprinklers or a round container divided into 3 or 4 compartments with a tiny spoon inside each. This should be made of plastic, china, or stainless steel.
26. A stainless steel or wooden churner or beater.
27. A stainless steel egg beater.
28. An electric beater.
29. Wire mesh lids to cover hot milk.
30. A big stainless steel sieve.
31. Two sieves, one big for wheat and other grains and a fine one for flour.
32. A pair of tongs—iron or stainless steel.
33. A small brass or iron mortar and pestle.
34. Kulfi moulds.
35. Moulds in different sizes and shapes for ice-creams, jellies, etc.
36. A pudding pan and a cake tin.
37. A pair of pincers.
38. An idli steamer.
39. A non-stick hand toaster.
40. A potato masher.
41. A can opener.
42. Electric sandwich toaster.
43. A pair of small scissors.

Crockery and Cutlery

1. A dinner set of china, plastic or stainless steel.
2. Stainless steel thalis and katoris of various sizes.
3. Insulated casseroles.
4. Serving bowls with serving spoons.
5. Plates and bowls of various sizes, made of china, plastic or stainless steel.
6. Fancy bowls with covers for serving pickles, jams, etc.

7. Glasses for drinking water made either of stainless steel or glass.
8. A teaset of china or stainless steel.
9. Cups and saucers.
10. Thermos flask.
11. A set of glasses for serving drinks.
12. Bottle opener.
13. Mugs for coffee, beer, etc.
14. A dessert set made of glass, plastic or stainless steel.
15. An ice pail and tongs.
16. Soup bowls with spoons either of plastic or china.
17. Trays for serving food and drinks.
18. Tablespoons, teaspoons, dessert spoons, forks and knives made of stainless steel.
19. Serviette sets.
20. Table Mats.
21. Coasters.

Miscellaneous Items
1. Toothpicks.
2. A picnic set (if necessary).
3. An insulated tiffin carrier.
4. Plastic buckets for storing water.
5. A big container for storing water.
6. *Big dekchis* for boiling and/or storing water.
7. A mop, a pail and a swab.
8. Brooms of two types; one with long sticks for washing floors and the other with softer bristles for sweeping.
9. A dustbin with a lid.
10. A kitchen scale.
11. Small swabs for wiping working area in the kitchen and the dining table.
12. A napkin for wiping hands.
13. Small napkins for wiping frying pans, griddle, etc.
14. Medium pieces of sponge.
15. Torch.
16. A few candles.
17. Match box.

2

VERNACULAR NAMES

English Names   *Indian Names*

Vegetables

English Names	Indian Names
Ash gourd	Petha or Bhopla (safed ya lal)
Bathua leaves	Bathua bhajee
Beetroot	Beet or Chukandar
Bitter gourd	Karela
Bottle gourd	Lauki, Ghia, Kaddu, Dudhi
Brinjal or Eggplant	Baigan
Broad bean	Papri
Cabbage	Bund gobhi
Calabash cucumber	Lauki, Ghia, Kaddu, Dudhi
Capsicum	Shimla mirch
Carrot	Gajar
Cauliflower	Phool gobhi
Celery	Silery, Ajwain ke patte
Cluster bean	Gavar phali
Colocasia	Arbi or Kachalu
Coriander leaves	Kothmir, Dhania
Corn	Makai
Cucumber	Kakri, Kheera
Curry leaves	Curry patta
Dill	Suva
Drumsticks	Singi, Sahjan ki phali
Fenugreek leaves	Methi
French bean	Flas bean or Fansi
Garlic	Lahsan
Gherkin	Tindli

Ginger	*Adrak*
Green chillie	*Hari mirch*
Green peas	*Watana, Matar*
Lady's finger	*Bhindi*
Lemon	*Neemboo*
Lettuce leaves	*Salad ke patte*
Lotus root	*Kamal kakri ka beej*
Lotus stem	*Kamal kakri, Bhein*
Mango (green)	*Kacha aam*
Mint	*Pudina*
Mushroom	*Goochi*
Mustard greens	*Rai or Sarson ki bhajee*
Onion	*Kandha or Pyaz*
Potato	*Alu or Batata*
Pumpkin	*Safed ya lal bhopla*
Radish	*Moolee*
Ridge gourd	*Torai*
Snakegourd	*Padval*
Spinach	*Palak*
Spring onion	*Hara pyaz*
Sweet potato	*Shakarkandi*
Tomatoes	*Tamatar*
Turnips	*Shalgam*
White gourd	*Tinda*
Yam	*Sooran, Jimikand*

Dry Fruits

Almond	*Badam*
Apricot (dry)	*Sookha jardalu or Khurmani*
Cashewnut	*Kaju*
Charoli	*Chironji*
Coconut (dry)	*Khopra or sookha narial*
Date (dry)	*Sookha khajoor*
Fig (dry)	*Sookha anjeer*
Peanut	*Mungphali, Singdana*
Pistachio nut	*Pista*
Prune (dry)	*Alubukhara*
Raisin	*Kishmish*
Walnut	*Akhrot*

Vernacular Names 9

Fresh Fruits
Apple	*Sev or Safarchand*
Apricot	*Khurmani or Jardalu*
Banana	*Kela*
Cashew fruit	*Kaju phal*
Cherry	*Cherry*
Coconut	*Narial*
Custard apple	*Sitaphal, Shareefa*
Date	*Khajoor*
Fig	*Anjeer*
Grapes	*Angoor*
Guava	*Amrood, Peru*
Jackfruit	*Phanas, Katahal*
Lemon	*Nimbu*
Mango	*Aam*
Melon	*Kharbooja*
Orange	*Santra or Narangi*
Papaya	*Papaiya, Papeeta*
Peach	*Aroo*
Pear	*Nashpati*
Pineapple	*Ananas*
Plantains	*Kacha kela*
Plum	*Alubukhara*
Pomegranate	*Anar*
Sweet Lime	*Mosumbi*
Watermelon	*Kalingar, Tarbooz*

Spices
Aniseed	*Saunf*
Asafoetida	*Hing*
Basil	*Tulsi*
Bay leaf	*Tej patta*
Caraway seeds	*Shahjeera*
Carbonate of potash	*Papad khar*
Cardamom	*Elaichi*
Celery seeds	*Ajwain*
Chilli powder	*Pisi lal mirch*
Chillies	*Sabut lal mirch*
Cinnamon	*Dalchini*
Cloves	*Lavang, laung*
Coriander seeds	*Sookha dhania*

Cumin seeds	*Jeera*
Dry fenugreek leaves	*Sookhi methi*
Dry garlic	*Sookha lahsan*
Dry ginger	*Sonth*
Fenugreek seeds	*Methi dane*
Mace	*Javitri*
Mango powder	*Amchur*
Mustard seeds	*Rai*
Nutmeg	*Jaiphal*
Pepper	*Pisi kali mirch*
Peppercorns	*Sabut kali mirch*
Pomegranate seeds	*Anardana*
Poppy seeds	*Khuskhus*
Saffron	*Kesar*
Salt	*Namak*
Sesame	*Til*
Soda-bi-carb	*Meetha soda*
Tamarind	*Imli*
Turmeric	*Haldi*

Pulses

Bengal gram	*Chana dal*
Black gram	*Urad dal chhilke ke saath*
Green gram	*Moong dal chhilke ke saath*
Red Lentils	*Masoor dal*
White gram	*Kabuli chana*
Yellow Lentils	*Tuvar dal, Arhar dal*

Cereals

Barley flour	*Jowar ka atta*
Gram flour	*Besan*
Maize flour	*Makai ka atta*
Millet flour	*Bajre ka atta*
Refined or Fine flour	*Maida*
Rice	*Chaval*
Rice flour	*Chaval ka atta*
Sago	*Sabudana*
Semolina	*Sooji*
Vermicelli	*Seviyan*
Wheat	*Gehoon*
Wheat flour	*Gehoon ka atta*

Vernacular Names

Oils
    Coconut oil   *Nariyal ka tel*
    Gingelly oil   *Til ka tel*
    Mustard oil   *Sarson ka tel*
    Peanut oil   *Mungphali ka tel*
    Sesame oil   *Til ka tel*

Miscellaneous
    Betel leaves   *Pan*
    Betelnut   *Supari*
    Cochineal   *Gulabi rang*
    Curd   *Dahi*
    Rind   *Chhilka*
    Sugar candy   *Misri*
    Vinegar   *Sirka*
    Yeast   *Khameer*
    Yoghurt   *Dahi*

3

COOKERY VOCABULARY

In order to follow the various methods used in cooking, it is important to be familiar with the terms used and their exact meaning. Here is a concise list.

Bake—cook by dry heat in an oven, pan or tawa.
Baste—dot with fat or butter.
Batter—ingredients beaten along with some liquid to a paste.
Beat—mix with a spoon or beater rendering the ingredients smooth.
Blend—mix together well.
Blanch—skin after putting in boiling water.
Boil—cook rapidly over high heat.
Broil—roast without fat.
Brush—apply butter or milk, etc, lightly.
Chill—cool over ice or in the refrigerator.
Chop—cut into small pieces.
Combine—mix.
Deep fry—cook in plenty of oil or fat in a pan.
Dice—cut into small cubes.
Dot—place a tiny piece of something, e.g., butter, on top of some other ingredients.
Dough—mixture of flour and liquid stiff enough to be rolled.
Drain—remove extra fat or liquid.
Dust—sprinkle.
Fry—cook in fat.
Fat—ghee, oil or butter.
Fold in—mix slowly and carefully.
Garnish—decorate.

Grate—reduce to short narrow pieces by rubbing through a grater.
Hors d'oeuvre—an appetizer served before a meal.
Knead—work dough with hand to make it smooth.
Mash—crush to pulp.
Mince—cut into very fine pieces.
Pare—peel or shave off the outer skin.
Parboil—half boil.
Peel—remove skin.
Poach—cook eggs without shells in boiling water (used in reference to eggs).
Puree—food materials reduced to a pulp and passed through a sieve.
Reheat—heat again.
Roast—same as bake.
Rub in—add fat to flour and combine the two.
Saute—fry lightly in a little fat over a medium fire.
Scald—cook or heat a liquid short of boiling.
Scrape—remove skin
Season—add spices.
Shallow fry—fry with a small quantity of fat, usually on a griddle or tawa.
Shred—cut into narrow, long strips.
Simmer—cook below the boiling point gently over low heat with an occasional bubble.
Sprig—bunch.
Steam cook—cook with steam as in a pressure cooker.
Steep—soak in liquid.
Stew—same as simmer.

4

PRELUDE TO A MEAL (SALADS)

Brinjal Salad

Cabbage Salad

Cucumber Boats

Chilled Yoghurt Salad

Golden Salad

Lettuce Salad

Onion Curls

Rose-shaped Tomato Salad

Shahi Salad

Sprouted Moong Salad

Tomato Cups

Stuffed Cabbage Salad

Salad Dressings

Prelude to a Meal

SALADS prepared from raw fruits and vegetables have high nutritive value. With effort and ingenuity, the simplest of salads can be made to look attractive. Eye-appealing garnishes stimulate appetite; so it is worthwhile for every housewife to learn the art of decorating salads. A variety of these mini-size nibblers and appetite-whetters are perfect party pick-ups.

BRINJAL SALAD

Ingredients

1 large brinjal
1 medium-sized onion (minced)
1 tbsp lemon juice
1 large tomato (diced)
1/4 cup coconut milk
2 green chillies (minced)
1 tbsp finely chopped coriander leaves
Salt to taste

Method
Roast the brinjal over an open flame until its peel turns black and the brinjal is cooked. Peel and mash to a pulp. Add the rest of the ingredients and blend thoroughly. Garnish with coriander leaves and tomato.

CABBAGE SALAD

Ingredients

Lettuce leaves
2 green chillies (cut into strips)
1 cup shredded cabbage
2 fresh red chillies (cut into strips)

1/2 cup apple pieces with skin   3 tbsps orange juice
Salt to taste

Method
Make a bed of lettuce leaves on a plate. Moisten the apple pieces with 1 tbsp orange juice. This prevents discolouration. Blend the apple and cabbage and place on lettuce leaves. Add the remaining orange juice. Sprinkle salt over it. Garnish with green and red chilli strips.

CUCUMBER BOATS

Ingredients

Lettuce leaves
1/2 cup shredded cabbage
1/4 cup apple pieces
1 large carrot (grated)
8 triangular pieces of paper (any colour)
Salt to taste

4 cucumbers
1/4 cup finely chopped celery (optional)
1 tbsp lemon juice
2 tbsps nuts (halved)
8 toothpicks

Method
Wash and cut the cucumbers in halves lengthwise. Make a hollow in the centre of each half and arrange on lettuce leaves on a plate. Combine the cabbage, celery, apple and cucumber (scooped out). Moisten with lemon juice or some dressing and fill the cucumber boats.

For a sail, glue a triangular piece of paper onto each toothpick and put one such toothpick into each cucumber piece. Garnish with grated carrots and nuts.

Prelude to a Meal

CHILLED YOGHURT SALAD

Ingredients

1 medium-sized carrot cut into cubes
1/4 cup shelled peas
1/2 cup fresh yoghurt (curd)
1 tsp chilli powder
1 tsp pepper powder
1/2 tsp garam masala
Salt to taste

1 medium-sized potato cut into cubes
1/4 cup shredded French beans
1 tbsp each of mint and coriander leaves (finely chopped)
1/2 tsp roasted cumin powder

Method
Boil all the vegetables. Beat the yoghurt (curd) and add the vegetables, along with the rest of the ingredients. Garnish with mint and coriander leaves. Chill and serve.

GOLDEN SALAD

Ingredients

Lettuce leaves
1/2 cup coconut milk
2 tbsps cashewnuts (coarsely pounded)

3 large carrots (grated)
2 tbsps raisins

Method
Moisten the carrots with coconut milk. Press into muffin cups. At the time of serving, turn these moulds out onto the lettuce leaves in the salad plate and garnish with cashewnuts and raisins.

LETTUCE SALAD

Ingredients

A few lettuce leaves
1 tbsp honey
1 tbsp sesame oil
1 hard-boiled egg (quartered)

Method
Wash the lettuce leaves and shake off the water. Wipe the leaves and cut them into small strips. Place them in a broad bowl. Mix sesame oil and honey and add to the lettuce leaves. Garnish with eggs.

ONION CURLS

Ingredients

2 medium-sized onions
(cut into thin curls)
1 tbsp coriander leaves
(finely chopped)
1 tbsp lemon juice
1 tbsp chilli powder
Salt to taste

Method
Wash the onion curls, sprinkle salt and set aside for 5 minutes. Wash and add the lemon juice, salt and chilli powder. Garnish with coriander leaves.

Prelude to a Meal

ROSE-SHAPED TOMATO SALAD

Ingredients

Lettuce leaves
2 medium-sized onions
   (cut into rings)
Salt to taste
1 cup finely chopped celery
   (optional)
1 tbsp lemon juice
1 large red tomato

Method
Make a bed of lettuce leaves on a plate. Cut a large tomato into 6 to 8 petal-like sections, taking care not to cut through the bottom. Open them a little and arrange like a rose. Place it in the centre of the plate. Fill the rest of the plate with celery and onion rings moistened with lemon juice to which a little salt has been added.

SHAHI SALAD

Ingredients

Lettuce leaves
2 medium-size cucumbers
   (cut into slices)
1/2 cup shelled peas (boiled)
1/4 cup shredded cabbage
1 tbsp lemon juice
1"-piece ginger
2 tbsps fresh coriander leaves
2 tbsps cashewnuts (halved)
2 medium-size onions
   (cut into rings)
2 medium-size potatoes
   (boiled and cut into slices)
1/4 cup shredded French
   beans (boiled)
2 green chillies
2 beetroots (boiled and grated)
2 tbsps raisins

Method
Make a bed of lettuce leaves on a plate. Add salt to the onion rings and keep aside for 5 minutes. Wash and arrange the onion and cucumber rings alternately all round the edge of the plate. Form the second circle with grated beetroots. Grind ginger, chillies and coriander leaves into a paste. In the centre of the plate, arrange the rest of the vegetables, mixed with the ground paste. Drizzle with lemon juice and garnish with cashewnuts and raisins.

SPROUTED MOONG SALAD

Ingredients

Lettuce leaves	1 cup sprouted moong
1"-piece ginger	1/2 cup fresh yoghurt (curd)
1 onion	1 tomato (cut into rings)
1 tbsp each finely chopped mint and coriander leaves	2 green chillies beginning to turn red (sliced)
1 tsp chilli powder	1 tsp pepper powder
1/2 tsp garam masala	1/2 tsp roasted cumin powder
Salt to taste	

Method
Make a bed of lettuce leaves on a plate. Grind ginger and onion to a paste. Beat the yoghurt, add the sprouted moong and ground paste together with the rest of the seasoning. Blend well. Garnish with tomato rings, mint and coriander leaves and sliced chillies. Chill and serve.

Prelude to a Meal

TOMATO CUPS

Ingredients

Lettuce leaves
1/2 cup shredded cabbage
1/4 cup apple pieces
1 large carrot (grated)
Salt to taste

4 large red tomatoes
1/2 cup finely chopped celery or mint leaves
1 tbsp lemon juice
2 tbsp peanuts (halved)

Method
Slice the tops of tomatoes and scoop out the pulp. Combine the tomato pulp, cabbage, celery, apple and add lemon juice and salt to taste. Fill the tomato cups with this mixture. Arrange the tomatoes on lettuce leaves in a salad plate and garnish with carrot and peanuts.

STUFFED CABBAGE SALAD

Ingredients

Lettuce leaves
1/2 cup shelled peas
1 medium-sized potato
1 medium-sized tomato
1 medium-sized onion
Mayonnaise sauce

1 medium-sized fresh cabbage
1/4 cup shredded French beans
1 medium-sized carrot
1 medium-sized cucumber
Salt and pepper to taste

Method
Cut potato and carrot into cubes. Cut tomato, onion and cucumber into rings. Cut the stalk of the cabbage carefully and

open the leaves, making sure that they do not come off from the base. The core should also be removed with a knife very carefully. Add salt and pepper to the peas, French beans, cubed potato and carrot. Fill up the cabbage with half the quantity of the mixture of vegetables, close the leaves and secure with a toothpick.

Steam the cabbage along with the remaining half of the vegetable mixture.

Wash the lettuce leaves and form a bed on a salad plate. Place the steamed cabbage in the centre. Arrange the remaining vegetables together with tomato, cucumber and onion rings around it, adding a little mayonnaise.

SALAD DRESSINGS

Most of the vegetable salads require garnishing. Cut thin slices of celery leaves or lettuce leaves and spread over the salad just before serving. Add red radishes, celery curls, carrot curls, cauliflorets, strips of green or red pepper and red tomato or sliced cucumber with a fancy edge.

Pieces of pineapple look very good, especially with cabbage salads; red apples or slices of orange give an attractive colour and flavour. For sweet garnishes, dry fruits like dates and figs are advisable as they too add colour, flavour and appeal to salads, apart from making them tastier.

Beetroot Garnish
Grate 2 beetroots, add 1 tbsp each of lemon juice and honey or 1 tbsp each of orange juice and honey. Store in a glass jar and use sparingly as a colour garnish.

Cabbage Relish
Mix 1 cup shredded cabbage, 1-1/4 cups orange juice and 2 tbsps honey. Place in a jar and cork tightly. This can be stored for a week.

Onion Relish
Mix 2 sliced onions, juice of 1 lemon, 1 tbsp honey and place in a glass jar. This can be stored indefinitely.

In this preparation, the onions lose their sharpness. It is good for health.

Coconut-honey Dressing
Mix 1 grated coconut, 6 tbsps honey and use as a topping for carrot salad. This is also good for fruit salads or fruit cup desserts.

Honey-sesame Dressing
Form an emulsion of equal quantities of sesame oil and honey. This forms a light dressing for lettuce.

5

SOUPS

Almond Soup

Cauliflower Soup

Cucumber Soup

Mulligatawny Soup

Peas Soup

Potato Soup

Spinach Cream Soup

South Indian Soup (Rasam)

Tomato Cream Soup

Mixed Vegetable Soup

Soups

Soup, the first course of a meal, should be nourishing, tasty and have an eye-appeal to enhance the appetite by holding out a promise of delicious things to follow.

ALMOND SOUP

Ingredients

2 cups blanched almonds
2 tbsps cream
1/4 tsp nutmeg powder
Salt and pepper to taste
1 cup milk
3 cups vegetable stock
A dash of saffron

Method

Make a paste of $1\frac{1}{2}$ cups almonds. Add the milk, saffron and nutmeg powder and simmer for 10 minutes. Add the stock, salt and pepper and simmer for 7 minutes.

Serve hot, garnished with whipped cream and the remaining almonds, finely sliced.

CAULIFLOWER SOUP

Ingredients

1 medium-sized cauliflower (chopped)
1 cup milk
1 sprig parsley or coriander leaves (finely chopped)
2 small onions (minced)
3 cups vegetable stock
2 tbsps butter
2 egg yolks (well beaten)
Salt and pepper to taste

Method
Heat the butter and saute onions. Add the cauliflower, mutton stock, salt and pepper and cook until the cauliflower turns tender. Mash and strain. Add milk and egg yolks. Cook 3 minutes longer.

The vegetarian cauliflower soup can be prepared by using water instead of stock and 1 tsp cornflour mixed with 1/4 cup water in place of egg yolks.

Serve hot garnished with parsley, or coriander leaves.

CUCUMBER SOUP

Ingredients

4 medium cucumbers (diced)	1 medium-sized onion
2 medium-sized tomatoes	4 cups water
2 tbsps butter	50 gms grated cheese
1 tsp cornflour	Salt and pepper to taste

Method
Heat the butter and saute the onions. Add the cucumbers, tomatoes, water, salt and pepper and cook till the vegetables turn tender. Mash and strain. Mix the cornflour with 1/4 cup cold water, add to the soup and cook for 3 minutes, stirring continuously.

Serve hot garnished with grated cheese.

MULLIGATAWNY SOUP

Ingredients

1 cup masoor dal
2 medium-sized carrots (diced)
2 medium-sized tomatoes (diced)
4 cups water
Salt to taste

2 medium-sized onions (minced)
2 tbsps butter
8 curry leaves
1/2 cup coconut milk
A slice of lemon

Roast and grind to a paste
1"-piece ginger
6 peppercorns
1 tsp coriander seeds

1/2"-piece turmeric
1 Kashmiri chilli

Method
Heat the butter and saute the onions. Add the dal, carrots, tomatoes, ground paste, curry leaves, salt and water and cook. When everything turns soft, mash to a pulp and strain. Add the coconut milk and cook 5 minutes longer.

Serve hot garnished with a slice of lemon.

PEAS SOUP

Ingredients

1 cup shelled green peas
1/2 cup milk
Salt and pepper to taste

4 cups water
Croutons (small pieces of crisp fried toast)

Method
Cook the green peas in 4 cups water until tender. Mash and strain. Add the milk, season and simmer for 3 minutes.
Serve hot garnished with croutons.

POTATO SOUP

Ingredients

5 medium-sized potatoes (diced)	1 medium-sized onion (minced)
4 cups milk	50 gms grated cheese
1 tbsp butter	Salt and pepper to taste

Method
Heat the butter and saute onion. Add the potatoes, water, salt, pepper and cook until potatoes are tender. Mash and strain. Add the milk and cook for 5 minutes.
Serve piping hot garnished with grated cheese.

SPINACH CREAM SOUP

Ingredients

3 medium-sized bunches spinach	1 medium-sized onion (minced)
3 cups water	2 medium-sized tomatoes (diced)
1 tsp cornflour	2 tbsps butter
1/2 cup cream	Salt and pepper to taste

Soups

Method
Saute the onion in 1 tbsp butter, add the spinach (finely chopped), tomatoes, water, salt and pepper. Cook until the spinach is tender. Mash and strain. Mix the cornflour with the remaining butter (melted) and add to the strained spinach. Reheat and cook 3 minutes longer, stirring continuously.
　　Serve piping hot topped with cream.

SOUTH INDIAN SOUP (RASAM)

Ingredients

1/2 cup tuvar dal
2 medium-sized tomatoes
　　(blanched and chopped)
10 curry leaves
5 cups water

1/2 cup tamarind juice
　　(medium consistency)
2 tbsps finely chopped
　　coriander leaves
Salt to taste

Roast and grind to a paste
1/2"-piece ginger
2 Kashmiri chillies
1 tsp cuminseeds
1 bay leaf

1/2"-piece turmeric
4 peppercorns
1 tsp coriander seeds

Method
Boil the dal in a little water, mash, strain and set aside. To the tamarind juice, add the salt, ground paste, curry leaves, tomatoes and water and boil. Simmer for 10 minutes. Add the dal and coriander leaves and simmer 5 minutes more.
　　Serve piping hot.

TOMATO CREAM SOUP

Ingredients

4 large tomatoes (diced)
2"-piece ginger (crushed)
1/2 cup cream
1 tbsp butter
Croutons
5 cups water
3/4 cup finely chopped coriander leaves
Salt and pepper to taste

Methods
Heat the butter, add the tomatoes and saute. Mash with a fork, add the ginger, coriander leaves, salt, pepper and water and boil. Simmer for 10 minutes. Strain. Reheat and add the cream.
 Garnish with croutons and serve hot.

MIXED VEGETABLE SOUP

Ingredients

1/2 cup moong dal (yellow)
1 medium-sized potato (diced)
1 medium-sized onion (minced)
5 cups water
1 tbsp butter
Croutons
2 medium-sized carrots (diced)
2 medium-sized tomatoes (diced)
1/4 cup shredded French beans
1 tbsp cornflour
Salt and pepper to taste

Methods
Wash all the vegetables and dal. Add water, salt and pepper and cook until tender. Mash and strain. Reheat the soup. Mix the cornflour with 1/4 cup water and add to the strained soup, stirring continuously. Simmer for 2 minutes.
 Serve hot garnished with croutons and butter.

6

PARATHAS

Potato Parathas

Cauliflower Parathas

Potato-Peas Parathas

Cabbage Parathas

Fenugreek Leaves Parathas

Radish Parathas

Whole Moong Parathas

Yellow Moong Dal Parathas

Sugar Parathas

PARATHAS can be served along with any meal, but they are usually preferred at breakfast time. They should be served with fresh curd or pickles.

POTATO PARATHAS

Ingredients

3 medium-sized potatoes (boiled and mashed)
1/2"-piece ginger
1 tbsp each of finely chopped mint and coriander leaves
1/2 tsp cumin seeds
Salt to taste
Ghee, oil or butter

2 cups wholewheat flour
2 green chillies
2 cloves garlic (optional)
1/2 tsp chilli powder
1/2 tsp mango powder
1/2 tsp turmeric powder
1/2 tsp garam masala

Method
Mince the ginger, garlic and chillies. Add all the ingredients (except wheat flour) to the boiled potatoes, blend well and keep aside.

Add a pinch of salt to the wheat flour and prepare a soft dough with water. Form small balls from the dough and roll out a little. Put a tablespoon of the potato mixture in the middle, cover and form into a ball again. Place on a wooden board and roll out as thin as possible, taking care that the filling does not come out. Bake on a hot griddle or tawa. Put a little ghee around the edges and fry until both sides turn golden brown.

Serve hot.

CAULIFLOWER PARATHAS

Ingredients

1 cup grated cauliflower   2 cups wholewheat flour
Rest of the ingredients are the same as for potato parathas.

Method
Add all the ingredients (except wheat flour) to the grated cauliflower, mix well and set aside. Remember, however, to squeeze the excess water before use.

Add a pinch of salt to the wheat flour and prepare a stiff dough with water. Take two small balls of the dough and roll out into two thin discs or chapaties on a wooden board. On one disc spread the cauliflower mixture evenly, apply a little water at the edges, cover with the other disc and press the edges. Bake on a hot griddle. Put a little ghee around the edges and turn over the paratha. Fry until both sides turn golden brown.
Serve hot.

POTATO-PEAS PARATHAS

Ingredients

2 medium-sized potatoes   1/2 cup shelled peas
   (boiled and mashed)   (boiled and mashed)
2 cups wholewheat flour
Rest of the ingredients are the same as for potato parathas.

Method
To the potatoes and peas add the rest of the ingredients except wheat flour, and blend thoroughly. Set aside.

Add a pinch of salt to the wheat flour and prepare a soft dough with water. Form small balls with the dough and roll out a little. Put a tablespoon of the mixture of peas and potatoes, cover and form into a ball again. Place on a wooden board and roll out as thin as possible. Bake on a hot griddle. Put a little ghee around the edges and turn over the paratha; fry until both sides turn golden brown.

Serve hot.

CABBAGE PARATHAS

Ingredients

1 cup grated cabbage   2 cups whole wheat flour
Rest of the ingredients are the same as for potato parathas.

Method
Add all the ingredients except the wholewheat flour to the grated cabbage, blend well and set aside. In this case also remember to squeeze out the excess water before use.

Add a pinch of salt to the wheat flour and prepare a stiff dough with water. Take two small balls of the dough and roll out into two thin chapaties on a wooden board. Take one disc, spread the cabbage mixture evenly on it, apply a little water at the edges, cover with the other disc and press the edges. Bake on a hot griddle. Put a little ghee around and turn over the paratha; fry until both sides turn golden brown.

Serve hot.

FENUGREEK LEAVES PARATHAS

Ingredients

1 medium sprig fenugreek leaves (finely chopped)
Ghee, oil or butter
2 cups wholewheat flour
1 tsp chilli powder
Salt to taste

Method
Add fenugreek leaves, salt, chilli powder, a little oil and water to the wheat flour and prepare a stiff dough. Form small balls from the dough and roll out as thin as possible on a wooden board. Place on a hot griddle and bake one at a time. Put a little ghee around the edges and turn over the paratha; fry until both sides turn golden brown.
   Serve hot.

RADISH PARATHAS

Ingredients

2 large radishes (grated)   2 cups wholewheat flour
Rest of the ingredients are the same as for potato parathas.

Method
Add all the ingredients except the whole wheat flour to the grated radish, blend well and set aside. Remember, however, to squeeze out the water thoroughly before use.

Add a pinch of salt to the wheat flour and prepare a soft dough by adding water. Form small balls from the dough and roll out a little. Put a tablespoon of the radish mixture in the middle, cover and form into a ball again. Place on a wooden board and roll out as thin as possible, taking care that the filling does not come out. Bake on a hot griddle. Put a little ghee around the edges and turn over the paratha; fry until both sides turn golden brown.

Serve immediately.

WHOLE MOONG PARATHAS

Ingredients

1 cup whole moong
2 tsps coriander powder
1/2 tsp mango powder
1/2 tsp turmeric powder
Ghee, oil or butter for frying

2 cups whole wheat flour
1 tsp chilli powder
1/2 tsp garam masala
Salt to taste

Method
Add salt and water to the whole moong and boil until soft. Strain, season, blend well and set aside.

Add a pinch of salt to the wheat flour and prepare a soft dough with water. Form into small balls. Take one ball, roll out a little. Put a tablespoon of the moong mixture in the middle, cover and form into a ball again. Place on a wooden board and roll out as thin as possible. Bake on a hot griddle. Put a little ghee around the edges and fry until both sides turn golden brown.

Serve hot.

YELLOW MOONG DAL PARATHAS

Ingredients

1 cup moong dal without skin	2 cups whole wheat flour
1 tsp chilli powder	1/2 tsp mango powder
1/2 tsp turmeric powder	1/2 tsp garam masala
Ghee, oil or butter for frying	Salt to taste

Method
Add salt and water to the moong dal and boil. Strain till no water is left. Season, blend well and set aside.

Add a pinch of salt to the wheat flour and prepare a soft dough with water. Form small balls from the dough and roll out a little. Put a tablespoon of the moong dal mixture in the middle, cover and form into a ball again. Place on a rolling board and roll out as thin as possible. Bake on a hot griddle. Put a little ghee around the edges and turn over the paratha; fry until both sides turn golden brown.

Serve hot.

SUGAR PARATHAS

Ingredients

4 tbsp sugar	2 cups wholewheat flour
Salt to taste	Ghee, oil or butter for frying

Method
Add a pinch of salt to the wheat flour and prepare a stiff dough with water. Take two small balls of the dough and roll out into

two thin discs on a rolling board. Take one disc, spread 1 tbsp sugar evenly on it, apply a little water at the edges, place the second disc on it and press the edges. Bake on a hot griddle. Put a little ghee around the edges and turn over the paratha; fry until both sides turn golden brown.

Serve hot.

Cucumber Boats (Salad)

South Indian Soup (Rasam)

Potato Parathas

Chinese Fried Rice

7

RICE PREPARATIONS

Chinese Fried Rice

Egg Fried Rice

Mughlai Biryani

Green Rice

Fried Khichdi with Vegetables

Amritsari Pulao

Shahi Pulao

Onion Pulao

Peas Pulao

Carrot Pulao

Bengal Gram Rice with Dates

Egg Curry

CHINESE FRIED RICE

Ingredients

1 cup long-grained rice
1/4 cup green peas, shelled and boiled
Salad oil or peanut oil
Salt and soya sauce to taste
10 spring onions (peel and slice onions and green tops)
1/4 cup cabbage, shredded and parboiled
A pinch of ajinomoto

Method

Prepare plain boiled rice in the usual way, but very slightly undercooked. Heat 4 tbsps oil, add the onions and fry on a high flame for 2 minutes, making sure that the onions do not change colour. Add the cabbage, salt and ajinomoto and stir. Add the rice, green peas, onion tops and soya sauce and stir carefully for 3 minutes till all the ingredients are well mixed and the rice has a light brown colour.
Serve hot with chillies in vinegar and chilli sauce.

EGG FRIED RICE

Ingredients

1 cup long-grained rice (boiled)
2 eggs (well beaten)
3 tbsps oil
8 spring onions (peel and slice onions and green tops)
A pinch of ajinomoto
Salt and soya sauce to taste

Rice Preparations

Method
Add salt to the beaten eggs and pour a thin layer on a greased griddle. Fry like an omelette. Cut the omelette into little squares and set aside.

Heat 3 tbsps oil and add the spring onions. Fry for 2 minutes on a high flame, making sure the onions do not change colour. Add salt, ajinomoto and onion tops and stir. Add the rice, omelette squares and soya sauce and stir fry the rice for 3 minutes till it is light brown in colour.

Serve hot with chillies in vinegar and chilli sauce.

MUGHLAI BIRYANI

Ingredients

1 cup long-grained rice
1/2"-piece ginger
1/2 cup sour curd
1/4 cup French beans
    (shredded and boiled)
2 tsps coriander powder
1/2 tsp chilli powder
3 tbsps raisins
Ghee

1 sprig coriander (chopped)
2 green chillies (minced)
1/2 cup shelled peas
1/4 cup carrots (diced)
2 medium-sized onions (sliced)
1/2 tsp turmeric powder
1/2 tsp garam masala
A little saffron
Salt to taste

Method
Prepare plain boiled rice in the usual way. Set aside.

Grind the coriander, ginger and green chillies. Add the curd and salt, blend well and set aside. This is the green chutney.

Heat 4 tbsps ghee, add the garam masala and onion and fry. Add the boiled vegetables and seasoning and fry for 5 minutes. Set aside.

Divide the rice into 3 portions and the vegetables into 2 portions. Tint one portion of the rice green by mixing it with chutney. Tint the second portion yellow by adding saffron. Keep the third portion white. Take a large serving dish and place a layer of white rice. Spread a layer of the vegetable mixture over it. Cover the vegetables with green rice. Then cover the green rice with vegetables and finally spread a layer of saffron rice.

Serve hot garnished with raisins.

GREEN RICE

Ingredients

1 cup long-grained rice
1/2"-piece cinnamon
2 cloves
2 cups water

1/2 cup shelled peas
1 cardamom
2 tbsps ghee
Salt to taste

Grind to a paste
1 large sprig coriander
1/2"-piece ginger
3 green chillies

1 medium-sized onion (optional)

Method
Wash and soak the rice in water for 20 minutes.

Heat the ghee, add the cloves, cardamom, cinnamon, green peas and 2 cups water and cook on a low fire until the green peas are half done. Add the rice, ground paste and salt. Continue cooking on a low fire until done. The green colour will be prominent.

Serve hot with a yoghurt curry.

FRIED KHICHDI WITH VEGETABLES

Ingredients

1 cup long-grained rice
1/4 cup moong dal without skin
1/4 cup diced carrots
1/4 cup shelled green peas
   boiled with salt
Salt to taste
1/4 cup moong dal with skin
1/2 cup melted ghee
1/4 cup shredded French beans
   boiled with salt
3 cups water

Method
Wash and soak the rice and the two dals together in water for half an hour.
   Heat the ghee, drain and add the rice and dals. Fry for five minutes, stirring continuously. Add water, vegetables and salt. Cover and cook until almost done. Place on a hot griddle and cook on a low fire until done.
   Serve hot with curd.

AMRITSARI PULAO

Ingredients

1 cup long-grained rice
2 medium-sized onions (sliced)
1 tsp coriander powder
1 tsp mango powder
1/2 tsp turmeric powder
1/2 tsp chilli powder
Ghee
3 wadis (made with urad dal, peppercorns, coriander seeds etc., available readymade in Sindhi and Punjabi shops)
2 cups water
Salt to taste

Method
Break the wadis into medium sized pieces, fry a little and parboil them. Drain and set aside.

Heat the ghee and fry the onions. Add the wadis, water, salt and other seasoning. When the water comes to a rolling boil, stir in the rice and cook on a low fire until done.

Serve steaming hot with a curry or vegetables.

SHAHI PULAO

Ingredients

- 1 cup long-grained rice
- 2 tomatoes (blanched and chopped)
- 1/2 cup shelled green peas
- 2 cardamoms
- 4 cloves
- 10 curry leaves
- 1 tbsp coriander leaves
- 1/2 tsp chilli powder
- 1/2 tsp garam masala
- 2 tbsps cashewnuts (broken into pieces)
- Salt to taste
- 3 medium-sized onions (sliced)
- 1/4 cup shredded French beans
- 1/4 cup diced carrots
- 1/2 cup cauliflower (broken into florets)
- 2 green chillies (minced)
- 1 tbsp mint leaves
- 1 tsp coriander powder
- 1/2 tsp pepper powder
- 1/2 tsp mango powder
- 2 tbsps raisins
- Ghee

Method
Prepare the plain boiled rice in the usual manner and set aside. Finely chop the mint and coriander leaves.

Heat the ghee and saute onions. Add the cardamoms, cloves, green chillies, cashewnuts and curry leaves and fry. Add the tomatoes and green peas and cook for 2 minutes. Add the rest of the vegetables and fry, stirring continuously till they are nearly done. Add the salt, seasoning, mint leaves and coriander leaves. Blend well. Add the cooked rice, and place the covered vessel on a hot tawa on a low fire. Cook 2 minutes longer. Garnish with raisins.

Serve hot with Raita.

ONION PULAO

Ingredients

1 cup long-grained rice
2 cups water
2 cloves
3 tsps coriander powder
1/2 tsp mango powder
1/2 tsp garam masala
Salt to taste

4 medium-sized onions (sliced)
6 tbsps ghee
1 cardamom
1/2 tsp turmeric powder
1 tsp chilli powder
2 tbsps fried cashewnuts

Method
Wash and soak the rice in water for 20 minutes.

Heat the ghee, add the cloves, cardamom and onions and fry. Toss in the seasoning and rice and fry for 5 minutes. Add water and salt. Cook on a low fire until done.

Serve hot garnished with cashew nuts.

PEAS PULAO

Ingredients

1 cup long-grained rice
1 medium-sized onion (minced)

1 cup shelled green peas
2 cloves

1 cardamom
1/2 tsp chilli powder
1/2 tsp garam masala
Ghee

2 cups water
1/2 tsp mango powder
3 tbsps grated coconut
Salt to taste

Method
Heat the ghee, add the cloves, cardamom and onions and fry. Toss in the green peas and seasoning and fry for 5 minutes. Add water and salt, and cook on a low fire. When the peas are half-cooked, add the rice and continue to cook on a low fire until done.
   Serve hot garnished with grated coconut.

CARROT PULAO

Ingredients

1 cup rice
4 large carrots (grated and water squeezed out)
1 cardamom
3 tsps coriander powder
1 tsp mango powder
1/2 tsp roasted cumin powder

2 cups water
4 spring onions (sliced)
2 cloves
6 tbsps ghee
1 tsp chilli powder
1/2 tsp garam masala
Salt to taste

Method
Prepare plain boiled rice in the usual manner and set aside.
   Heat the ghee, add the cloves, cardamom and onions and fry. Add the seasoning, carrots and salt and fry for 2 minutes, so that the colour of carrots is visible. Stir in the rice and blend well.
   Serve hot.

Rice Preparations

BENGAL GRAM RICE WITH DATES

Ingredients

1 cup long-grained rice	1/2 cup Bengal gram
3 cups water	100 gms dates
3 tbsps ghee	A dash of asafoetida
Salt to taste	

Method
Wash and soak the Bengal gram and rice separately in water for 30 minutes.

Heat 1 tbsp ghee, toss in the asafoetida, chana dal and water. When the chana dal is half cooked, add the rice and salt to taste and cook on a low fire until it is almost done. Place the vessel on a hot griddle on a low fire. Add 2 tbsps ghee and also the washed dates. Cook covered until the rice is done by which time the dates will also turn a little soft.

Serve hot.

EGG CURRY

Ingredients

4 hard-boiled eggs (halved)	1/4 cup grated coconut
1 onion (sliced)	2 tbsps melted ghee or oil
2 cups water	

Grind to a paste

1 tsp raw rice	4 cloves garlic
1"-piece ginger	2 Kashmiri chillies
1/2 tsp peppercorns	1 tsp cumin seeds
A small piece of turmeric	Salt to taste

Method
Heat the ghee and lightly fry the onion. Add the ground masala and coconut. Fry for 2 minutes. Add water and cook for 5 minutes or until the gravy thickens a little. Put in the eggs and cook uncovered for 2 minutes more.

Serve hot.

8

CURRIES

Vegetable Curry
Brinjal Curry with Curd
Tomato Curry
Sindhi Curry (1)
Sindhi Curry (2)
Gujarati Yoghurt Curry

VEGETABLE CURRY

Ingredients

1 kg vegetables (washed and cut into pieces)
1/2 tsp garam masala
2 onions (sliced)
6 cups water
Salt to taste

5 tbsps curd (sour)
1 tsp turmeric powder
2 tsps sugar
1 bay leaf
Ghee or oil

Grind to a paste
2 onions
6 Kashmiri chillies
2"-piece ginger
2 tsps cumin seeds

Method

Heat the ghee, add the onion and bay leaf (broken into bits) and fry. Add the vegetables together with the ground paste mixed with curd and fry for 7 minutes. Add water, turmeric powder, salt and sugar. Cook until done. Sprinkle garam masala and a little ghee.

Serve hot with rice.

BRINJAL CURRY WITH CURD

Ingredients

1/2 kg brinjals (washed and cut into pieces)
2 medium-sized onions (sliced)
1 tsp turmeric powder (1/2 tsp for fish and 1/2 tsp for curry)
Salt to taste

2 cups water
2 Kashmiri chillies (broken into bits)
6 tbsps curd (sour)
1 tsp sugar
Ghee or oil

Curries

Method

Mix the salt, turmeric powder and curd together.

Heat some ghee and fry the onions. Put the brinjals and Kashmiri chillies in it and fry for 7 minutes. Sprinkle water, turmeric powder, salt and sugar. Cook until done.

Serve hot with plain boiled rice.

TOMATO CURRY

Ingredients

- 4 large tomatoes
- 6 tbsps ghee or oil
- 2 green chillies (chopped)
- 2 Kashmiri chillies
- 1 tsp fenugreek seeds
- 1 tsp turmeric powder
- 100 gms cluster beans (gavar)
- 15 curry leaves
- 3 tbsps gram flour
- 1"-piece ginger (minced)
- 3 tbsps coriander leaves (finely chopped)
- 1 tsp cumin seeds
- 6 cups water
- 150 gms lady's fingers (bhindi)
- Salt to taste

Method

Boil the tomatoes, mash and pass through a sieve. Set aside.

Heat the ghee, add the gram flour and keep stirring continuously until it is almost brown. Toss in the green chillies, Kashmiri chillies, cumin and fenugreek seeds and continue stirring until the gram flour is dark brown in colour. Stir in the tomato juice along with 6 cups of water. Add the salt, turmeric powder, ginger and curry leaves. Wash and cut the gavar and lady's fingers lengthwise. Add these to the curry and cook uncovered until they are tender.

Garnish with coriander leaves and serve hot with plain boiled rice.

SINDHI CURRY (1)

Ingredients

3/4 cup tuvar dal
6 tbsps ghee or oil
2 green chillies (chopped)
2 Kashmiri chillies
1 tsp fenugreek seeds
8 cups water
1/2 cup tamarind juice
150 gms lady's fingers (diced)
2 medium-sized white gourds (optional)
Salt to taste
3 tbsps gram flour
1 tbsp ginger (minced)
3 tbsps coriander leaves (finely chopped)
1 tsp cumin seeds
1 tsp turmeric powder
100 gms cluster beans
2 medium-sized potatoes
10 drumstick pieces (3" long)
15 curry leaves
10 black cocums

Method

Boil the tuvar dal, pass through a sieve and keep it aside.

Heat the ghee and brown the gram flour. Add the green chillies, Kashmiri chillies, cumin and fenugreek seeds and cook a little. Pour the dal water, 8 cups of water, salt, turmeric powder, ginger, curry leaves, cocums, cluster beans, white gourds and drumsticks. When these are half done add the lady's fingers and potatoes and cook on a low fire until the vegetables are tender. Add tamarind juice.

Garnish with coriander leaves and serve piping hot with

Curries 53

SINDHI CURRY (2)

Ingredients

3/4 cup gram flour
1"-piece ginger (minced)
3 tbsps coriander leaves
   (finely chopped)
1 tsp cumin seeds
8 cups water
1 tsp turmeric powder
15 curry leaves

1/3 cup melted ghee or oil
4 green chillies (chopped)
2 Kashmiri chillies
1 tsp fenugreek seeds
1/2 cup tamarind juice
1/2 cup jaggery
Salt to taste
10 black cocums

Vegetables same as for Sindhi Curry No. 1

Method
Heat the ghee, add the gram flour and stir continuously until it is almost brown. Toss in the green chillies, Kashmiri chillies, cumin and fenugreek seeds and stir until the gram flour turns dark brown in colour. Add water, seasoning and vegetables in the same order as in Sindhi Curry No. 1. Lastly, add the tamarind juice and jaggery and cook for 5 minutes.
    Garnish with coriander leaves and serve piping hot with plain boiled rice.

GUJARATI YOGHURT CURRY

Ingredients

1 cup sour curd
1 tsp turmeric powder
2 cloves

3 tbsps gram flour
6 cups water
4 peppercorns

2 Kashmiri chillies
2 tbsps melted ghee or oil
2 tbsps coriander leaves
   (finely chopped)
1 tsp mustard seeds
1/2 tsp fenugreek seeds
10 curry leaves
Salt to taste

Method
Beat the curd, add the gram flour, blend well, pass through a sieve and set aside.

Heat the ghee, toss in the fenugreek seeds and mustard seeds and when they splutter, add the Kashmiri chillies, cloves, peppercorns, curd-gram flour mixture, water, curry leaves, turmeric powder and salt. Cook till it comes to a boil. Stir continuously, otherwise it will overflow. After it stops bubbling, cook for 5 minutes longer.

Garnish with coriander leaves and serve piping hot with plain boiled rice.

9

KOFTAS

Pumpkin Koftas

Carrot Koftas

Mixed Vegetable Koftas

Yam Koftas

Potato Koftas

Dal Koftas

Kofta Curry

KOFTAS can be served as 'chaat' by immersing them in seasoned tamarind chutney or as a snack with a mint/coconut chutney or ketchup. You can also use koftas to make delicious Kofta Curry.

PUMPKIN KOFTAS

Main ingredients

300 gms pumpkin   1 small potato

Common ingredients for all koftas

2 tbsps gram flour
1/2"-piece ginger (ground)
2 green chillies (ground)
1/2 tsp each of turmeric and mango powder
2 tsps coriander powder
Salt to taste

1 tsp ghee (melted)
3 cloves garlic (ground)
1 tsp each of pomegranate seeds, pepper powder, and chilli powder
2 tbsps each of finely chopped mint and coriander leaves

Method
Wash and grate the pumpkin and potato and squeeze out the water. Add the rest of the ingredients and blend well. Form into round balls or koftas and deep fry a few at a time. When golden brown, remove from the oil.

CARROT KOFTAS

Main ingredients

300 gms carrots   1 small potato

Other ingredients

Same as those common for all koftas.

Method
Wash and grate the carrots and potato and squeeze out the water. Add the rest of the ingredients and blend well. Form into round koftas and deep fry a few at a time. Remove from the oil when golden.

MIXED VEGETABLE KOFTAS

Main ingredients

100 gms peas, shelled and boiled
100 gms grated carrots
2 slices bread (soak in water and squeeze)
100 gms French beans, shredded and boiled
2 small potatoes, boiled and mashed

Other ingredients

Those common for all koftas except gram flour and 1 tsp ghee.

Method
Combine the main ingredients. Add the remaining ingredients and blend. Form into round koftas and deep fry until golden. Take out from the oil and drain.

YAM KOFTAS

Main ingredients

300 gms yam, boiled and mashed

Other ingredients

Same as those common for all koftas.

Method
Blend well the mashed yam and the rest of the ingredients. Form into round koftas. Deep fry until golden. Drain and keep aside.

POTATO KOFTAS

Main ingredients

300 gms potatoes, boiled and mashed

1/2 cup chana dal boiled with a pinch of salt

2 slices bread (soak in water and squeeze)

Other ingredients

Same as those common for all koftas except gram flour and 1 tsp ghee.

Method
Combine the potatoes and bread. Add the remaining ingredients except chana dal and blend. Take a little of the mixture, flatten on your palm, place a little chana dal in the centre and form into a ball. In this manner form the rest of the koftas. Deep fry until golden.

DAL KOFTAS

Main ingredients

300 gms green moong dal

Koftas

Other ingredients

Same as those common for all koftas except reduce the gram flour to 1 tbsp.

Method

Soak the moong dal for at least 4 hours. Rub it with the palms of your hands and remove some of the outer green skin.

Drain and grind it coarsely. Add the rest of the ingredients and blend well. Form into round koftas and deep fry until golden.

Dal koftas are equally delicious in all the three forms, i.e., as a snack with chutney, as chaat immersed in tamarind chutney and in kofta curry.

KOFTA CURRY

It is very simple to turn out a delicious kofta curry. Simply prepare anyone of the following three curries and when it is ready, add any one of the kofta preparations, i.e., pumpkin koftas or mixed vegetable koftas or dal koftas, and cook for 2 minutes more. If you cook longer, the koftas will break.

CURRY 1

Ingredients

2 onions (sliced)
4 tbsps ghee or oil

2 tomatoes (chopped)
4 cups water

Seasoning

2 green chillies (minced)
2 tsps coriander powder
3 tbsps coriander leaves
   (finely chopped)
10 curry leaves

1/2"-piece ginger (minced)
1/2 tsp each of turmeric and
   mango powder
1/2 tsp each of garam masala
   and chilli powder

Method
Heat 4 tbsps ghee and brown the onion in it. Add the tomatoes and cook. Add the remaining ingredients except the fresh coriander. Also add 4 cups of water (this can be varied if you prefer a curry of thick/thin consistency) and when it comes to a boil, cook on a low fire for 5-7 minutes. Add the koftas and cook for 2 minutes more.
Serve hot garnished with coriander leaves.

CURRY 2
This is mainly for people who do not eat onions or dislike them.

Ingredients

4 medium-sized tomatoes (chopped)
4 cups water

1 tsp cumin seeds
3 tbsps ghee or oil

Seasoning
Same as for Curry 1

Method
Heat the ghee and toss in the cumin seeds. Add the tomatoes and cook. Mash with a fork and add the remaining ingredients except the fresh coriander. Also add 4 cups of water and when it comes to a boil, cook on a low fire for 5-7 minutes. Add the koftas and cook for 2 minutes more. Serve hot garnished with coriander leaves.

CURRY 3

Ingredients

2 tomatoes (chopped)
2 tbsps fresh coriander (finely chopped)

4 tbsps ghee or oil
4 cups water
A dash of asafoetida

Grind to a paste
2 Kashmiri chillies
2 cloves garlic
1 bay leaf
1 tsp cumin seeds
A small piece of turmeric

2 cloves
1/2"-piece ginger
2 tsps coriander seeds
1/4 coconut

Koftas

Method

Heat the ghee, toss in the asafoetida and tomatoes and cook. Add the ground masala and cook for a while. Add 4 cups water and when it comes to a boil, cook on a low fire for 5 to 7 minutes. Put in the koftas and cook for 2 minutes more.

Serve hot garnished with coriander leaves.

10

VEGETABLE TREATS

Mashed Ash gourd

Ash gourd with Tomatoes

Sauted Bitter gourds

Masala Bitter gourd

Bitter gourd and Onion Curry

Fried Bitter gourds

Curried Brinjals

Sauted Brinjals

Bhurtha Treat

Sauted Cabbage

Cabbage Onion Relish

Cabbage with Green Peas

Masala Capsicum

Capsicum Vegetable Treat

Carrot Potato Mix

Carrots with Peas

Carrots with Spinach

Vegetable Treats

- Fried Cauliflower
- Cauliflower with Tomatoes
- Cauliflower Peas Curry
- Sauted Cauliflower
- Savoury Cauliflower Hash
- Sauted Cluster Beans
- Savoury Cluster Beans
- Cluster Beans with Coconut
- Colocasia Fingers
- Colocasia Cutlets
- Colocasia Straws
- Colocasia Dip
- Curried Drumsticks
- Drumsticks with Coconut Gravy
- Drumstick Vegetable Mix
- French Beans with Coconut
- French Beans Saute
- Curried French Beans
- Gherkin Straws
- Gherkins with Onions
- Gherkin Vegetable Saute
- Savoury Spinach
- Dhansak
- Spinach Curry
- Savoury Lady's Fingers

Sauted Lady's Fingers

Masala Lady's Fingers

Fried Lady's Fingers

Potato Fingers

Double-fried Potatoes

Potatoes with Brinjals

Sauted Potatoes

Curried Potatoes

Sweet and Sour Potatoes

Curried Pumpkin

Pumpkin with Bengal Gram

Savoury Ridge Gourd

Ridge Gourd with Bengal Gram

Fried White Gourds

White Gourds with Yoghurt

White Gourds with Lotus Stem

Yam Keema

Fried Yam

Yam Cutlets with Yoghurt

Savoury Yam

Crunchy Yam

MASHED ASH GOURD

Ingredients

250 gms ash gourd
1 medium-sized tomato (diced)
2 green chillies
1/2 tsp turmeric powder
1/4 tsp garam masala
Salt and chilli powder to taste
2 medium-sized onions (sliced)
2 tbsps melted ghee or oil
2 tsps coriander powder
1/2 tsp mango powder
1 lemon (sliced)

Method

Peel and cut the ash gourd into small cubes.

Heat the ghee and saute the green chillies and onions to a pale golden colour. Add the tomato and cook covered, until it turns soft. Wash and stir in the ash gourd together with the seasoning. Cook covered on a low fire, stirring occasionally, until the vegetable is done. Mash and cook uncovered for a minute longer, stirring continuously.

Serve hot garnished with lemon wedges.

ASH GOURD WITH TOMATOES

Ingredients

250 gms ash gourd
1 tsp fenugreek seeds
2 tsps coriander powder
1/2 tsp chilli powder
1/4 tsp garam masala
Salt to taste
2 medium-sized tomatoes (diced)
3 tbsps melted ghee or oil
1/2 tsp turmeric powder
1/2 tsp mango powder
A dash of asafoetida

Method

Peel and cut the ash gourd into small cubes.

Heat the ghee and toss in the fenugreek seeds together with asafoetida. Stir. Then wash and add the ash gourd, tomatoes and seasoning. Cover and cook on a low fire, stirring occasionally, until the vegetable is done.

Serve hot with chapaties.

SAUTED BITTER GOURDS

Ingredients

4 large bitter gourds	2 medium-sized onions (sliced)
1 medium-sized tomato (diced)	2 green chillies (minced)
2 tsps coriander powder	1/2 tsp turmeric powder
1/4 tsp garam masala	1/4 tsp mango powder
Salt and chilli powder to taste	Oil for frying

Method

Scrape the bitter gourds. Chop into 1/2"-pieces, sprinkle with salt and set aside for 3 to 4 hours or, if possible, overnight to get rid of the bitterness. Wash thoroughly in running water and set aside.

Heat the oil and deep fry the bitter gourd pieces to a pale golden colour. Drain.

Heat 2 tbsps oil and fry chillies and onions to a golden colour.

Add the tomatoes and salt and cook until they turn soft. Stir in the bitter gourds together with seasoning. Cook covered, stirring occasionally, until the bitter gourds turn soft and no moisture is left.

Serve hot.

MASALA BITTER GOURD

Ingredients

6 medium bitter gourds
4 tsps coriander powder
1 tsp chilli powder
1 tsp mango powder
6 tbsps oil
1/2 tsp turmeric powder
Salt to taste

Method
Scrape the bitter gourds, slit them lengthwise, sprinkle salt inside the slits and set aside for 3 to 4 hours to get rid of the bitterness. Wash the bitter gourds well in water and squeeze. Combine seasoning with 1 tbsp oil. Fill them with the seasoning mixture. Secure with threads. Heat the remaining oil and place the bittergourds in it. Cook covered on a low fire, stirring occasionally, until the gourds are done.
    Serve hot.

BITTER GOURD AND ONION CURRY

Ingredients

4 small bitter gourds
1 tbsp gram flour
2 green chillies (minced)
2 cups water
2 tsps coriander powder
1/2 tsp turmeric powder
Salt and chilli powder to taste
4 small onions
1 tsp mustard seeds
2 tbsps finely chopped coriander leaves
4 cocums
Oil for frying

Method
Scrape the bitter gourds, sprinkle with salt and set aside for 3 to 4 hours. Wash thoroughly in water. Peel the onions, slit into fours, sprinkle with salt and set aside for 15 minutes. Heat the oil and deep fry the bitter gourds and onions separately to a pale golden colour. Drain and set aside together.

Heat 1 tbsp oil and toss in green chillies and mustard seeds. When they splutter, add the gram flour and fry, stirring continuously, until it turns golden. Add 2 cups of water together with seasoning and cocum. When the water comes to the boil, stir in the bitter gourds and onions and cook for another 5 minutes.

Serve hot garnished with coriander leaves.

FRIED BITTER GOURDS

Ingredients

6 medium bitter gourds
2 tsps coriander powder
1/2 tsp mango powder
Salt and chilli powder to taste
1/2 cup water
1/2 tsp turmeric powder
Oil for frying

Method
Scrape the bitter gourds, slit them lengthwise, sprinkle salt in the slits and set aside for 3 to 4 hours to remove the bitterness. Wash thoroughly in water. Heat the oil and deep fry to a golden colour. Drain in a frying pan. Stir in 1/2 cup water together with seasoning and cook covered, stirring occasionally, until the gourds turn soft.

Serve hot.

CURRIED BRINJALS

Ingredients

3 medium-sized brinjals (cut into 3/4" x 3/4" cubes)
1 medium-sized tomato (diced)
3 tbsps oil
2½ cups water
Salt to taste

1 medium-size potato (cut into 3/4" x 3/4" cubes)
3 tbsps finely chopped coriander leaves
A dash of asafoetida

Grind to a paste
2 medium-sized onions
3 cloves garlic
2 tbsps grated coconut
1 tsp cumin seeds
A small piece of turmeric

1"-piece ginger
2 Kashmiri chillies
1 tsp coriander seeds
1 bay leaf

Method
Heat the oil. Slightly fry the asafoetida and the ground paste. Wash and stir in the vegetables and fry for 3 minutes. Add the tomatoes, water and salt. Cover and cook on a low fire until the vegetables are done.
 Serve hot garnished with coriander leaves.

SAUTED BRINJALS

Ingredients

2 large brinjals
1"-piece ginger (minced)
1 tbsp finely chopped coriander leaves

2 green chillies (minced)
2 medium onions (sliced)
Oil for frying

Seasoning

3 tsps coriander powder
1/2 tsp turmeric powder
1/2 tsp garam masala

1 tsp chilli powder
1/2 tsp mango powder
Salt to taste

Method
Cut the brinjals into 3/4"-thick round slices. Score them crisscross on both sides. Sprinkle with salt and keep aside for 10 minutes. Heat the oil and deep fry them. Drain and arrange in a frying pan. Keep the frying pan aside.

Heat a little oil separately and saute the onions, ginger and green chillies. Add the seasoning and coriander leaves. Blend well and sprinkle evenly on fried brinjal slices. Cover the pan and cook for 3 minutes on a low fire.

Serve hot.

BHURTHA TREAT

Ingredients

1 large brinjal
1"-piece ginger (minced)
2 green chillies (minced)
1 lemon (sliced)

1 large onion (grated)
2 medium-sized tomatoes (diced)
3 tbsps oil
A dash of asafoetida

Seasoning

3 tsps coriander powder
1/2 tsp turmeric powder
Salt to taste

1 tsp chilli powder
1/2 tsp garam masala

Method
Roast the brinjal over an open flame until its peel turns black and the brinjal is sufficiently cooked inside. Peel and mash with a fork. Keep aside.

Vegetable Treats 71

Heat the oil and add asafoetida. Stir in the onion, ginger and green chillies and fry. Add the tomatoes and cook. Add the mashed brinjal. Season and simmer for 5 minutes, stirring frequently.

Serve hot garnished with lemon wedges.

SAUTED CABBAGE

Ingredients

1 medium-sized cabbage head (shredded)	6 tbsps oil
	1 tsp mustard seeds
1"-piece ginger (minced)	2 green chillies
3 tsps coriander powder	1/2 tsp turmeric powder
1/2 tsp mango powder	1/2 tsp chilli powder
Salt to taste	

Method
Heat the oil and toss in the mustard seeds. When they splutter, wash and put in the cabbage together with the green chillies, ginger, salt and turmeric powder. Cook covered on a low fire, stirring occasionally, until the cabbage turns tender. Add the remaining seasoning and cook, uncovered, for 5 minutes, stirring often.

Serve hot.

CABBAGE ONION RELISH

Ingredients

3 cups shredded cabbage
2 green chillies (minced)
2 medium-sized tomatoes (diced)
1/2 tsp turmeric powder
1/2 tsp mango powder
Salt to taste

3 medium onions (grated)
1"-piece ginger (minced)
3 tbsps oil
2 tsps coriander powder
1/2 tsp chilli powder
1/4 tsp garam masala

Method
Heat the oil and fry the onions, ginger and green chillies slightly. Wash and add the cabbage, together with the tomatoes, salt and turmeric powder. Cover and cook on a low fire until the cabbage is done. Add the seasoning and cook, uncovered, for 3 minutes more, stirring often.
Serve hot.

CABBAGE WITH GREEN PEAS

Ingredients

2 cups shredded cabbage
1 medium potato (cut into small cubes)
2 tbsps coriander powder
1/2 tsp pepper powder
A dash of asafoetida

1 cup shelled peas (boiled)
1 tsp mustard seeds
2 tbsps oil
1/2 tsp chilli powder
1/2 tsp turmeric powder
Salt to taste

Vegetable Treats

Method
Heat the oil and add the asafoetida. After a little while add the mustard seeds. When they splutter, wash and add the cabbage, potato, salt and turmeric powder. Cook covered until the vegetables are almost ready. Add the green peas together with the remaining seasoning and cook, uncovered, 5 minutes longer, stirring often.
  Serve hot.

MASALA CAPSICUM

Ingredients

6 medium-sized capsicums   4 tbsps oil

Masala
4 tsps coriander powder   1/2 tsp chilli powder
1/2 tsp turmeric powder   1/2 tsp mango powder
1/2 tsp pepper powder   1/4 tsp garam masala
$1^1/_2$ tbsps chopped coriander   Salt to taste
  leaves

Method
Wash the capsicums and slit into four, half-way. Add 1-1/2 tsps oil to the masalas and blend well. Fill the capsicums with this masala. Heat the remaining oil and place the capsicums in it. Cover and cook on a low fire, stirring occasionally, until the capsicums are done.
  Serve hot.

CAPSICUM VEGETABLE TREAT

Ingredients

4 capsicums
1 medium-size cucumber
3 tbsps oil
3 tsps coriander powder
1/2 tsp chilli powder
1/2 tsp mango powder
A dash of asafoetida

1 medium-size carrot
1/2 cup shredded cabbage
1 tsp mustard seeds
1/2 tsp turmeric powder
1/2 tsp pepper powder
1/4 tsp garam masala
Salt to taste

Method
Remove the seeds from the capsicums and cut into small pieces. Scrape the carrots, pare the cucumber and cut both into small cubes. Wash the vegetables.

Heat the oil and add a dash of asafoetida. Then toss in the mustard seeds and when they splutter, put all the vegetables together with salt and turmeric powder. Cover and cook on a low fire until the vegetables are done. Season and cook uncovered for 3 minutes stirring often.

Serve hot.

CARROT POTATO MIX

Ingredients

3 medium-sized carrots
   (scraped and cut into
   thin sticks)
2 green chillies (minced)
3 tbsps oil

3 medium-sized potatoes (pared
   and cut into small cubes)
2 medium-sized tomatoes (diced)
1"-piece ginger (minced)
1 tsp cumin seeds

Vegetable Treats

Seasoning

3 tsps coriander powder
1/2 tsp turmeric powder
Salt to taste

1 tsp chilli powder
1/2 tsp garam masala

Method

Heat the oil and toss in the cumin seeds. When they splutter, add the tomatoes, vegetables, green chillies, ginger, salt and turmeric powder. Cover and cook on a low fire until the vegetables are done. Add the remaining seasoning and cook uncovered 2 minutes longer, stirring often.
 Serve hot.

CARROTS WITH PEAS

Ingredients

3/4 cup shelled green peas
2 medium-sized onions (sliced)
2 medium-sized tomatoes (diced)
1 tsp mint leaves
    (finely chopped)
4 cups water

3 medium-sized carrots
    (scraped and diced)
4 tbsps oil
1 tbsp coriander leaves
    (finely chopped)
Salt to taste

Grind to a paste

1"-piece ginger
3 cloves garlic
2 tsps coriander seeds
A small piece of turmeric

2 Kashmiri chillies
2 tsps grated coconut
1 tsp cumin seeds
A small piece of cinnamon

Method

Heat the oil and saute the onions. Add the tomatoes, cover and cook until they turn soft. Add the ground paste and vegetables and fry for 5 minutes. Add water and salt and cook on a low fire until the vegetables turn tender and the gravy is thick. Serve hot garnished with mint and coriander leaves.

CARROTS WITH SPINACH

Ingredients

1 medium-sized bunch spinach (chopped)
2 green chillies (minced)
2 medium-sized onions (sliced)
3 tbsps oil
1/2 tsp garam masala
1/2 tsp turmeric powder
Salt to taste
3 medium-sized carrots (scraped and cut into thin sticks)
1"-piece ginger (minced)
1/2 cup water
2 medium-sized tomatoes (diced)
2 tsps coriander powder
1/2 tsp chilli powder

Method
Heat the oil and add the onions, ginger and green chillies and saute. Toss in the carrots and fry for 5 minutes. Stir in the spinach, water, tomatoes and seasoning. Cover and cook until the vegetables are tender.
Serve hot.

FRIED CAULIFLOWER

Ingredients

500 gms cauliflower (cut into florets)
3 medium-sized onions (sliced)
2 medium-sized tomatoes

Vegetable Treats

2 green chillies (minced)
1-1/2 tbsps coriander leaves (finely chopped)
Oil for frying
1"-piece ginger (minced)
1-1/2 tbsps mint leaves (finely chopped)

Seasoning

3 tsps coriander powder
1/2 tsp mango powder
1/2 tsp pepper powder
Salt to taste
1/2 tsp turmeric powder
1/2 tsp chilli powder
1 tsps garam masala

Method

Wash the cauliflower, sprinkle with salt and set aside for 10 minutes. Heat the oil and deep fry the cauliflower pieces to a pale colour. Drain and set aside.

Heat 3 tbsps oil and saute the onions, ginger and green chillies. Add the tomatoes and cook covered until they turn soft. Add salt. Stir in the fried cauliflower along with the remaining seasoning. Cover the pan and simmer for 5 minutes.

Serve hot garnished with mint and coriander leaves.

CAULIFLOWER WITH TOMATOES

Ingredients

300 gms cauliflower (broken into florets and the green stem chopped fine)
2 green chillies (minced)
2 tbsps oil
1 tbsp chopped mint leaves
3 tsps coriander powder
1/2 tsp chilli powder
1/2 tsp garam masala
2 medium-sized potatoes (diced)
4 large tomatoes (diced)
1"-piece ginger (minced)
1 tsp cumin seeds
1 tbsp chopped coriander leaves
3/4 cup water
1/2 tsp turmeric powder
1/2 tsp pepper powder
Salt to taste

Method

Heat the oil, add the cumin seeds and when they splutter add the tomatoes: Cover and cook on a low fire until they turn soft. Mash with a fork. Wash and add the florets and potatoes. Fry for 3 minutes. Add the seasoning and water. Cover and cook on a low fire until the vegetables turn tender.

Serve hot garnished with coriander leaves.

CAULIFLOWER PEAS CURRY

Ingredients

300 gms cauliflower (cut into florets)
100 gms shelled peas
2 medium-sized tomatoes (diced)
2 medium-sized onions (sliced)
3 tbsps melted ghee or oil
2 cups water
1 tbsp chopped coriander leaves
1 tbsp chopped mint leaves
Salt to taste

Seasoning
Fry in 1 tsp oil and grind
2 tsps coriander seeds
2 Kashmiri chillies
1/2 tsp peppercorns
1 tsp cumin seeds
A small piece of cinnamon
2 cloves
1 cardamom
A small piece of turmeric

Grind separately
2 tbsps grated coconut
1"-piece ginger
4 cloves garlic

Method

Heat the ghee and saute the onions. Toss in the tomatoes and cook covered until they turn soft. Wash and add the vegetables together with the ground masalas and fry for 5 minutes. Add water and salt. Cover and cook on a low fire, stirring occasionally. When the vegetables turn soft and very little gravy is left, garnish with coriander leaves.

Serve hot with chapaties.

Vegetable Treats

SAUTED CAULIFLOWER

Ingredients

300 gms cauliflower (broken into florets)
1"-piece ginger (minced)
1 tsp cumin seeds
1-1/2 tbsps chopped coriander leaves
1 medium-sized potato (diced)
2 green chillies (minced)
1 medium-sized tomato (diced)
4 tbsps oil

Seasoning
2 tsps coriander powder
1/2 tsp turmeric powder
Salt to taste
1/2 tsp chilli powder
1/4 tsp garam masala

Method
Heat the oil and toss in the cumin seeds. When they splutter, wash and add the florets, potato, green chillies, ginger, salt and turmeric powder. Cover and cook on a low fire. When it is half-cooked, add the tomatoes and cook covered until the vegetables are done. Add the remaining seasoning and cook uncovered for 3 minutes more, stirring often.

Serve hot garnished with coriander leaves.

SAVOURY CAULIFLOWER HASH

Ingredients

250 gms cauliflower (broken into florets)
2 tbsps melted ghee or oil
2 tsps coriander powder
1"-piece ginger
2 green chillies
1/2 cup water
1/2 tsp turmeric powder

1/4 tsp garam masala
1/2 tbsp pepper
Salt to taste

1 tbsp curd (beaten)
A dash of asafoetida

Method
Add the salt, 1/2 cup water and turmeric powder to the cauliflower and pressure cook.

Drain and mash coarsely.

Heat the ghee and add the asafoetida, ginger and green chillies. Stir in the mashed cauliflower together with the rest of the ingredients and cook 5 minutes longer, stirring often.

Serve hot.

SAUTED CLUSTER BEANS

Ingredients

20 gms cluster beans
2 tbsps oil
1/2 tsp turmeric powder
1/2 tsp chilli powder

1 tsp mustard seeds
1 tsp coriander powder
1/2 tsp mango powder
Salt to taste

Method
String and chop the cluster beans into 1/2"-pieces. Add the salt and turmeric powder and boil with sufficient water to cook the beans. Heat the oil, toss in the mustard seeds and when they start spluttering, stir in the boiled cluster beans. Season and cook uncovered 3 minutes longer, stirring often.

Serve hot.

Vegetable Treats

SAVOURY CLUSTER BEANS

Ingredients

1 medium-sized potato
1 medium-sized onion (sliced)
2 tbsps melted ghee or oil
2 cups water
1 tsp coriander powder
1/2 tsp chilli powder
Salt to taste

200 gms cluster beans
2 medium-sized tomatoes (diced)
2 tbsps finely chopped coriander leaves
1/2 tsp turmeric powder
1/4 tsp garam masala

Method
Chop the cluster beans into 1/2"-pieces. Pare and cut the potato into medium-sized cubes.

Heat the ghee and fry the onion to a pale golden colour. Add the tomatoes and saute. Wash and add the cluster beans, potato pieces and seasoning. Fry for 3 minutes. Pour water and cook covered on a low fire until the vegetables turn soft and the gravy is thick.

Serve hot garnished with coriander leaves.

CLUSTER BEANS WITH COCONUT

Ingredients

200 gms cluster beans
1 tsp mustard seeds
1 tsp coriander powder
1/2 tsp mango powder

1/4 cup grated coconut
2 tbsps oil
1/2 tsp turmeric powder
Salt and chilli powder to taste

Method
Chop the cluster beans into 1/4"-pieces. Add the salt and turmeric powder and boil with water just sufficient to cook them.

Heat the oil, toss in the mustard seeds and when they splutter, stir in the cluster beans, seasoning and coconut. Cover and cook 3 minutes longer, stirring often.

Serve hot.

COLOCASIA FINGERS

Ingredients

250 gms colocasia
1/2 tsp turmeric powder
1/2 tsp mango powder
Oil for frying

3 tsps coriander powder
1/2 tsp chilli powder
Salt to taste

Method
Scrape and cut the colocasia into 1/2"-thick fingers. Wash, sprinkle salt over them and set aside for 10 minutes.

Heat the oil and deep fry to a golden colour. Drain and season. Toss.

Serve hot as an accompaniment to a main meal.

COLOCASIA CUTLETS

Ingredients

250 gms colocasia
1/2 tsp turmeric powder

3 tsps coriander powder
1/2 tsp chilli powder

1/2 tsp mango powder Salt to taste
Oil for frying

Method
Boil the colocasia. Drain, peel and sprinkle salt all over. Set aside for 10 minutes.
 Heat the oil and deep fry to a pale golden colour. Drain. When slightly cool, flatten the pieces and re-fry until crisp and golden. Add the seasoning and toss.
 Serve hot.

COLOCASIA STRAWS

Ingredients

250 gms colocasia 1 tsp cuminseeds
6 tbsps oil 3 tsps coriander powder
1/2 tsp turmeric powder 1/2 tsp chilli powder
1/2 tsp mango powder Salt to taste

Method
Scrape and cut the colocasia into 1/4" thick straws.
 Heat the oil, add the cumin seeds and when they splutter, wash and add the colocasia together with salt and turmeric powder. Cook covered, stirring occasionally until the colocasia turn tender. Add the remaining seasoning and cook uncovered for 5 minutes, stirring often.

COLOCASIA DIP

Ingredients

1 cup colocasia (boiled, peeled and diced)
1 tbsp coriander leaves (finely chopped)
Salt and chilli powder to taste
2 cups tamarind juice mixed with sugar or jaggery to taste
1 tbsp mint leaves (finely chopped)

Method
Immerse the colocasia in tamarind juice. Add salt and chilli powder. Mix well. Garnish with mint and coriander leaves. Serve cold as a side dish or a snack.

CURRIED DRUMSTICKS

Ingredients

3 drumsticks (scraped and cut into 3"-long pieces)
1/2"-piece ginger (minced)
2 green chillies (minced)
2 tbsps melted ghee or oil
3 cups water
2 tsps coriander powder
1/2 tsp mango powder
Salt and chilli powder to taste
1 medium-sized onion (diced)
2 medium-sized onions (minced)
2 medium-sized tomatoes (diced)
2 tbsps finely chopped coriander leaves
1/2 tsp turmeric powder
1/4 tsp garam masala

Vegetable Treats

Method
Heat the ghee and saute the ginger, green chillies and onions. Add the tomatoes. Cover and cook until they are tender. Add the drumsticks and potatoes and fry for 5 minutes. Pour water and season. Cover and cook on a low fire until the vegetables are cooked.
Serve hot garnished with coriander leaves.

DRUMSTICKS WITH COCONUT GRAVY

Ingredients

3 drumsticks (scraped and cut into 3"-long pieces)
2 medium-sized tomatoes (pureed)
3 cups water
1/4 tsp garam masala
Salt and chilli powder to taste

1 medium-sized potato (diced)
1/4 cup grated coconut
1 tsp cumin seeds
2 tbsps melted ghee or oil
1 tsp coriander powder
1/2 tsp turmeric powder
A dash of asafoetida

Method
Heat the ghee and add the asafoetida and cumin seeds. When the latter splutter, toss in the coconut and fry a little. Add the tomato puree together with the rest of the ingredients. Cover and cook on a low fire until the vegetables are tender.
Serve hot.

DRUMSTICK VEGETABLE MIX

Ingredients

2 drumsticks (scraped and cut into 3"-long pieces)
1 medium-sized brinjal (cut into small cubes)
10 cluster beans (cut lengthwise)
1/2 tsp turmeric powder
1/2 tsp mango powder
Salt and chilli powder to taste

8 lady's fingers (cut full length and slit)
1 medium-sized potato (cut into small cubes)
8 tbsps oil
3 tsps coriander powder
1/4 tsp garam masala
1/2 tsp pepper powder

Method
Heat the oil and fry all the masalas for 2 minutes. Wash and add the vegetables. Cover and cook on a low fire, stirring occasionally and carefully, until the vegetables are tender.
Serve hot.

FRENCH BEANS WITH COCONUT

Ingredients

200 gms French beans
2 tbsps grated coconut
2 tbsps oil
1 tsp coriander powder
Salt and chilli powder to taste

2 tbsps tuvar dal
1 tsp mustard seeds
1/2 cup water
1/2 tsp turmeric powder

Method
Soak the tuvar dal in hot water for 2 minutes. String and cut the beans into 1/4"-pieces.

Gujarati Yogurt Curry

Kofta Curry

Green Peas with Paneer

Stuffed Brinjals

Vegetable Treats

Heat the oil and toss in the mustard seeds. When they splutter, wash and add the French beans and tuvar dal. Fry for 2 minutes. Add water and seasoning. Cook covered on a low fire, stirring occasionally, until the vegetables are cooked.

Serve hot garnished with grated coconut.

FRENCH BEANS SAUTE

Ingredients

200 gms French beans
3 tbsps oil
1/2"-piece ginger (minced)
1 tsp coriander powder
Salt and chilli power to taste

1 medium-sized tomato (diced)
2 green chillies (minced)
1 tsp cumin seeds
1/2 tsp turmeric powder

Method
String and cut the beans into 1/2"-pieces.

Heat the oil and toss in the cumin seeds. When they splutter, wash and add the beans, turmeric powder and salt. Cook covered, stirring occasionally. When the vegetable is half-cooked, add the tomato and cook until it is almost done. Season and cook uncovered 3 minutes longer, stirring often.

Serve hot.

CURRIED FRENCH BEANS

Ingredients

200 gms French beans
1/2 cup water

1 medium-sized onion (sliced)
3 tbsps oil

Grind to a paste

2 Kashmiri chillies	1 tsp coriander seeds
1/2 tsp peppercorns	A small piece of turmeric
1/2"-piece ginger	2 cloves
A small piece of cinnamon	4 cloves garlic
Salt to taste	

Method
String and cut the French beans into 1/2"-long pieces.

Heat the oil and fry the ground masala and French beans for 5 minutes. Add water and cook covered on a low fire, stirring occasionally, until the vegetable is done.

Serve hot.

GHERKIN STRAWS

Ingredients

1 cup gherkins (cut into 1/4"-straws)	1 tsp coriander powder
	1/2 tsp chilli powder
1/4 tsp turmeric powder	1/4 tsp mango powder
Salt to taste	Oil for frying

Method
Wash the gherkins, sprinkle salt over them and set aside for 10 minutes.

Heat the oil and deep fry the gherkins until they turn golden in colour. Drain and season. Blend well.

Serve hot as a side dish.

GHERKINS WITH ONIONS

Ingredients

1 cup gherkins
   (cut into small cubes)
1 tbsp finely chopped
   coriander leaves
1/2"-piece ginger (minced)
1 tsp coriander powder
1/4 tsp garam masala

2 medium-sized onions (sliced)
2 medium-sized tomatoes
2 tbsps oil
1/2 cup water
2 green chillies (minced)
1/2 tsp turmeric
Salt and chilli powder to taste

Method
Heat the oil and saute the ginger, green chillies and onions until the latter turn pale golden in colour. Add the tomatoes and cover. Cook until they turn soft. Stir in the gherkins and fry for 3 minutes. Add water and seasoning. Cover and cook on a low fire until the gherkins are cooked.
   Serve hot garnished with coriander leaves.

GHERKIN VEGETABLE SAUTE

Ingredients

1 cup gherkins
   (cut into 1/4"-straws)
1/2 cup pieces of cauliflower
2 medium-sized tomatoes
   (diced)
1/2"-piece ginger (minced)
2 tsps coriander powder
1/4 tsp garam masala
Oil for frying

2 medium-sized potatoes
   (peeled and cut into 1/2"-fingers)
2 medium-sized onions (sliced)
1 tbsp finely chopped
   coriander leaves
2 green chillies (minced)
1/2 tsp turmeric powder
Salt and chilli powder to taste

Method
Wash all the vegetables, sprinkle with salt and set aside for 10 minutes. Heat the oil and deep fry all the vegetables separately. Drain and mix the vegetables.

Heat 3 tbsps of oil and saute the green chillies, ginger and onion to a pale golden colour. Add the tomatoes, cover and cook until they turn soft. Stir in the fried vegetables together with the rest of the ingredients. Cover and cook on a low fire for 5 minutes, stirring occasionally.

Serve hot.

SAVOURY SPINACH

Ingredients

1 bunch spinach (chopped)
1 bunch khatta bhaji (chopped)
1 small potato (cut into cubes)
2 medium-sized tomatoes (diced)
1 medium-sized onion (minced)
1/2 cup chana dal
2 green chillies (minced)
1 tsp cumin seeds
3 tbsps melted ghee
2 tsps coriander powder
A dash of asafoetida
1 bunch suva (chopped)
1 small brinjal (cut into cubes)
1/2 cup small cubes of bottle gourd
1 medium-sized carrot (scraped and cut into small cubes)
1 medium-sized white gourd (cut into cubes)
1/2 cup water
1/2 tsp turmeric powder
1/4 tsp garam masala
Salt and chilli powder to taste

Method
Wash and soak the dal in water for half an hour.

Heat 2 tbsps ghee and add the asafoetida. Wash and add the greens, dal, vegetables, seasoning and water. Cover and cook until all the ingredients turn soft. Remove from the fire and mash well with a wooden spoon. Reheat and cook 5 minutes longer. Heat the remaining ghee, toss in the cumin

seeds and when they splutter pour into the prepared vegetable.
Serve hot.

DHANSAK

Ingredients

1 cup mixed dals (tuvar, masoor and moong)
1 tbsp mint leaves
1/2 cup chopped red pumpkin
2 large onions (sliced)
6 cloves ground garlic
4 cups water
1/2 tsp turmeric powder
Salt to taste

1 bunch methi leaves
1 tbsp coriander leaves
1 brinjal (cut into cubes)
1 potato (cut into cubes)
1"-piece ginger (ground)
4 cloves
2 tbsps melted ghee
1 large tomato (diced)

Grind to a paste
2 cardamoms
8 peppercorns
1 tsp coriander seeds
A small piece of dried coconut

4 Kashmiri chillies
1 tsp cumin seeds
A small piece of cinnamon
A small piece of turmeric

Method
Pick and wash the dals. Add one onion, ginger, garlic, cloves, turmeric powder, salt, greens and the rest of the vegetables (except tomatoes) and 4 cups water. Cover and cook until the vegetables turn soft. Mash and pass through a sieve.

Fry separately the remaining one onion, ground masala and tomato. Add to the strained vegetables and simmer for 10 minutes.

Serve hot with fried rice.

SPINACH CURRY

Ingredients

1 bunch spinach
1 cup curd (fresh)
1/4 cup groundnuts
1 tsp cumin seeds
1/2 tsp sugar
Salt to taste

1/2 cup gram flour
1 tsp chana dal
1/2 tsp turmeric powder
2 green chillies (slit)
2 tbsps melted ghee or oil

Method
Soak the groundnuts and chana dal in water for 1/2 hour. Cook the spinach, dal and groundnuts until soft. Mash.

Combine the gram flour with curd, beat well and add to the mashed spinach. Also add the salt and turmeric powder. Put it on the fire. When it comes to the boil, stir in the sugar and cook for 10 minutes on a low fire stirring often. Heat the ghee separately, add the slit chillies and cumin seeds, and when the latter splutter, pour over the spinach mixture.

Serve hot.

SAVOURY LADY'S FINGERS

Ingredients

200 gms lady's fingers (small ones)
1/2"-piece ginger (minced)
1/4 tsp mango powder
1/2 tsp turmeric powder
Salt and chilli powder to taste

2 medium-sized onions (sliced)
2 green chillies (minced)
4 tbsps oil
2 tsps coriander powder
1/4 tsp garam masala

Method
Wash and cut the lady's fingers lengthwise. Heat the oil and fry the onions, green chillies and ginger until the onions become transparent. Add the lady's fingers, salt and turmeric powder. Cook covered on a low fire, stirring occasionally, until the lady's fingers are almost done. Increase the heat. Season and cook 5 minutes longer, stirring often but taking care not to break the lady's fingers.
Serve hot.

SAUTED LADY'S FINGERS

Ingredients

200 gms lady's fingers
1/2"-piece ginger (minced)
1 tsp cumin seeds
1/2 tsp turmeric powder
Salt and chilli powder to taste

2 green chillies (minced)
4 tbsps oil
1 tsp coriander powder
1/2 mango powder

Method
Wash and cut the lady's fingers into 1/2"-pieces. Heat the oil, toss in the cumin seeds and when they splutter, stir in the lady's fingers, ginger, green chillies, salt and turmeric powder. Cook covered on a low fire, stirring occasionally, until the lady's fingers become soft. Increase the heat. Season and cook uncovered 3 minutes longer, stirring often.
Serve hot.

MASALA LADY'S FINGERS

Ingredients

200 gms lady's fingers
4 tbsps oil
1/2 tsp turmeric powder
1/4 tsp garam masala
Salt to taste

1 tsp cumin seeds
4 tsps coriander powder
1/2 tsp mango powder
1/2 tsp chilli powder

Method
Wash and cut the lady's fingers lengthwise, slitting on one side. Combine seasoning with 1 tsp oil and stuff the lady's fingers with it.

Heat the oil, toss in the cumin seeds and when they splutter, add the lady's fingers together with the leftover masala mixture, if any. Cook covered on a low fire, stirring occasionally, until the lady's fingers are done.

Serve hot.

FRIED LADY'S FINGERS

Ingredients

200 gms lady's fingers
1/2 tsp mango powder
Oil for frying

1 tsp coriander powder
1/2 tsp chilli powder
Salt to taste

Method
Wash and cut the lady's fingers into 1/2"-pieces. Sprinkle with salt and set aside for 5 minutes.

Vegetable Treats

Heat the oil and deep fry until they are pale golden in colour. Drain. Season and toss.
Serve hot.

POTATO FINGERS

Ingredients

4 medium-sized potatoes
   (cut into 1/2"-fingers)
1/2 tsp turmeric powder
Salt to taste

1/2 tsp chilli powder
1 tsp coriander powder
1/2 tsp mango powder
Oil for frying

Method
Wash the potatoes, sprinkle with salt and set aside for 10 minutes.
Heat the oil and deep fry until golden. Drain and season. Blend well.
Serve hot as a side dish. Without the seasoning, serve the potato fingers as a snack with sauce or chutney.

DOUBLE-FRIED POTATOES

Ingredients

4 medium-sized potatoes
   (halved)
1/2 tsp turmeric powder
Salt to taste

1 tsp coriander powder
1/2 tsp chilli powder
1/2 tsp mango powder
Oil for frying

Method
Wash the potatoes, sprinkle salt over them and set aside for 10 minutes. Heat the oil, add the potatoes, cover and deep fry on a low fire until they turn soft. Drain and cool a little. Flatten them and re-fry until they turn crisp and golden in colour. Drain, season and blend well.

Serve hot as a side dish.

POTATOES WITH BRINJALS

Ingredients

2 medium-sized potatoes (cut into cubes)	1 medium-sized brinjal (cut into cubes)
1 medium-sized tomato (diced)	1 tsp cumin seeds
	1 tbsp melted ghee
2 cups water	1 tbsp finely chopped coriander leaves
2 green chillies (minced)	
1 tsp coriander powder	1/2 tsp turmeric powder
Salt and chilli powder to taste	Oil for frying

Method
Wash the potatoes and brinjals, sprinkle with salt and set aside for 10 minutes. Heat the oil and deep fry. Drain and set aside.

Heat 1 tbsp ghee, toss in the cumin seeds and when they splutter, add the green chillies and tomatoes. Cover and cook until the tomatoes are soft. Add water and seasoning. When the water comes to the boil, stir in the vegetables and cook 5 minutes longer.

Serve hot garnished with coriander leaves.

SAUTED POTATOES

Ingredients

4 medium-sized potatoes (cut into cubes)
1/2"-piece ginger
2 tsps coriander powder
1/4 tsp garam masala
Oil for frying

2 medium-sized onions (sliced)
1 medium-sized tomato (diced)
2 green chillies
1/2 tsp turmeric powder
Salt and chilli powder to taste
2 tbsps finely chopped coriander leaves

Method
Wash the potatoes, sprinkle salt over them and set aside for 10 minutes. Heat the oil and deep fry. Drain and set aside.

Heat 2 tbsps oil and saute the ginger, green chillies and onions to a golden colour. Add the tomato. Cover and cook until it turns soft. Add the seasoning together with the fried potatoes. Cover and cook for 2 minutes.

Serve hot garnished with coriander leaves.

CURRIED POTATOES

Ingredients

4 medium-sized potatoes (cut into cubes)
1 medium-sized tomato (diced)
10 curry leaves
Salt to taste

3 tbsps melted ghee or oil
$1^1/_2$ cups water
1 tbsp finely chopped coriander leaves

Grind to a paste

1 medium-sized onion
2 green chillies
1/2 tsp peppercorns
1 bay leaf
1/2 tsp coriander seeds
A small piece of cinnamon
1/2"-piece ginger
1 tbsp coconut (grated)
2 cloves
1 tsp cumin seeds
A small piece of turmeric

Method
Heat the ghee and fry the potatoes and ground paste for 5 minutes. Add the tomato, water, salt and curry leaves. Cover and cook on a low fire until the potatoes are done.

Serve hot garnished with coriander leaves.

SWEET AND SOUR POTATOES

Ingredients

4 medium-sized potatoes (boiled, peeled and cubed)
1/2 tsp sugar
1 tbsp finely chopped coriander leaves
1 tsp coriander powder
1/4 tsp garam masala
Salt and chilli powder to taste
3 tbsps oil
1 tsp mustard seeds
10 curry leaves
3 green chillies (minced)
1/2"-piece ginger (minced)
1/2 tsp turmeric powder
Juice of 1 lemon

Method
Heat the oil and toss in the mustard seeds. When they splutter, add the ginger, green chillies and curry leaves. Fry for a minute and add the potatoes together with the rest of the ingredients. Cook uncovered on a low fire, stirring continuously, until all the ingredients are well blended.

Serve hot.

CURRIED PUMPKIN

Ingredients

250 gms pumpkin
1 tsp cumin seeds
1/2"-piece ginger (minced)
1/2 cup water
2 tsps coriander powder
1/2 tsp turmeric powder
2 tomatoes (diced)
2 green chillies (minced)
2 tbsps melted ghee or oil
1 tbsp finely chopped coriander leaves
Salt and chilli powder to taste

Method
Peel and cut the pumpkin into small cubes.

Heat the ghee and toss in cumin seeds, green chillies and ginger. When cumin seeds splutter stir in the pumpkin. Fry for 5 minutes. Add the tomatoes together with seasoning and water. Cover and cook until the pumpkin is done.

Serve hot garnished with coriander leaves.

PUMPKIN WITH BENGAL GRAM

Ingredients

250 gms pumpkin
2 medium-sized tomatoes (diced)
1 tsp cumin seeds
1/2 cup water
2 tsps coriander powder
1/2 tsp turmeric powder
1/2 cup chana dal
2 green chillies (minced)
1/2"-piece ginger (minced)
2 tbsps melted ghee or oil
2 tbsps finely chopped coriander leaves
Salt and chilli powder to taste

Method
Peel and cut the pumpkin into small cubes. Wash and soak the chana dal in water for 1/2 hour.

Heat the ghee and toss in the green chillies, ginger and cumin seeds. When the cumin seeds splutter, add the tomatoes and cook covered until they turn soft. Stir in the pumpkin, dal, seasoning and water. Cover and cook until everything is done. Blend well.

Serve hot garnished with coriander leaves.

SAVOURY RIDGE GOURDS

Ingredients

250 gms ridge gourd	2 medium-sized onions (sliced)
2 medium-sized tomatoes (diced)	1/2"-piece ginger (ground)
	2 green chillies (ground)
2 tbsps melted ghee or oil	4 cloves garlic (ground)
1 tbsp finely chopped coriander leaves	2 tsps coriander powder
	1/2 tsp turmeric powder
1/4 tsp garam masala	Salt and chilli powder to taste

Method
Peel and cut the ridge gourd into small cubes.

Heat the ghee and lightly fry the onions. Add the ground ginger, green chillies and garlic and fry along with the onions. Stir in the tomatoes together with the ridge gourds and seasoning. Cook covered until the vegetable is done and very little water is left.

Serve hot garnished with coriander leaves.

RIDGE GOURDS WITH BENGAL GRAM

Ingredients

250 gms ridge gourds
2 medium-sized tomatoes (diced)
1/4 cup water
1 tsp cumin seeds
2 tsps coriander powder
1/4 tsp garam masala
1/2 cup chana dal
2 green chillies (minced)
2 tbsps melted ghee or oil
2 tbsps finely chopped coriander leaves
1/2 tsp turmeric powder
Salt and chilli powder to taste

Method
Peel and cut the ridge gourd into small cubes. Wash and soak the chana dal in water for 1/2 hour.

Heat the ghee and toss in the cumin seeds. When they splutter, wash and add the ridge gourd together with the green chillies, tomatoes, seasoning and water. Cook covered until everything is done. Blend well.

Serve hot garnished with coriander leaves.

FRIED WHITE GOURDS

Ingredients

8 medium-sized white gourds (scraped and sliced into rings)
1/2 tsp turmeric powder
1/2 tsp mango powder
1 tsp cumin seeds
6 tbsps oil
2 tbsps coriander powder
1/2 tsp chilli powder
Salt to taste

Method
Heat the oil and toss in the cumin seeds. When they splutter, wash and add the white gourds together with the rest of the ingredients. Cover and cook on a low fire, stirring occasionally, until the gourds are done.
Serve hot.

WHITE GOURDS WITH YOGHURT

Ingredients

4 medium-sized white gourds (scraped and cubed)
1 medium-sized potato (peeled and cubed)
2 tbsps melted ghee or oil
1"-piece ginger (minced)
2 green chillies (minced)
1/2 tsp turmeric powder
1/4 tsp garam masala
1 medium-sized carrot (scraped and cubed)
3 tbsps curd (beaten)
1 medium onion (sliced)
1 tbsp coriander powder
Salt and chilli powder to taste
1 tbsp finely chopped coriander leaves

Method
Combine the white gourds, carrot and potato. Add salt and sufficient water to cover them. Boil and set aside.
  Heat the ghee and saute the onion, ginger and green chillies. When the onions turn golden, add the curd together with the seasoning. Stir for a minute. Add the vegetables with 1/4 cup water and cook 5 minutes longer on a low fire.
  Serve hot garnished with coriander leaves.

WHITE GOURDS WITH LOTUS STEM

Ingredients

250 gms white gourds
4 medium-sized
 tomatoes (diced)
1 tsp cumin seeds
2 tbsps finely chopped
 coriander leaves
1/2 tsp turmeric powder
Salt and chilli powder to taste

250 gms lotus stem
1"-piece ginger (minced)
2 green chillies (minced)
3 cups water
2 tbsps ghee
2 tsps coriander powder
1/4 tsp garam masala
Oil for frying

Method
Wash and scrape the lotus stem. Cut them slanting into 1" thick slices and boil. Drain and set aside.

Scrape the white gourds, cut into halves, sprinkle with salt and set aside for 10 minutes. Deep fry on a low fire until they turn soft. Drain and set aside.

Heat 2 tbsps ghee and toss in the cumin seeds. When they splutter, add the ginger, green chillies and tomatoes; cover and cook until the tomatoes turn soft. Add water and seasoning. When the water comes to a boil, stir in the vegetables and cook 7 minutes longer.

Serve hot garnished with coriander leaves.

YAM KEEMA

Ingredients

250 gms yam
2 medium-sized tomatoes

2 medium-sized onions
 (minced)

(diced)
2 green chillies (minced)
2 tbsps coriander leaves (finely chopped)
1/2 tsp turmeric powder
1/2 tsp roasted cumin powder
1"-piece ginger (minced)
3 tbsps melted ghee
1/2 cup water
2 tsps coriander powder
1/2 tsp garam masala
Salt and chill powder to taste

Method
Peel and grate the yam. Parboil and drain.

Heat the ghee and fry the onions, ginger and green chillies to a golden colour. Add the yam and fry for 5 minutes. Stir in the tomatoes, 1/2 cup water, and the rest of the ingredients except coriander leaves. Cover and cook on a low fire, stirring occasionally, until the yam is sufficiently tender.

Serve hot garnished with coriander leaves.

FRIED YAM

Ingredients

250 gms yam
1/2 tsp chilli powder
1/2 tsp mango powder
Oil for frying
3 tsps coriander powder
1/2 tsp turmeric powder
Salt to taste

Method
Peel and cut the yam into medium-sized cubes. Wash, sprinkle with salt and set aside for 10 minutes.

Heat the oil and deep fry on a low fire until the yam pieces turn soft and pale golden in colour. Drain. When slightly cool, flatten and re-fry to a golden colour. Season and toss.

Serve hot.

YAM CUTLETS WITH YOGHURT

Ingredients

250 gms yam
1/2"-piece ginger (ground)
1/4 tsp garam masala
Salt and chilli powder to taste
1 cup yoghurt
2 green chillies (ground)
1/2 tsp roasted cumin powder
Oil for frying

Method
Peel and cut the yam into medium-sized cubes. Wash, sprinkle salt over them and set aside for 10 minutes. Heat the oil and deep fry on very low fire until the yam pieces turn soft and pale golden in colour. Drain and when slightly cool, flatten with your palm and set aside.

Beat the yoghurt well. Add the seasoning and mix. Arrange the fried yam pieces in a broad dish and pour the yoghurt over them.

Serve cold as a snack or side dish for lunch or dinner.

SAVOURY YAM

Ingredients

250 gms yam
2 medium-sized tomatoes (diced)
2 cups water
2 medium-sized onions (sliced)
Oil for frying
1-1/2 tbsps finely chopped coriander leaves

Grind to a paste
2 Kashmiri chillies
A small piece of turmeric
4 cloves garlic
1"-piece ginger
A small piece of cinnamon
1 tbsp grated coconut

1 tsp cumin seeds
Salt to taste

1 tsp coriander seeds

Method
Peel and cut the yam into medium-sized cubes. Wash, sprinkle salt over them and set aside for 10 minutes. Heat the oil and deep fry on a low fire until the yam pieces turn soft and pale golden in colour. Drain and set aside.

Heat 2 tbsps oil and saute the onions. Add the tomatoes and ground masala and fry for 5 minutes. Add the fried yam, water, salt and cook on a low fire until the yam is sufficiently tender and the gravy is thick.

Serve hot garnished with coriander leaves.

CRUNCHY YAM

Ingredients

250 gms yam
1 tsp lemon juice
2 tbsps gram flour
Salt and chilli powder to taste

1 tsp garam masala
2 tbsps rice (soaked or 1/2 hr and ground)
Oil for frying

Method
Peel and cut the yam into thin broad pieces. Boil the pieces in salted water. Drain and set aside.

Combine the rest of the ingredients, except the yam and oil. Beat the mixture well. Coat each yam piece with the mixture and deep fry to a golden colour. Drain.

Serve hot as a side dish or a snack with mint chutney or tomato ketchup.

11

MISCELLANEOUS VEGETABLES

UNDHIA (GUJARATI)

RADISH SPECIAL

FENUGREEK LEAVES BHAJEE

GREEN PEAS WITH PANEER

TURNIP HASH

SAVOURY URAD DAL WADIES

UNDHIA (GUJARATI)

Ingredients

300 gms tender papri
100 gms green peas
100 gms small brinjals
2 raw bananas
50 gms kandh
1 sprig fenugreek leaves (chopped fine)

100 gms papri beans
100 gms small potatoes
100 gms sweet potatoes
50 gms yam
$1\frac{1}{2}$ cups gram flour
Oil

Masala
Salt to taste
1 tsp mustard seeds
2"-piece ginger ground
2 tsps sugar
1 tsp turmeric powder
2 tsps garam masala

1/2 tsp asafoetida
8 green chillies (ground)
1 sprig coriander leaves (chopped fine)
1/2 coconut (grated)
1 tbsp sesame seeds

Method
Mix all the masalas except asafoetida and mustard seeds. Add 1/4 of the masala, gram flour, fenugreek leaves, a little oil and water and prepare a stiff dough. Make $1\frac{1}{2}$"-long rolls (muthias) and deep fry until light brown. Drain and set aside.

Slit the brinjals, potatoes and sweet potatoes into fours. Fill some of the masala mixture in them. Also cut the remaining vegetables. Heat 6 tbsps of oil in a large dekchi and toss in the asafoetida and mustard seeds. When they splutter, arrange a layer of half the quantity of papri beans and sprinkle a little masala. Over this arrange all the other vegetables and finally arrange a layer of the remaining papri beans. Sprinkle a little masala over every layer. Add a little water and cover the dekchi. Cook on a low fire shaking the pan occasionally. When the vegetables are half-cooked, add the muthias over the vegetables. Continue cooking in the same way until the vegetables are done.
   Serve hot.

RADISH SPECIAL

Ingredients

2 medium-radishes with leaves	1 tsp mustard seeds
1 tsp coriander powder	2 tbsps oil
1/2 tsp chilli powder	1/2 tsp turmeric powder
	Salt to taste

Method

Peel and cut the radishes and the leaves into small pieces. Heat the oil and toss in the mustard seeds. When they splutter, stir in the washed vegetable together with the turmeric powder and salt. Cook covered, stirring occasionally, until the vegetable turns tender. Season and cook uncovered 3 minutes longer, stirring often.

Serve hot.

FENUGREEK LEAVES BHAJEE

Ingredients

1 bunch fenugreek leaves (chopped)	1 medium-sized potato (peeled and cut into cubes)
A dash of asafoetida	2 tbsps oil
1 tsp coriander powder	1/2 tsp turmeric powder
1/2 tsp chilli powder	Salt to taste

Method
Heat the oil and add the asafoetida. Next wash and stir in the chopped fenugreek leaves and potatoes, together with the salt and turmeric powder. Cook covered on a low fire, stirring occasionally, until the vegetables are almost done and the water has dried up. Season and cook uncovered for 3 minutes, stirring often.

Serve hot.

GREEN PEAS WITH PANEER

Ingredients

200 gms green peas (shelled)
2 medium-sized onions (sliced)
1/2"-piece ginger (minced)
3 tbsps oil
1 tbsp finely chopped coriander leaves
1/4 tsp garam masala
10 cubes of paneer (fried)
2 medium-sized tomatoes (diced)
2 green chillies (minced)
2 cups water
1 tsp coriander powder
1/2 tsp turmeric powder
Salt and chilli powder to taste

Method
Heat the oil and fry the green chillies, ginger and onions to a pale golden colour. Add the tomatoes and fry. Wash and stir in the green peas, water and seasoning. Cook covered, stirring occasionally, until the peas are tender. Add the paneer and cook covered for 3 minutes.

Serve hot garnished with coriander leaves.

TURNIP HASH

Ingredients

200 gms turnips (peeled and cubed)
1 medium-sized tomato (diced)
1/2"-piece ginger (minced)
1/4 cup water
1/2 tsp turmeric powder
Salt and chilli powder to taste
2 medium-sized onions (minced)
2 green chillies (minced)
2 tbsps oil
1 tsp coriander powder
1/4 tsp garam masala
1 tbsp finely chopped coriander leaves

Method
Heat the oil and fry green chillies, ginger and onions to a pale golden colour. Add the tomatoes and fry. Wash and add the turnips, water and seasoning. Cook covered on a low fire until turnips are done. Mash with a fork.
Serve hot garnished with coriander leaves.

SAVOURY URAD DAL WADIES

Ingredients

3 medium-sized wadies (each broken into 4 pieces)
1 medium-sized white gourd (peeled and cubed)
1 medium-sized onion (sliced)
2 green chillies (minced)
2 tbsps finely chopped coriander leaves
1 medium-sized potato (peeled and cubed)
1 brinjal (cubed)
3 tbsps melted ghee or oil
2 medium-sized tomatoes (diced)
1/2"-piece ginger (minced)
2 tsps coriander powder
1/2 tsp turmeric powder

1/4 tsp garam masala 4 cups water
Salt and chilli powder to taste

Method
Heat the ghee and quickly fry the wadies to a red colour. Drain and boil in a little water until they are nearly soft. Set aside.

Heat the remaining ghee and fry the ginger, chillies and onion to a pale golden colour. Add the tomatoes and fry. Wash and stir in the vegetables and fry for 3 minutes. Add water, seasoning and wadies. Cook covered until the vegetables are done.

Serve hot garnished with coriander leaves.

12

STUFFED SURPRISES

General Stuffing

Stuffed Lady's Fingers

Stuffed Tomatoes

Stuffed Capsicums

Stuffed Cucumbers

Stuffed White Gourds

Stuffed Potatoes

Stuffed Brinjals

Stuffed Bitter gourds

STUFFED surprises are prepared by using whole vegetables, i.e., without cutting them into pieces, and then stuffing them. You can turn out delectable stuffed surprises from the following:
1. Lady's Fingers
2. Tomatoes
3. Capsicums
4. Cucumber
5. White Gourds
6. Potatoes
7. Brinjals
8. Bittergourds

Mostly, the stuffing remains the same. This has, therefore, been referred to below as the 'general stuffing'. However, in one or two cases, the general stuffing is used with a slight variation.

GENERAL STUFFING

Ingredients

4 medium-sized onions (washed and grated)
2 green chilles (minced)
2 tsps coriander powder
1/2 tsp garam masala
1 tbsp each of finely chopped mint and coriander leaves
Salt to taste

1 medium-sized potato (boiled and mashed)
1/2"-piece ginger (minced)
1 tsp each of turmeric, chilli and mango powder
4-6 tbsps oil
A dash of asafoetida

Method
Heat the oil and toss the asafoetida. Add the grated onion and fry to a light brown colour on a low fire. Stir in the mashed potato and the rest of the seasoning and fry for 2 to 3 minutes. Put the mint and coriander leaves and blend well.

STUFFED LADY'S FINGERS

Ingredients

300 gms lady's fingers   6 tbsps oil

Method
Wash the lady's fingers. Chop off the heads and ends and slit them lengthwise. Fill them tightly with the general stuffing, keeping about 1 tbsp of it aside.

Heat the oil in a skillet or a frying pan and add the stuffed lady's fingers. Sprinkle the remaining general stuffing and cover tightly with a lid. Allow the lady's fingers to cook on a low fire until done.

Stirring should be kept to a minimum, otherwise the lady's fingers will break.

STUFFED TOMATOES

Ingredients

300 gms half-ripe tomatoes   6 tbsps oil (approx)

Method
Wash the tomatoes and scoop out the seeds and pulp, keeping the outer shells intact. Blend the seeds and pulp with the general stuffing and stuff the tomatoes tightly with this mixture. If necessary, secure the tomatoes with a thread. Cook like lady's fingers, taking care not to break them while turning.

STUFFED CAPSICUMS

Ingredients

300 gms capsicums		8 tbsps oil

Method
Wash the capsicums and scoop out the seeds, keeping the outer shells intact. Discard the seeds and stuff the capsicums with the general stuffing. The method of cooking remains the same as for lady's fingers and tomatoes.

STUFFED CUCUMBERS

Ingredients

300 gms cucumbers		6 tbsps oil

Method
Peel the cucumbers and wash them. Make 2 slits and remove a piece lengthwise from one side of each cucumber. Fill them with the general stuffing, put back the removed pieces and fasten with a thread. Cook like lady's fingers.

STUFFED WHITE GOURDS

Ingredients

300 gms white gourds (small)   Oil for frying

Method
Scrape the white gourds, slit vertically into four from the top, keeping intact at the bottom and sprinkle salt on them. Keep aside for 5 minutes. Heat the oil and fry slightly. Drain and fill with the general stuffing. The method of cooking remains the same as for lady's fingers.

STUFFED POTATOES

Ingredients

300 gms small potatoes   6 tbsps oil

Method
Peel the potatoes, slit them vertically into four from the top, keeping intact at the bottom and sprinkle salt on them. Keep aside for 5 minutes and fill them with the general stuffing. The method of cooking remains the same as for lady's fingers.

STUFFED BRINJALS

Ingredients

300 gms brinjals (small, preferably without seeds)

6 tbsps oil

Method
Wash the brinjals, slit vertically into four, from the top, retaining the stalks. Fill tightly with the general stuffing and cook like lady's fingers.

STUFFED BITTER GOURDS

Ingredients

300 gms bitter gourds (large)
1 tbsp tamarind juice

Oil for frying
1 tbsp water

Method
Scrape the bitter gourds and slit them lengthwise, from one side only, scooping out the seeds. Sprinkle or rub salt into them and keep aside for 2 to 3 hours to remove their bitterness. Discard hard and red seeds. Wash and deep fry the bitter gourds to a golden colour. Drain and set aside.

Take the tender seeds, pound them a little and fry with the general stuffing. Blend well and fill the bitter gourds with this stuffing. Secure them with a thread. Add the tamarind juice and cook on a low fire until they become a little soft.

Stuffed Capsicums

Hamburgers

Dried Red Beans & Toast

Mint Chutney with Cutlets

13

FROM ODDS AND ENDS (LEFTOVERS)

- Mixed Vegetables Delight
- Hamburgers
- Palak Pakoras
- Palak Omelette
- Palak Alu
- Pakoras
- Mini Pakoras
- Samosas
- Vegetable Toast
- Wadas
- Patties
- Vegetable Rolls
- Pan Rolls
- Chapati Rolls
- Parathas
- Pulaos
- Curry

MASALA BREAD
LEFTOVER CURD
RICE PATTIES
PULAO
PORRIDGE
SWEET TOAST
BREAD PORRIDGE
BREAD ROLLS
BREADCRUMBS AND CROUTONS

From Odds and Ends

To HAVE leftovers is quite a frequent occurrence in the home. Of course, with high prices it is better to cook in measured quantities to reduce leftovers to a bare minimum.

It is common to find many people in a fix when they are down to the last potato or onion or a handful of dal. One can always get more, but with imagination and a little effort, delicious meals can be turned out with bits and pieces of leftovers.

To make cooked leftovers appear on the dining table in a different form at the next meal is an art in itself worth acquiring, as it will not only win you accolades but will also help in avoiding wastage of food. The art consists mainly in "eking out" dishes with suitable accompaniments.

MIXED VEGETABLE DELIGHT

If you have bits and pieces of raw vegetables, all you do is to brown an onion in oil, add 2 green chillies (minced), add bits and pieces of vegetables, etc., season with spices like coriander, chillies and garam masala powders and cook until done. Garnish with finely chopped coriander leaves.

HAMBURGERS

If you have leftover vegetables, make delicious cutlets by using fresh seasoning and place between hamburger buns along with a slice each of tomato and onion. Serve with a sauce and garnish with beet curls. (For cutlets, see chapter on 'Snacks').

PALAK PAKORAS

Take some gram flour, add salt, a pinch of soda-bicarbonate, leftover palak bhaji and just a little water and make a thick batter. Drop spoonfuls of this batter in smoking oil and deep fry until golden. Serve hot with chutney.

PALAK OMELETTE

Prepare a batter of gram flour and palak bhaji using the same ingredients as in palak pakoras. To this, also add one small finely chopped onion. Let the batter be of thinner consistency. Pour a little oil on a hot griddle, spread a ladleful of the batter evenly on it and pour oil on top. Fry for a minute or so, on a low fire and turn with a flat spatula. Remove when both sides are done. Spread a little sauce on the omelette and serve hot.

PALAK ALU

Take 2 or 3 potatoes, boil and cut into slices.

Cut a raw mango into tiny bits as also 2 green chillies and add to the leftover palak. Also add 1/4 cup of water and cook until the mango bits are soft. Mash the palak. Add potatoes, salt to taste, coriander powder, turmeric powder and garam masala. Blend well. Take 2 tablespoons of ghee; add a dash of asafoetida and 1 tsp cumin seeds. When the cumin seeds splutter, pour these into the vegetable.

From Odds and Ends

Left-over vegetables can be utilised to make the following delicacies:

PAKORAS

Prepare a batter of gram flour with water adding salt, a pinch of soda-bicarbonate, chopped green chillies and chopped coriander along with 1 tsp ghee. Add the leftover vegetables and/or fish, prawns (chopped) to the batter and blend well. Drop spoonfuls of the batter in hot oil and fry until golden. Serve hot with mint chutney or sauce.

MINI PAKORAS

Prepare a batter with leftover vegetables as for pakoras. Drop spoonfuls in hot oil and fry until light brown. Break into small pieces and fry these again until they turn golden. Drain and serve hot with mint chutney, sauce or tamarind chutney. Mini pakoras are more crisp.

SAMOSAS

Prepare a dough out of maida by adding salt, a little oil and water. Or you can prepare a dough of one part maida and one part semolina to which salt should be added. Take a little dough and roll out on a board into a round disc. Cut into two. Fold each portion in the shape of a cone by applying water on the sides and fill the cooked leftover vegetables to which fresh spices have been added. Seal the edges firmly by applying water. Deep fry until golden. Drain and serve with coriander chutney or tomato ketchup.

VEGETABLE TOAST

Take the sandwich toaster, spread a little ghee on one side and place a slice of bread on it. Spread a little of the cooked leftover vegetable (after checking for seasoning) on it. Cover with another slice. Spread a little ghee on top of the second slice. Close the toaster and hold it on a low fire until both sides are brown. Serve hot with chutney or sauce.

WADAS

Prepare a batter of gram flour with water, adding salt, a dash of soda-bicarbonate, chilli powder and set aside.
    Take a little oil, i.e., 2 or 3 tbsps in a frying pan, add mustard seeds and when they splutter, add curry leaves, a few pomegranate seeds and the leftover vegetables. Season with garam masala, pepper powder, salt (if necessary), coriander and mango powder. Blend well. Take a little of this mixture, flatten on your palm, dip in gram flour batter and deep fry until golden. Drain and serve hot with coconut or mint chutney.

PATTIES

Boil 2 or 3 potatoes, peel and mash. Add this to the leftover vegetables. Soak 2 slices of bread in water, squeeze and mix well with the vegetable mixture. Season with chopped green chillies, coriander, mango powder, garam masala powder and salt. Take a little of this mixture, flatten on your palm and shallow fry on a hot griddle. Drain and serve hot with mint chutney.

VEGETABLE ROLLS

Prepare a mixture, as in the case of patties, with potatoes, leftover vegetables and bread. Prepare finger-rolls and deep fry 3 or 4 at a time. Drain when golden and serve with chutney or sauce.

PAN ROLLS

Make a batter of 1 egg and maida to which salt has been added. The batter should be of thin consistency like the omelette. Put a little oil on a hot griddle and spread this batter with a ladle. Remove with a flat spatula. Please note that only one side should be cooked. Season the leftover vegetables with fresh spices and coriander leaves and place a little of this in the centre of the pan roll. Roll up and fold it up like an envelope.

The uncooked side should hold the vegetables. Seal the edges with egg and deep fry. Serve hot with ketchup.

CHAPATI ROLLS

Brown an onion, add spices, chopped coriander leaves together with the leftover vegetables. Blend well. Prepare a chapati, place a little of this mixture in the centre and roll it up. Secure the contents with a piece of thick thread and deep fry on a low fire. Drain and serve hot.

PARATHAS

Prepare a dough of wheat flour to which salt has been added. Roll out two equal-sized discs on a board. Place a little of the leftover vegetables on one disc, cover with the second disc and seal the sides by using water. Press the paratha lightly with your palm and bake on a hot griddle. Pour a little oil on the sides and fry until both sides turn brown. Serve with curd or pickles.

PULAOS

Prepare white rice (plain rice) and when it is almost done, add the leftover vegetables and season with spices. Garnish with fresh coriander, grated coconut and serve hot.

CURRY

Brown 2 chopped onions in a little oil, add 2 chopped tomatoes and saute. Add the leftover vegetables, a little water and season with spices. Cook for a few minutes and garnish with fresh coriander leaves.

MASALA BREAD

Take 4 slices of bread and cut them into 2" x 2" squares. Brown 2 onions in a little oil, add 2 chopped tomatoes and a little tamarind juice. Add the leftover vegetables, bread pieces and finely chopped coriander leaves. Season with spices and add a little water. Cook on a low fire until the bread pieces turn soft and no water is left.

LEFTOVER CURD

This can be used to make Dhoklas (see chapter on 'Snacks') and Gujarati Curry (see chapter on 'Curries').

RICE PATTIES

Mash the leftover rice and season. Apply a little oil on your palm and form round patties. Put a little oil on a hot griddle and shallow fry the patties until golden and crisp. Serve hot with chutney.

PULAO

Boil chopped French beans, carrots, potatoes and shelled peas, with a little salt. Take 2 tbsps ghee, add mustard seeds, and when they splutter, add the boiled vegetables and $1/2$ cup beaten curd. Add rice and cook for about 5 minutes on a low fire. Garnish with grated coconut and coriander leaves.

PORRIDGE

Take 2 cups of milk, add $2^1/_2$ tsps of sugar (or as required), 1 cardamom, a dash of saffron, 1 clove, 1/2 cup of leftover rice and boil until it becomes slightly thick. Serve piping hot.

SWEET TOAST

Make a syrup of sugar and set aside. Take a slice of bread, dip in milk (boiled and cooled to room temperature and without sugar) and deep fry until golden. Drain and immerse in the syrup. Remove from the syrup after 2 minutes and serve hot.

BREAD PORRIDGE

This can be prepared in the same manner as rice porridge. Rice is to be replaced by bread.

BREAD ROLLS

Boil peas, carrots, potatoes and French beans and season with salt and other spices. Also add finely chopped coriander and mint leaves. Take a slice of bread, dip it in salted water and squeeze out the water by pressing between your palms. Place a little of the vegetable mixture on half of the slice, fold the remaining half, crimp and seal the edges by pressing together. Deep fry until golden. Serve with ketchup or coriander chutney.

BREADCRUMBS AND CROUTONS

Leftover bread can be dried in the sun and turned into breadcrumbs by pounding it. These breadcrumbs can be used for making cutlets, rolls, patties and other items. Leftover bread can also be cut into small squares or rounds and deep fried for use in soups as a garnish.

14

SNACKS

Khandwi

Patra

Dhokla

Batata Poha

Savoury Peanuts

Salted Peanuts

Salted Almonds

Dried Red Beans on Toast

Idli

Sambar

Sada Dosa

Masala Dosa

Rava Idli

Uppama

Sago Treat

Chhole

Chhole on Bread

PATTIES
MOONG DAL TIKKIES
POTATO TIKKIES
SAMOSAS
CUTLETS
BARFI SAMOSA
BATATA WADAS
PAKORAS
BRINJAL PAKORAS
CAULIFLOWER PAKORAS
CAPSICUM PAKORAS
POTATO PAKORAS
TOMATO PAKORAS
WHITE GOURD PAKORAS
BREAD PAKORAS
TRICOLOUR BREAD PAKORAS
CABBAGE PAKORAS
BAKED EGG BURGERS

Snacks

KHANDWI

Ingredients

1 cup gram flour
2 cups water
1/2 tsp turmeric powder
1 tsp mustard seeds
3 tbsps finely chopped coriander leaves

1 cup sour curd
2 green chillies (minced)
2 tbsps oil
1/4 coconut (grated)
Salt to taste

Method
Beat the curd. Add the gram flour and water and blend well till there are no lumps. Add the green chillies, salt and turmeric. Pour into a saucepan and keep on a low fire. Boil the mixture until it becomes thick. Add 1 tsp oil, mix well and place a little of the mixture on a thali and if it comes off easily, the consistency is correct. Remove the mixture and quickly spread it into thin layers on the thalis with a spoon. When cool, cut into 1"-broad strips and roll up. Place the rolls in a serving dish. Heat the remaining oil, toss in the mustard seeds and when they splutter, pour over the khandwi rolls. Garnish with coriander leaves and grated coconut.

PATRA

Ingredients

6 arbi leaves
1 tsp chilli powder
2 cloves garlic (ground)
2 tbsps thick tamarind juice

2 cups gram flour
1/2 tsp garam masala
4 green chillies (ground)
1/4 coconut (grated)

3 tbsps finely chopped
   coriander leaves
Water as required

Oil for frying
Salt to taste

Method

To the gram flour, add all the ingredients except the arbi leaves, coconut and coriander leaves and make a thick batter. Wash the arbi leaves and string the backs.

    Spread one leaf, apply a thin layer of the gram flour batter on it, cover with another leaf and apply the batter and repeat with the third leaf. Roll the three leaves into a tight roll. Prepare another roll of 3 leaves in the same manner. Heat water in a large dekchi, place a sieve above the water and steam-cook the rolls. Cut into 1/4"-thick pieces and deep fry until crisp. Drain and garnish with coriander leaves and grated coconut.

    Instead of deep frying, you may follow this procedure, if you wish. Take 2/3 tbsp hot ghee in a frying pan, add 1 tsp mustard seeds. When they splutter, add the steamed patra pieces and lightly fry until they become crisp. Garnish with coriander leave and grated coconut.

DHOKLA

Ingredients

250 gms coarse rice flour
3 cups sour lassi or
   buttermilk
1 tsp mustard seeds
1 sprig coriander leaves
   (chopped fine)
Salt and chilli powder to taste

50 gms gram flour
1 tsp turmeric powder
1/2 coconut (grated)
5 tbsps melted ghee or oil
A dash of asafoetida
A dash of soda bicarb

Grind to paste
1"-piece ginger 2 green chillies

Method
Mix the rice flour and gram flour with warm lassi and make a smooth batter. Keep aside for 8 hours or till it ferments. Add salt, soda bicarb, turmeric powder, chilli powder and ground masala. Mix well. Spread the batter, about 1"-thick, on a greased thali and steam. Remove from the fire and cut into 2" x 2" squares.

Heat the ghee separately and add the asafoetida and mustard seeds. When the latter splutter, pour over the cut squares. Garnish with grated coconut and coriander leaves.

Serve hot with dhokla chutney.

BATATA POHA

Ingredients

2 cups beaten rice
1/4 cup shelled peas
2 green chillies (minced)
2 tbsps ghee or oil
3/4 cup grated coconut
1 lemon
A dash of asafoetida
Salt and chilli powder to taste

1 cup potato cubes
1"-piece ginger (minced)
1 tsp cumin seeds
2 tbsps finely chopped
   coriander leaves
1 tsp turmeric powder
1/2 cup water

Method
Heat the ghee and fry the asafoetida, cumin seeds, green chillies and ginger. Add the potatoes and peas together with 1/2 cup water. Also add turmeric powder, salt and chilli powder. Cook covered, stirring occasionally, until the vegetables are done. Wash the beaten rice and squeeze out the

excess water. Combine with the vegetables and cook on a low fire, stirring occasionally, until done. While serving, squeeze the lemon juice on the beaten rice. Garnish with coconut and coriander leaves.

SAVOURY PEANUTS

Ingredients

1/2 cup gram flour
1 cup roasted peanuts
Oil for frying
1 tsp chilli powder
Salt to taste
A dash of soda bicarb

Method
Prepare a batter with the gram flour (of medium consistency) adding salt, soda bicarb and chilli powder and set aside for 10 minutes.

Heat the oil to smoking point. Dip each peanut in batter and deep fry until brown. Drain.

Serve hot with coriander chutney.

SALTED PEANUTS

Ingredients

1/2 cup peanuts
2 tbsps water
1 tsp oil
Salt to taste

Snacks

Method
Heat the oil in a frying pan and toss in the peanuts. Place a tight-fitting lid over the pan and shake evenly over the fire for 5 minutes. Check in between. Keep covered and cool. The nuts will be roasted and their skins will peel off easily. Discard the skins and add the salt dissolved in water. Place on the fire and stir until water dries up.

Serve hot.

SALTED ALMONDS

These can be prepared in the same way as salted peanuts.

DRIED RED BEANS ON TOAST

Ingredients

1 cup red beans (boiled)
1"-piece ginger (minced)
1/2 tsp pepper powder
1/2 tsp garam masala
1 tbsp coriander leaves (finely chopped)
Salt to taste
A dash of asafoetida
2 large tomatoes (chopped)
1 tsp roasted cumin powder
1 tsp chilli powder
2 tbsps ghee or oil
4 slices of bread (lightly toasted)
1/2 cup water

Method
Heat the ghee, add the asafoetida and ginger and saute for a few seconds. Add the tomatoes and cover. Cook on a low fire until they turn soft. Mash with a fork and stir in the beans

along with the rest of the ingredients. Cook for 3 minutes. Serve hot on toast garnished with coriander leaves.

IDLI

Ingredients

2 cups rice 1 cup urad dal
Salt to taste

Method
Soak the rice and dal separately in water overnight. Grind the rice coarsely. Grind the dal to a fine paste. Mix them and make a thick batter. Add salt and keep aside for 12 hours to ferment. Grease the idli moulds, pour some batter into each mould and steam till done. If you are using a thali, make round idlis by using katoris.
    Serve hot with coconut chutney and/or sambar.

SAMBAR

Ingredients

1 cup tuvar dal 1 tbsp chana dal
1 tbsp urad dal 8 pieces of 3"-long drumsticks
2 medium-sized potatoes 1 medium-sized onion (sliced)
  (peeled) 1 medium-sized brinjal (cubed)
1 tsp mustard seeds 6 lady's fingers (cut into halves)
1 sprig curry leaves 2 tbsps oil
2 tbsps finely chopped 1/4 cup tamarind juice

Snacks

coriander leaves
Salt to taste

A dash of asafoetida

Roast and grind
3 Kashmiri chillies
1/2 tsp fenugreek seeds
2 tsps coriander seeds
A small piece of coconut
1/2 tsp cumin seeds
1/2 tsp mustard seeds
A small piece of turmeric

Method
Roast and grind the chana and urad dals finely. Add a little hot water and strain. Keep the strained liquid aside.

Add 6 cups of water and salt to the tuvar dal and boil until it turns soft. Mash it lightly. Add the vegetables, chana and urad dal liquid, ground paste, curry leaves and salt (if required). Cook on a low fire until the vegetables are done. Add the tamarind juice. Heat the oil separately, add the asafoetida and mustard seeds and when they splutter, pour over the sambar.

Serve hot with idlis or dosas.

SADA DOSA

Ingredients

2 cups rice
Ghee for frying
1 cup urad dal
Salt to taste

Method
Steep the dal and rice separately in water. Grind them separately to smooth pastes. Mix them together, add the salt and keep aside for 10-12 hours to ferment. Spread a ladleful evenly in a thin layer on a hot greased griddle and fry until both sides turn crisp and golden. Repeat with the remaining batter.

Serve hot with coconut chutney and sambar.

MASALA DOSA

Ingredients

Prepare dosas as described for the sada dosa. Prepare the filling as follows:

- 2 medium-sized potatoes (boiled and diced)
- 1 tsp urad dal
- 1/2 tsp turmeric powder
- 10 curry leaves
- Salt to taste
- 2 medium-sized onions (sliced)
- 2 green chillies (minced)
- 1/2 tsp mustard seeds
- 1 tsp chilli powder
- 2 tbsps oil

Method

Heat the oil, add the mustard seeds, dal and curry leaves. When the mustard seeds splutter, add the onions and green chillies and fry them lightly. Add the potatoes and seasoning. Cook on a high flame for 3 minutes, stirring continuously.

On each dosa, place 2 tbsps of the filling in the centre, fold over both the sides and serve immediately with coconut chutney and sambar.

RAVA IDLI

Idlis can also be prepared using rava.

Ingredients

- 1 cup urad dal
- 2 green chillies (minced)
- 10 curry leaves
- 2 tbsps cashewnuts (broken into small bits)
- Salt to taste
- 2 cups rava
- 1 tsp mustard seeds
- 1 tsp chana dal
- 2 tbsps oil
- Juice of 1 lemon

Method

Soak the urad dal in water overnight. Next morning grind it to a very fine paste. Mix with the rava and make into a thick batter. Stir in the salt. Keep the batter aside for 6 to 8 hours to ferment.

Heat the oil in a frying pan and toss in the mustard seeds. When they splutter, add the remaining ingredients except the lemon juice. Pour these into the batter. Add the lemon juice and mix. Grease the idli moulds, pour some batter into each mould and steam until the idlis are cooked.

Serve hot with coconut chutney and sambar.

UPPAMA

Ingredients

2 cups semolina
1 tsp mustard seeds
3 Kashmiri chillies (broken into bits)
2 tbsps ghee
A dash of asafoetida
1 tbsp urad dal
15 curry leaves
4 cups water
1/2 cup cashewnuts (broken into small pieces)
Salt to taste

Method

Heat 1 tbsp ghee, fry the semolina lightly and set aside. Heat the remaining ghee, add the asafoetida and mustard seeds and when the latter splutter, add the dal, cashewnuts, Kashmiri chillies and curry leaves and fry. Stir in the semolina, water and salt. Cook on a low fire until all the water is absorbed.

Serve hot with coconut chutney.

SAGO TREAT

Ingredients

1 cup sago
2 green chillies (chopped)
1 tsp cumin seeds
3 tbsps melted ghee
1/3 cup grated coconut
1/3 cup peanuts without skin (coarsely pounded)
1 medium-sized potato (small cubes)
Salt to taste

Method
Wash, drain and spread the sago in a broad vessel. After 2 hours, mix it with peanuts, green chillies and salt. Keep aside.

Heat the ghee and add the cumin seeds. When they splutter, add the potato cubes. Cover and fry until they are half cooked. Stir in the sago and peanut mixture. Cover and cook on a low fire, stirring occasionally, until the sago is ready. Garnish with grated coconut.

CHHOLE

Ingredients

250 gms Kabuli chana
2 green chillies
1"-piece ginger (minced)
3 tbsps melted ghee
4 tsps coriander powder
1 tsp chilli powder
3 tbsps tamarind juice
A dash of soda bicarb
Salt to taste
3 medium-sized onions (sliced)
4 cloves garlic (minced)
2 medium tomatoes (diced)
5 cups water
1/2 tsp turmeric powder
1 tsp garam masala
1 tbsp each of finely chopped mint and coriander leaves

Method
Soak the Kabuli chana in water overnight.
Pressure cook with salt, soda bicarb and 5 cups water. Keep aside.
Heat the ghee and fry the green chillies, ginger, garlic and 2 onions. Add the tomatoes and cook. Stir in the chana along with the water used to boil them. Add the rest of the ingredients except the mint and coriander leaves. Mash a few chanas to make the gravy thick. Cook on a low fire for 5 minutes.
Serve hot garnished with mint, coriander leaves and onion rings.

CHHOLE ON BREAD

Chhole should be prepared as given in the above recipe.
Place a slice of bread in a plate and pour a ladleful or more of chhole on it. Garnish with onion. If desired, serve 1 tsp coriander chutney with each slice of bread.

PATTIES

Ingredients

4 medium-sized potatoes (boiled and mashed)	1/4 cup peas (shelled and boiled)
2 green chillies (minced)	1/4 cup chana dal (boiled)
4 slices of bread (soaked in water, squeezed and mashed)	2 tsps coriander powder
	1 tsp chilli powder
	1/2 tsp garam masala
Oil for frying	Salt to taste

Method

Add the salt and mashed bread to the potatoes. Mix the peas and chana dal with the rest of the ingredients. Divide the potato mixture and the other mixture into equal portions. Flatten a portion of the potato mixture in the palm, place a portion of peas and chana dal mixture on it and cover with the potato mixture. Shallow fry on a hot griddle until golden. Drain.

Serve hot with coriander chutney. Chhole and patties can also be served together.

MOONG DAL TIKKIES

Ingredients

1 cup moong dal with skin
3 cloves garlic (minced)
1 tsp chilli powder
2 tsps coriander powder
1/2 tsp garam masala
1 tbsp gram flour
Oil for frying

1"-piece ginger (minced)
2 green chillies (minced)
1/2 tsp dry mango powder
1/2 tsp turmeric powder
1 tsp melted ghee
Salt to taste

Method

Soak the moong dal in water for at least 4 hours. Rub it with fingers and remove some of the skin. Drain and grind it coarsely. Stir in the rest of the ingredients. Take two tablespoons of the mixture, flatten on your palm and form round tikkies. Deep fry until golden in colour. Drain.

Serve hot with coriander chutney.

POTATO TIKKIES

Ingredients

4 large potatoes (boiled and mashed)
6 slices of bread
1 tsp chilli powder
1/2 tsp pepper powder
1/2 tsp garam masala
Salt to taste
3 green chillies (minced)
1/4 cup finely chopped mint and coriander leaves
3 tsps coriander powder
1/2 tsp turmeric powder
1/2 tsp mango powder
Oil for frying

Method
Soak the bread in water. Squeeze and mix it with the potatoes along with the rest of the ingredients. Take a little of the mixture, flatten on the palm and form round tikkies. Deep fry until golden. Drain.
   Serve hot with mint and coriander chutney.

SAMOSAS

Ingredients

1 cup refined flour
1/2 cup shelled peas (boiled)
2 tbsps cashewnuts (broken into small pieces)
1 tbsp each of mint and coriander leaves
1/2 tsp garam masala
1/2 tsp mango powder
Water as required
4 medium potatoes (boiled and cubed)
2 tbsps raisins (washed)
2 green chillies (minced)
3 tsps coriander powder
1 tsp chilli powder
1/2 tsp turmeric powder
Salt to taste
Oil for frying

Method

Add the salt and 2 tbsps oil to the maida and rub with fingers. Add a little water and prepare a stiff dough. Set aside.

Heat 3 tbsps oil and add the green chillies and cashewnuts. Fry them lightly and stir in the rest of the ingredients. Fry for 5 minutes until they are well blended. Keep aside.

Take small portions of the dough and roll out into thin, round discs. Cut each disc into two, so that each portion looks like a semi-circle. Apply a little water on the edges and shape each semi-circle into a cone with the top open. take 1 tbsp of the vegetable mixture, place it in the cone and seal the edges firmly. Deep fry until golden. Drain.

Serve hot with mint and coriander chutney or tomato ketchup.

CUTLETS

Ingredients

- 2 medium-sized potatoes (cubed)
- 1 medium-sized carrot (small cubes)
- 3/4 cup breadcrumbs
- 1 tsp gram flour
- 2 tsps chilli powder
- 1/2 tsp turmeric powder
- 1/2 tsp dry mango powder
- Salt to taste
- 1 beetroot (peeled and chopped)
- 1/4 cup shelled peas
- 1/4 cup cabbage (shredded)
- 1/4 cup French beans (shredded)
- 1 tbsp each of finely chopped mint and coriander leaves
- 1 tsp pepper powder
- 1/2 tsp garam masala
- 3 tsps coriander powder
- Oil for frying

Method

Boil all the vegetables. Drain and stir in the rest of the ingredients. Blend well and form into oblong shapes on your palm and deep fry until golden. Drain.

Serve hot with mint chutney or tomato ketchup.

BARFI SAMOSA

Ingredients

1 cup refined flour
Salt to taste
Water as required

250 gms barfi
Oil for frying

Method
Add salt and 2 tbsps oil to the maida and rub with fingers. Add a little water and prepare a stiff dough. Take small portions of the dough and roll out into thin, round discs. Cut each disc into two, so that each portion looks like a semi-circle. Apply a little water on the edges of the semi-circle and form into a cone with the top open. Take small helpings of the barfi, place in the cone and seal the edges firmly. Deep fry until golden. Drain.
Serve hot.

BATATA WADAS

Ingredients

1 cup gram flour
12 curry leaves
2 green chillies (minced)
2 tbsps finely chopped
 coriander leaves
1/2 tsp turmeric powder
1/2 tsp mango powder
Salt and chilli powder to taste
A dash of soda bicarb

4 medium-sized potatoes
 (boiled, peeled and coarsely
 mashed)
1 tsp mustard seeds
2 tsps coriander powder
1/4 tsp garam masala
Oil of frying
Water as required

Method
Add the salt, soda bicarb and water to the gram flour, and prepare a batter of medium consistency. Set aside.

Heat 3 tbsps of oil and toss in the mustard seeds. When they splutter, add the curry leaves and green chillies. Thereafter, stir in the potatoes together with the remaining ingredients and fry for 5 minutes, stirring often. Remove from the fire, cool and form into round balls. Dip each ball in the gram flour batter and deep fry to a golden colour. Drain.

Serve hot with mint or coconut chutney.

PAKORAS

There are several types of pakoras one can make.

Batter for Pakoras

Ingredients

1 cup gram flour
A dash of soda bicarb
Salt and chilli powder to taste
1 tsp ghee
A dash of asafoetida

Method
Mix all the above ingredients and prepare a batter of medium consistency. Test for lightness by dropping 1 tsp in a glass of water. If it floats, it is ready for use.

Snacks

BRINJAL PAKORAS

Ingredients

2 medium-sized brinjals
A dash of soda bicarb
Salt and chilli powder to taste
Oil for frying

Method

Cut the brinjals into 1/3"-thick slices. Score them criss-cross on both the sides. Wash and sprinkle salt, chilli powder and soda bicarb. Set aside for 5 minutes.

Heat the oil, dip each brinjal slice in the gram flour batter and deep fry until golden. Drain.

Serve hot with mint chutney or tomato sauce.

CAULIFLOWER PAKORAS

Ingredients

1 small cauliflower cut into florets
Oil for frying
Salt and chilli powder to taste
A dash of soda bicarb

Method

Wash the florets. Sprinkle them with salt, chilli powder and soda bicarb. Set aside for 10 minutes. Heat the oil, dip each piece into the gram flour batter and deep fry until golden. Drain.

Serve hot with mint chutney or tomato sauce.

CAPSICUM PAKORAS

Ingredients

4 capsicums (cut into halves through the stalk)
Salt and chilli powder to taste
Oil for frying

1 potato (boiled)
1/4 cup shelled green peas (boiled)

Method
Mash the potatoes and green peas. Season. Take a little of this mixture and fill the hollow of each capsicum piece. Carefully dip the portion with the potato mixture in the gram flour batter and deep fry until golden. Drain.
    Serve immediately with chutney or sauce.

POTATO PAKORAS

Ingredients

2 medium-sized potatoes
A pinch of soda-bicarb

Salt and chilli powder to taste
Oil for frying

Method
Peel and cut the potatoes into 1/8"-thin slices. Sprinkle salt, chilli powder and soda bicarb. Set aside for 10 minutes.
    Heat the oil, dip each potato slice in the gram flour batter and deep fry until golden. Drain.
    Serve hot with chutney or sauce.

TOMATO PAKORAS

Ingredients

3 red tomatoes
Oil for frying
Salt and chilli powder to taste

Method
Wash and cut the tomatoes into thin rings. Sprinkle salt and chilli powder and set aside for 5 minutes.

Heat the oil, dip each tomato ring in gram flour batter and deep fry until golden. Drain.

Serve hot with chutney.

WHITE GOURD PAKORAS

Ingredients

3 white gourds
A dash of soda bicarb
Salt and chilli powder to taste
Oil for frying

Method
Scrape and cut the white gourds into thin slices. Sprinkle salt, chilli powder and soda bicarb over them. Set aside for 5 minutes.

Heat the oil, dip each slice into gram flour batter and deep fry to a golden colour. Drain.

Serve hot with chutney or sauce.

BREAD PAKORAS

Ingredients

3 slices of bread
Salt and chilli powder to taste
1/2 cup tamarind juice
Oil for frying

Method

Cut each slice of bread into four pieces. Add the salt and chilli powder to the tamarind juice.

Heat the oil. Dip each bread piece in tamarind juice, then in gram flour batter and deep fry until golden. Drain.

Serve hot with chutney or tomato ketchup.

TRICOLOUR BREAD PAKORAS

Ingredients

4 slices of bread
1 tbsp tomato sauce
Oil for frying
1 tbsp mint chutney
1 tbsp butter

Method

Apply the mint chutney to one slice of bread. Cover with the second slice. Apply the tomato sauce to the top of the second slice. Cover with the third slice. Apply butter to the third slice. Cover with the fourth slice. Press the four slices together. Hold them carefully, dip in gram flour batter and deep fry until golden. Drain and cut into four pieces.

Serve hot with chutney.

CABBAGE PAKORAS

The method here is slightly different. The gram flour batter used in other pakoras is not necessary.

Ingredients

1 cup shredded cabbage
1/4 cup fresh curd
1 tbsp finely chopped coriander leaves
Soda bicarb (a pinch)
Oil for frying
1/2 cup gram flour
1/2 tsp pomegranate seeds, coarsely powdered
Salt and chilli powder to taste
A dash of Asafoetida

Method
Combine all the ingredients and form a thick batter. Use a little water if the curd is insufficient to prepare the batter.

Heat the oil, drop spoonfuls of the batter and deep fry to a golden colour. Drain.

Serve hot with chutney or sauce.

BAKED EGG BURGERS

Ingredients

6 hamburger rolls
2 tbsps butter (unmelted)
3 tsps cheese (grated)
4 tbsps butter (melted)
6 eggs
Salt to taste

Method
Remove the centres of the rolls. Bake the centres at 325°F in an oven. Crumble and keep the crumbs aside.

Rub the bread shells from inside as well as outside with melted butter. Sprinkle the cheese and break an egg directly in each bread shell. Add salt. Sprinkle the toasted breadcrumbs, and dot with unmelted butter. Bake at 325°F for 15 to 20 minutes.

Serve hot.

15

CHUTNEYS

Dosa Chutney

Dhokla Chutney

Onion Chutney

Mint Chutney

Coconut Chutney

DOSA CHUTNEY

Ingredients

1/4 coconut
4 green chillies
2 Kashmiri chillies
   (broken into two)
Salt to taste

1 tbsp urad dal (fried)
1/2"-piece ginger
1/2 tsp mustard seeds
1 tsp oil
Tamarind juice (as required)

Method
Grind to a paste the coconut, urad dal, green chillies and ginger. Heat the oil and fry the mustard seeds and Kashmiri chillies. Add to the ground chutney. Season with salt and tamarind juice.

DHOKLA CHUTNEY

Ingredients

1/2 cup roasted chickpeas
1 small sprig fresh coriander
1/4 tsp sugar
Lemon juice (as required)

1/2 cup groundnuts
4 green chillies
Salt to taste

Method
Grind the chickpeas, groundnuts, fresh coriander, green chillies and sugar. Season with salt and lemon juice.

ONION CHUTNEY

Ingredients

4 onions
3 green chillies
Salt to taste
Tamarind juice (as required)

1"-piece ginger
2 tbsps chopped coriander leaves

Method
Grind the onions, ginger, green chillies and coriander leaves. Season with salt and tamarind juice.

MINT CHUTNEY

Ingredients

1 sprig mint leaves
3 onions
Salt to taste

1 sprig coriander leaves
8 green chillies
Tamarind juice (as required)

Method
Grind the green chillies and onions separately. Set aside. Then grind the mint and coriander leaves. Combine these with green chillies and onions. Season with salt and tamarind juice.

COCONUT CHUTNEY

Ingredients

1/2 coconut
4 green chillies
Salt to taste

2 tbsps chopped coriander leaves
Tamarind juice (as required)

Method
Grind the coconut, coriander leaves and green chillies to a fine paste. Season with salt and tamarind juice.

16

DESSERTS

Carrot Cake

Falooda Ice-cream

Sponge Cake Delight

Punjabi Kulfi

China Grass

Rabri with Crushed Ice

Dry Fruit Whip

Pink Apple Whip

Banana Boats

Apple Basket

CARROT CAKE

Ingredients

500 gms dates (seeds removed and sliced)
1 coconut (grated)
2 tbsps honey

1 kg carrots (scraped and grated, water squeezed out)

Method
Mix well half the dates, half coconut and the entire grated carrots. Take a pudding bowl and press this mixture in it. This forms the first layer. Mix the remaining half coconut with honey and spread on the first layer. Decorate with the remaining dates and place in the refrigerator till firm and chilled.
 Cut into slices and serve.

FALOODA ICE-CREAM

Ingredients

50 gms Chinese falooda (fine variety)
1 slab pista ice-cream (readymade)
Crushed ice

2 cups milk
2 tbsps sugar
Sugar to taste
A little rose water

Method
Boil the falooda in water until it is nearly cooked. Drain out the water leaving only 1 tbsp and continue cooking on low fire

after adding sugar, until the falooda turns tender and a little syrupy liquid remains. Set aside.

Add 2 tbsps sugar to the milk and cook on a low fire until it is reduced to half. This is called 'rabri'. Set aside.

Serve in ice-cream cups by putting a little falooda first, then 'rabri' and finally the ice-cream. Sprinkle rose water and add the crushed ice.

SPONGE CAKE DELIGHT

Ingredients

1 sponge cake
1 orange
1 apple
1/2 cup custard powder
2 tbsps sugar
2 chikoos
2 bananas
1/2 packet raspberry jelly crystals
2 cups milk

Method
Prepare the jelly as per instructions on the packet and set. Keep 1/2 cup milk for sprinkling on the cake. Now prepare the custard. Heat $1\frac{1}{4}$ cups milk and add the sugar. Mix 1/4 cup milk with the custard powder and add to the hot milk, stirring continuously for 2 minutes. Cool and chill in the refrigerator. Peel and cut all the fruits into small pieces. Mix and set aside.

Cut the cake into three layers. Take the first layer, sprinkle a little milk over it. Then spread the custard, fruits and finally the jelly. Cover these with the second layer of cake. Cover the second layer with the same ingredients, i.e., first milk, then custard, fruits and lastly jelly. Cover these with the third layer of cake. Now place the cake with the filling in the refrigerator.

Cut and serve when chilled.

PUNJABI KULFI

Ingredients

1 litre full cream milk
2 cardamoms
Sugar to taste
A dash of saffron

2 tsps cornflour
10 almonds (blanched and sliced)

Method
Add the sugar to the milk and boil. Mix the cornflour in a little cold water and add to the boiling milk. Stir continuously for a minute. Dissolve saffron in a little warm milk and add to the boiling milk together with the cardamoms and almonds. Continue to cook on a low fire until it is reduced to half its quantity. Remove from the fire. Cool and pour into individual kulfi moulds. Screw on the lids and place in the freezer.
When set, serve in plates or wafer cones.

CHINA GRASS

Ingredients

4 cups full cream milk
4 tbsps china grass
    (chopped fine)

6 tbsps sugar
2 tbsps pistachio nuts
    (chopped fine)

Method
Place the milk on the fire. When it comes to a boil, add the china grass and continue cooking on a low fire, stirring

occasionally until the china grass dissolves. Add the sugar and continue to cook until the milk is reduced to 3/4 its original quantity. Cool. Pour into individual dessert cups, sprinkle pistachio nuts in each and place in the refrigerator.

Serve when set.

RABRI WITH CRUSHED ICE

Ingredients

2 cups full cream milk
2 cardamoms (pounded)
A dash of saffron (kesar)
Crushed ice

2 tbsps sugar
1 tbsp pistachio nuts (chopped fine)

Method
Dissolve the saffron in a little warm milk. Place 2 cups of milk on fire. Stir in all the ingredients except the pistachio nuts and leave on a low fire until the milk is reduced to half of its original quantity. Stir in the pistachio nuts and blend.

Chill and serve in individual dessert cups with crushed ice.

DRY FRUIT WHIP

Ingredients

1 cup mixed dry fruits
    (dates, figs, raisins, apricots)

1 cup water
1/4 grated coconut
1 tsp honey

Method
Wash and chop the dry fruits. Add water and honey and set aside for 1 hour. Blend well in a mixer and pour into small glasses. Top with grated coconut and place in the refrigerator. It will turn into a jelly like consistency. As it is very rich, only small quantities should be served.

PINK APPLE WHIP

Ingredients

1 medium apple (small cubes)
1 tbsp beetroot juice
A dash of honey
1 cup pineapple juice
Chopped celery (optional)
A little powdered cinnamon

Method
Combine the apple, beetroot and pineapple juice and celery. Celery has been included to give a tangy flavour. Pour into small glasses and chill. Serve topped with honey and cinnamon powder.

BANANA BOATS

Ingredients

4 bananas
3/4 cup halved black grapes
8 toothpicks
3/4 cup chopped walnuts
8 triangular pieces of paper
(any colour)

Desserts

Method
Peel and split the bananas into halves. Sprinkle walnuts on each half. Garnish with halved grapes. For a sail, glue a triangular piece of paper to each toothpick and put one such toothpick into each halved banana. If desired, use some salad dressing.

APPLE BASKET

Ingredients

4 medium-sized apples
1/4 cup pineapple cubes
1 tsp honey or sugar
1/4 cup seedless grapes
1/4 cup orange slices

Method
Wash the apples and slice off a piece from the top of each apple. Scoop out 2/3 pulp from each without damaging the outer skin. Combine the scooped out apple pulp with the rest of the fruits and honey. Fill the apples with the fruit mixture. The apple top may be used as a handle.

17

JAMS AND MARMALADES

ORANGE MARMALADE

MANGO MARMALADE

GREEN MANGO JAM

RIPE MANGO JAM

TOMATO JAM

RASPBERRY JAM

BANANA JAM

Sponge Cake Delight

Pink Apple Whip

Tomato Jam

Lemon Squash

ORANGE MARMALADE

Peel and extract the juice of a few oranges. Strain and measure the juice. If it is 2 cups, take 2 cups of sugar and boil together until a thick syrup is formed. Keep removing the scum that will form on the surface. Cool to room temperature and bottle.

Soak peels in salt water for 2 days. Drain and boil in fresh water until they turn tender. Drain and put them in cold water. Scrape the white pith from the peels. Wipe and cut them into thin short strips. Measure the peel and take an equal quantity of sugar and water and boil until a thick syrup is formed. Add the bottled syrup prepared 2 days earlier and simmer until the marmalade consistency is obtained.

MANGO MARMALADE

Ingredients

1 cup pulp of green mangoes   2 cups sugar

Pare and grate the green mangoes. For 1 cup pulp, add 2 cups of sugar and cook on a low fire. Remove the scum that will be formed. When it thickens to the marmalade consistency, cool to room temperature, pour into sterilised bottles and cork.

GREEN MANGO JAM

Pare and cut the green mangoes into pieces. Add water just sufficient to cover them and cook on a low fire until the mangoes turn soft. Mash and strain. Measure the quantity of pulp. If it is one cup, add 2 cups sugar. Simmer the mixture until it reaches the jam consistency. Cool to room temperature, pour into sterilised bottles and cork them.

RIPE MANGO JAM

Take fully ripe mangoes. Peel and cut them into pieces. Reduce them to a pulp. Measure the pulp. If it is one cup, take 3/4 cup sugar and 1/4 tsp citric acid. Mix well and simmer till the jam consistency is reached. Cool, pour into sterilised bottles and cork them.

TOMATO JAM

Add 1/4 cup water to 4 red tomatoes and boil until they turn soft. Mash and strain. Measure the pulp. If it is 1 cup, add 3/4 cup sugar and simmer until it reaches the jam consistency. Cool, pour into sterilised bottles and cork them.

Jams and Marmalades

RASPBERRY JAM

Remove the seeds and measure the chopped berries. For 1 cup, add 3/4 cup sugar and simmer until it reaches the jam consistency. Cool, pour into sterilised bottles and cork them.

BANANA JAM

Take fully ripe bananas and mash them. Measure the pulp and for every 1 cup add 3/4 cup sugar and 1/4 tsp citric acid. Simmer until the bananas reach the jam consistency. Cool, pour into sterilised bottles and cork them.

18

SQUASHES AND SYRUPS

Lemon Squash

Pineapple Squash

Orange Squash

Sweet Lime Squash

Ripe Mango Squash

Raspberry Syrup

Rose Syrup

Mogra Syrup

Sandalwood Syrup

Orange Syrup

LEMON SQUASH

Wash the lemons and extract the juice. Measure the quantity of juice. For one cup, take 2-1/2 cups sugar and 3/4 cup water. Mix the sugar and water and boil. When the sugar dissolves, stir in 1 tbsp milk and boil. Remove the scum that forms on the surface. As soon as the syrup turns a little thick, remove from the fire, strain and cool to room temperature. Then add the lemon juice, a little lemon essence and yellow colour. For preserving, stir in $1/4$ tsp citric acid. Transfer into sterilised bottles and cork them.

PINEAPPLE SQUASH

Peel, core and slice a pineapple. Remove the core and cut into small pieces. Boil the pieces in a little water till soft, rub and pass through a sieve. Measure the juice. For one cup, take $1 1/4$ cups sugar and $3/4$ cup water. Add the sugar to the water and place on fire. When the sugar dissolves, add 1 tbsp milk and boil. Remove the scum that forms on the surface. As soon as the syrup turns a little thick, remove from the fire, strain and cool to room temperature. Then add the pineapple juice, a little pineapple essence and yellow colour. For preserving, stir in $1/2$ tsp citric acid. Transfer into sterilised bottles and cork them.

ORANGE SQUASH

Peel oranges and extract their juice. Measure the juice. For one cup, take $1\frac{1}{4}$ cups sugar and $\frac{3}{4}$ cup water. Cook the sugar and water together. When the sugar dissolves, stir in 1 tbsp milk and boil. Remove the scum that forms on the surface. As soon as the syrup turns a little thick, remove from the fire, strain and cool to room temperature. Then add the orange juice, a little orange essence and orange colour. For preserving, stir in $\frac{1}{2}$ tsp citric acid. Transfer into sterilised bottles and cork them.

SWEET LIME SQUASH

Peel sweet limes and extract the juice. Measure the juice. For one cup, take $1\frac{1}{4}$ cups sugar and $\frac{3}{4}$ cup water. Cook the sugar and water together. When the sugar dissolves, stir in 1 tbsp milk and boil. Remove the scum that forms on the surface. As soon as the syrup turns a little thick, remove from the fire, strain and cool to room temperature. Then add the sweet lime juice, a little yellow colour and 1/2 tsp citric acid. Mix well, transfer into sterilised bottles and cork them.

RIPE MANGO SQUASH

Wash and peel the mangoes. Stone, dice and reduce to pulp. Measure the pulp. For one cup of pulp, take 1 cup each of sugar and water. Cook sugar and water together. When the sugar dissolves, add 1 tbsp milk and boil. Remove the scum that forms on the surface. As soon as the syrup turns a little thick, remove from the fire, strain and cool to room temperature. Then add the mango pulp, a little mango essence and yellow colour. For preserving, stir in 1 tsp citric acid. Transfer into sterilised bottles and cork them.

RASPBERRY SYRUP

Take 2 cups each of sugar and water, mix and place on the fire. When the sugar dissolves, add 1 tbsp milk and boil. Remove the scum that forms on the surface. When the syrup is sufficiently thick, remove from the fire, strain and cool to room temperature. Stir in the raspberry essence and cochineal colour. Transfer into sterilised bottles and cork them.

ROSE SYRUP

Take 2 cups each of sugar and water and boil them together. When the sugar dissolves, add 1 tbsp milk and boil again. Remove the scum that forms on the surface. When the syrup is sufficiently thick, remove from the fire, strain and cool to room temperature. Stir in the rose essence and cochineal colour. Transfer into sterilised bottles and cork them.

MOGRA SYRUP

Take 2 cups each of sugar and water and boil them together. When the sugar dissolves, add 1 tbsp milk and boil again. Remove the scum that forms on the surface. When the syrup is sufficiently thick, remove from the fire and stir in 3/4 cup fresh mogra flowers. Cover the dekchi and place a heavy weight on it. Keep aside for at least 3 hours. Strain and add some tiny bits of silver foil. Transfer into sterilised bottles and cork.

SANDALWOOD SYRUP

Take 2 cups each of sugar and water and boil them together. When the sugar dissolves, add 1 tbsp milk and boil again. Remove the scum that forms on the surface. Stir in 2 tbsps sandalwood powder and boil until the syrup turns sufficiently thick. Remove from the fire and strain. Cool and stir in yellow colour. Transfer into sterilised bottles and cork.

ORANGE SYRUP

Take 2 cups each of sugar and water and cook together. When the sugar dissolves, add 1 tbsp milk and boil. Discard the scum that forms on the surface. When the syrup is sufficiently thick, remove from the fire, strain and cool. Stir in some orange essence and orange colour. Pour into sterilised bottles and cork them.

19

HANDY HINTS

1. To peel apples faster use a potato peeler.
2. To add taste and eye appeal to fresh lemon juice, add a drop of rose or raspberry essence.
3. Always ensure that the frying pan is dry before pouring oil into it to avoid spluttering.
4. To determine whether the batter for pakoras is perfect, pour 1/2 tsp in a bowl of water. If it floats, it is done. Otherwise, it needs further beating.
5. After extracting juice from lemons, save the skins to rub over hands or to clean pressure cooker and other utensils.
6. To prevent discolouration of apple slices, sprinkle them with lemon juice or salt.
7. To stone raisins quickly, rub a little butter on the fingers.
8. Your bottle of honey will not attract ants if you keep it in a container filled with water.
9. To keep ants at bay, sprinkle turmeric powder in the vicinity.
10. When making syrups, always add about one tablespoon of milk while cooking, to remove dirt.
11. If you require tamarind juice immediately, boil it with a little water instead of soaking it in cold water.
12. Your chapatis will remain hot for some time if you keep them in a container and place the latter on the hot tawa after you finish preparing them.

13. To preserve spices, keep a piece of asafoetida in the container.
14. Lemon juice added to pulaos will help to keep the rice grains separate and prevent formation of lumps.
15. Food colouring added to pulaos makes them look attractive.
16. Worms and insects will not attack lentils if you rub a little castor oil on them.
17. To prevent beetroot from 'bleeding', always ensure that its skin is not damaged.
18. To obtain a deep red colour while making tomato delicacies, add a slice of cooked beetroot.
19. To avoid tears while chopping onions, stick a small pared potato to the end of the knife.
20. To prevent discolouration of potatoes and brinjals, cut them directly into a bowl of cold water.
21. To get the "Espresso" coffee effect, just churn the coffee (after addition of milk and sugar) with a churner and you will see froth on the surface.
22. To prevent patties from soaking oil, always fry a few at a time and also allow a gap of a minute or so between each batch so that the oil gets heated to the right temperature.
23. To quicken shaping of patties, etc., apply a little water to your hands.
24. While making coconut milk gravy, always leave the vessel uncovered, otherwise the milk will curdle and spoil the taste.
25. Your cooking time will be drastically reduced if you cook rice, dal and vegetable together in a pressure cooker.
26. Sago wafers will come off easily if you spoon them on a plastic sheet instead of a cloth sheet.
27. Insects will not attack your rava or sooji if you roast it a little before preserving in airtight containers.
28. Dry vegetables will cook faster if you keep them in a tightly covered pan on a low fire.
29. Lentils will cook faster if you add ghee and turmeric powder at the beginning.
30. If you add soda bicarb while boiling green vegetables, they will lose some of their important vitamins, especially vitamin C.

Handy Hints

31. Add a teaspoon of lemon juice or vinegar while boiling cauliflower, it will retain its whiteness.
32. Greens will remain fresh for a longer time if they are wrapped in polythene bags before placing them in the refrigerator.
33. Bitterness of cucumber can be removed by chopping off about $1/2$" from the two ends and rubbing the surfaces with the chopped pieces until froth is visible.
34. Bitterness of bitter gourds can be removed by rubbing them with salt, setting aside for 2 to 3 hours, then boiling in fresh water and rubbing the bitter gourds on a piece of cloth.

20

A BALANCED DIET

CARBOHYDRATES

FATS

PROTEINS

VITAMINS

MINERALS

A Balanced Diet

A BALANCED diet contains all the elements of food required by the body in the right proportion. Our body needs a variety of foods from which it obtains the necessary elements for growth and repair. Deficiency of any one of these adversely affects one's health. Among the elements of food carbohydrates, fats, proteins, vitamins and minerals are important and should form part of the daily diet.

CARBOHYDRATES

Called the instant energy giver, carbohydrates satisfy the daily energy requirements of the body. When in excess, they are converted into fats and kept as reserves.

Sources: dry fruits, honey, potatoes, sweet potatoes, rice, sago, sugar.

FATS

Fats give the most concentrated form of heat and energy, that is, twice as much as provided by an equal amount of carbohydrates. It takes longer to digest fats, so they should be taken in moderate quantities. Fats are more sustaining, giving heat and energy over extended periods.

Sources: oils, ghee, meat, fish, nuts, milk and milk products.

PROTEINS

Yet another essential nutrient of diet is protein. Proteins are body builders and are indispensable for physical and mental development. Children, pregnant women and nursing mothers should take a protein-rich diet. Deficiency of protein leads to stunted growth, low resistance to diseases and general debility.

Sources: eggs, meat, fish, milk and milk products, peas, beans, pulses.

VITAMINS

Vitamins are called the 'helpers' as they help other nutrients in keeping the body healthy.

VITAMIN A is necessary for healthy eyes and a healthy skin. It helps in the normal growth of the body. Its deficiency leads to night blindness, improper growth and a rough skin.

Sources: eggs, milk, fish, butter, cheese, spinach, cauliflower, drumsticks and its leaves, mango, papaya, carrots, dates, liver.

The **VITAMIN B-COMPLEX** group assists the body in its activity, digestion, functioning of the nervous system and maintaining a healthy heart. Deficiency of this vitamin leads to constipation, insomnia, loss of appetite, blisters in the mouth, a red tongue, watering of the eyes, fatigue and irritability.

Sources: whole grains, liver, eggs, mutton, yeast, groundnuts, almonds, soyabean and pulses.

VITAMIN C develops resistance to diseases and aids in healing wounds fast. It is essential for healthy eyes and skin.

A Balanced Diet

Deficiency of this vitamin results in skin diseases, bleeding gums, lustreless eyes, premature greying of hair, sore throat, frequent colds, brittle bones and general weakness.

Sources: fresh fruits and vegetables are rich sources of this vitamin. To name a few—capsicums, mustard greens, mangoes, pears, papaya, citrus fruits, sprouted beans, cabbage, pineapple and green chillies.

MINERALS

Many people take vitamins conscientiously but neglect the less glamorous minerals, which are equally important for a healthy body. In fact, vitamins and minerals work together to regulate the body functions, for example, maintain water in the body, influence gland secretions and preserve acid balance in the body.

Minerals are present as soluble salts in all the fluids of the body, supplying power of movement and assisting in digestion. Their lack in diet leads to poor health and growth of the body and serious diseases. The most important minerals are calcium, iron and iodine.

CALCIUM builds strong bones, teeth and nails. Rickets, skin disorders, tooth decay, cramps, nervousness and brittle bones indicate its deficiency.

Sources: milk, yoghurt, green leafy vegetables, cabbage, egg yolk and molasses.

IRON is needed for the formation of blood cells in the body. Healthy blood cells give a rosy complexion, a good memory and sound health. Insufficient iron in the blood is the cause of anaemia and other related problems.

Sources: kidney, liver, spinach, tomatoes, almonds, eggs, dry fruits and soyabeans.

IODINE aids the functioning of the thyroid gland and builds stamina for work. Its deficiency leads to mental depression, goitre and excessive weight gain.

Sources: sea fish and green vegetables. Iodised salt is another method of providing iodine in the diet.

Besides, traces of minerals such as **Phosphorous, Copper, Manganese** and **Potassium** and **Sodium chloride** are essential for a healthy diet.

Glyn and Clare Court

First Edition printed in 1975
Second Edition printed in 2018
ISBN: 9781982900847
Edited & Published by Michael Harper

To the happy memory of my parents William George and Ada Palser Court

— Glyn Court

This book is a joint venture, but not to the extent of the authors writing alternate words. To save lengthy explanations, each chapter is prefaced with the name of the author.

About the Authors

Glyn Court

Dr Glyn Court is a historian, linguist, musician, local preacher, former County Councillor, Liberal Parliamentary candidate, and winner of BBC Brain of Britain 1973.

He was brought up and educated in West Somerset, where he developed a strong connection with the history and heritage of the county. He began studying French and German at University College Exeter in 1942, before pausing his study to serve in Burma between 1943-1947. After returning from the war, he completed his degree in 1950, and continued his studies with a PhD in music and languages in 1961.

With an unusually wide range of interests he has written about military history, music, languages, and on Somerset life and characters, ranging from famous to little-known. He excels in bringing to life the stories and lost cultures of everyday characters and traditional societies.

He was the chairman of Somerset County Libraries and Museums Committee between 1973-1977, 83-91, a District councillor between 89-93, and vice-chairman of the County Council, 1991-93. In recognition of his distinguished service to Somerset, he was awarded the title of Honorary Alderman of Somerset County Council in February 2018.

Clare Court

Clare Carpenter, later to become Clare Court, was born in South Devon in 1928.

She was educated at Exmouth Grammar School and the University College of the South West, Exeter, where she studied Modern Languages. The end of the war brought in an influx of students from the forces, two years after it had ended for most servicemen. So in 1948 Clare met Glyn Court, who had only recently returned from Burma.

After marrying, they lived in France for two years, Clare teaching while Glyn researched for his PhD. They returned to the UK in 1953 to raise a family, which became a full-time occupation for some years.

Clare had always liked writing and produced articles and stories, and in 1995, when the village of Roadwater was commemorating the end of the war, she produced a short history of those years with 'A Somerset Village in Wartime'. Clare continued writing articles for the Village History Society, founded by herself and Glyn in 1987, and in 2005 she collaborated with Glyn to bring out 'The Book of Roadwater'.

Contents

1	Starting Points	1
2	Our Parish	5
3	Roadwater	15
4	My Father	23
5	My First Visit	29
6	Times Remembered	37
7	The Building of the House	43
8	Of Oaken Things	59
9	An Artist at Home	65
10	The Garden	71
11	An Artist Abroad	87
12	The Business as I remember it	95
13	The Bakehouse	109
14	The Women of the Family	113
15	We Inherit the Property	131
16	Brief Flirtation with Commerce	141
17	Times Best Forgotten	151
18	Problems	155
19	Making the Museum	165
20	Treasure Trove	179
21	Men and Their Monuments	189
22	Epilogue	211
23	A New Chapter	213

1 Starting Points

Clare Court

The story really begins quite a few years before either of us was born - in fact one would be hard put to it to name a date or a place, to fix on one particular event, a birth, death, marriage or building of a house, as having an overwhelming and supreme significance in one's own particular portion of history. For we are all, whether we like it or not, inextricably and forever woven into an infinitely complex pattern of history involving many people and places unknown to us. The delicate web of family connections, for example, knows no end when once a diligent search is made. Social upheavals of major or minor importance such as the rise and fall of the iron ore industry on the Brendon Hills, the coming of the railway, the Bible Christian movement, the advent of the telephone, the Great Depression of the 1930s, all these have had tremendous repercussions one way and another on the life of our family and helped shape many of its members.

It is usual when beginning a work of this sort (one hesitates to use such a grand title as "autobiography") to fill the first few pages with a detailed account of all the known members of the family, their dates of birth, what they did far a living, how many children they had and so forth; but not only will much of this information come to light in the course of our narration, it will fill a large part of the ensuing pages. Suffice it to say therefore that my husband and I were married in 1950 at the respective ages of twenty-six and twenty-two years, and we came from very different backgrounds.

My father and family were draughtsmen and engineers in the gas industry and I had grown up very happily and pleasantly by the seaside on the South Devon coast where my father had charge of a small and not very onerous gas company. There was always plenty of time to play tennis, go sailing, camping, take part in amateur dramatic productions, and generally enjoy life. On my mother's side of the family I come from Cumberland farmers in the neighbourhood of Penrith. Although not rich by the standards of pre-1940, we were comfortably off and the life we led certainly seems pleasant and rather easy when compared with the frantic existence of 1975. I had never left my home, apart from occasional shopping trips and Sunday School outings, and this rural calm continued even throughout the war years. Horizons began to widen a little with the preparations for D-Day, when large numbers of American soldiers were posted in our area for several months. These were the first foreigners that I had ever met. Then at the end of the war, I progressed to University College, Exeter, where (apart from having my mind broadened just a little more) I met my future husband.

Glyn (as he is always known, discarding the other two grandparental names of Albert and William lovingly bestowed on him by his parents) came from a very different background. He has in his veins the blood of Somerset yeomen, rural craftsmen and bootmakers, with a strong dash of the Great Western Railway on his mother's side, the whole nicely seasoned with a generous sprinkling of Post Office ink. One could no doubt find all sorts of interesting analogies or even, if so inclined, and with time and interest to spare, theories to account for this and that. Heredity after all has it exponents and I would be the last one to decry its merits. But for the time being I merely give the information for what it is worth.

I find myself back once again at the starting point, which I have almost convinced myself is going to be our wedding day, 23rd September 1950; the day when two fairly opposite poles suddenly came together seems as good a moment as any to call the beginning. In fact, I am almost ready to convince myself of the validity of the argument and take that date, namely twenty-five years ago, as the beginning, focal point, hub or radius, or whatever one likes to call it, of this story. If I decide on this course, a flashback technique will be inevitable.

Looking back to that day in 1950, not so very long after the war, when skirts were calf length and girls looked pretty (in my husband's opinion), I think it would be perfectly true to say that I had not the slightest idea what I was taking on. In common with most young brides, I quite sincerely

CHAPTER 1. STARTING POINTS

believed that I was beginning a life of unequivocal bliss and happiness. I mention this not to contradict the belief but merely to stress the fact that I have had a very good share of both of those enviable commodities, but also quite unimagined practical problems which few people would expect to have to deal with in a normal married life in such quiet backwaters of Devon and Somerset.

2

Our Parish

Glyn Court

The parish of Old Cleeve, in which most of this story of ours takes place, is the largest in West Somerset, apart from those few which take in vast tracts of the Quantocks and Exmoor. Its five thousand acres admittedly make something less than a Texas, but they contain a variety of scenery rarely to be equalled, marshland and mountain, moorland, forest and meadow. Our northern boundary is the Bristol Channel, our southern, five miles distant, the prehistoric ridgeway running along the Brendon Hills. Seen on a map (Figure 2.1), the parish has the shape on an hour-glass, being two miles wide in the south, narrowing to little more than three furlongs in the middle, and again broadening to two miles in the north. No one knows how, or under what monarch, the parish was given its peculiar shape; but it comprises the valley of a nameless stream and its tributaries which rise on the precipitous northern slopes of the Brendon Hills, and in the north it takes in the old Saxon manor of Wecetford or Washford, which may indeed have formed the original nucleus of the parish. This little plot of earth, with the seaport of Watchet lying at the mouth of the stream, was the scene in which most of the men and women who figure in these pages lived their strenuous lives.

Little enough room for the energies of vigorous characters to have play, one might think; but surprisingly ample if the energy is of the mind and spirit, for who knows then to what unexplored recesses of the world such radiant energy can find its way?

I hope I am not labouring the obvious when I insist on the beauty of the scenery of our parish, the freshness of the meadows and woodlands, the harmonious lines of the green hillsides, the stately heights of the Brendons on which one's gaze rests in the south, the houses which seem to grow out of the rich soil, and all down along the valley the stream, alive with trout,

A VILLAGE INHERITANCE

Figure 2.1: A map of Old Cleeve Parish in 1838

which hurries rippling and murmuring over its stone to find its way at last in gentle meanders to the pearl-grey sea. Even the monks of the Middle Ages, who too often saw in earthly beauty a snare for the spirit, could not hold out against the charm, and they named the place "Vallis florida". And even the forces of modern progress the speculative builder, the county surveyor or his minions, the river board, and the "industrial farmer" – though they have attacked this age-old beauty, have not destroyed it.

Nature here is on the human scale; the beauty has come from man's unconscious partnership with Nature, and for a thousand years and more they have been getting on pretty well together. In the nineteenth century and Old Cleeve Parish is unique in the distribution of its people, certainly in West Somerset, and probably in all the rural county - the parish supported a population of fifteen or sixteen hundred, living in three sizeable villages, Old Cleeve, Washford, Roadwater, three hamlets, Bilbrooke, Golsoncott and Leighland, and in more than a score of farms and cottages spread along the stream or upon the hillsides. Industries flourished, yet they did not disturb this delicate balance of economy and beauty, for they derived from the life of the country and served essential not artificial needs. Each was an industry of craftsmen, of smiths, millers, wheelwrights, sawyers, carpenters, cordwainers, harnessmakers, and saddlers, lime burners, charcoal burners. Their methods changed little in five hundred years, and they could never have imagined that their crafts might ever pass into oblivion. Men needed food, food must be grown by farmers, farmers needed horses: these things could never change.

Justifiably they thought so; the Industrial Revolution which had struck the North of England had left the West practically unscathed; and since West Somerset had no coal, there seemed no reason that the new kind of industry should come and break the mould of their contented days- for contented they were, on the whole, despite the hunger. But come it did, and though in the form it assumed it did not break the mould of village life, it made an indelible impression on the minds of the people.

Up on the Brendon Hills, long out of living memory, the "old men" had mined iron ore. Who they were, no one is certain. Germans in Queen

Elizabeth's time, perhaps, for it is known that German miners brought their skills to other parts of the country, notably Cumberland, and it may be more than coincidence that the German word for "iron", "Eisen", is found in the name of one tract of the Brendon range, Eisen Hill. More likely, though, it was the Romans or the Roman Catholics (for to most of the old country people they were one and the same) and they had interestingly confused ideas on the origins of some of the archaeological monuments; and it was all very, very long ago.

But in the 1840s, the commercial value of the ore began to be appreciated, when Sir Thomas Lethbridge of Luxborough started to mine black haematite ore (with over fifty percent metallic content) on a small scale on Withiel Hill. and two samples of this ore were displayed at the Great Exhibition of 1851. Soon a company was formed, based on Ebbw Vale, and for a quarter of a century mines were being sunk or driven in thirty different sites over hills and three quarters of a million tons were taken out. Miners and their families came from Cornwall, South Wales and the North of England, and new communities sprang into life at Brendon Hill and Gupworthy. Few local men worked in the mines, and the farm labourers' wage did not rise, but the coming of the miners did bring a modest prosperity to the tradesmen of the valley and to the cottagers with whom they lodged until houses were built for them up on the hills as near as possible to their work. From two to three hundred were employed in the mines, and it is reasonable to assume that the mining families numbered from six to eight hundred persons; two hundred of whom lived in our parish and in the new village of Brendon Hill.

To this day the spoil heaps are clearly to be seen; and here and there lumps of iron ore can be found; but the haematite was generally of high grade too valuable to waste, and I have a sample, once used as a door stop, the size of a melon, with a noded surface as smooth as if polished by an emery wheel. Many of the workings are flooded, and must hold tens of millions of gallons of water; but others are explored from time to time by cavers, and one of these has brought to me a collection of minerals which is remarkably varied for such a small area as ours.

CHAPTER 2. OUR PARISH

Stemming directly from this enterprise was another, more vital to the life of the parish, and more exciting - I use that much-abused word advisedly - to my forebears. The mines were, in the strictest sense, marginal to their life; this enterprise was central. It was the "mineral line".

The mine heads are mostly situated at twelve hundred feet above sea level, and the ore had to be carted between six and ten miles to the port of Watchet for shipment to the company's smelting works in Barry, and the roads the carts had to negotiate were not only execrably rutted but also included Sticklepath Hill, a mile long gradient of one in six. Sometimes they would return from Watchet laden with lime or sand for the farms, but by and large the transport threatened to make the mining economically unattractive when the best veins were exhausted.

Legend has it that the head of the company, Charles Edward Rowcliffe, was so moved by seeing an old horse labouring up Sticklepath that he determined to press for a railway. Immediately the surveyors got to work and a line was marked from Watchet up along the banks of the stream for six miles through Washford, Torre and Roadwater to the foot of the hills at Comberow, and thence up the hillside, continuing along the top at a height of 1200 feet for four miles to Gupworthy. The land was bought, and in July, 1855, the first sod was cut at Roughmoor, half-way between Watchet and Comberow, and the gangs of navvies set to work.

They made swift progress, for the line as far as Comberow follows the easy natural gradient of the valley; but the leap of eight hundred feet from Comberow to the top of the hill was accomplished in a feat of imaginative daring which, if not unique, was essentially Victorian.

But first I must describe the line as if we were travelling in the "wrong" direction, up from Watchet. For six miles we rise gently enough, pausing at the stations of Washford and Roadwater and the halts of Torre and Clitsome, rarely exceeding a gradient of one on 100 and never straying more than a landyard or two from the bank of the river, until we stop at Comberow, six hundred feet above sea level, in the shadow of the Brendon Hills, where the northern slopes are steepest. We alight and seven hundred feet above us we see the brow of the hill where the mines begin and where

Figure 2.2: The Incline, Cumberow. Built as part of the West Somerset Mineral Line to transport ore to the port of Watchet

CHAPTER 2. OUR PARISH

Figure 2.3: Pontypool Train Locomotive at Whitehall shed, Watchet, in 1893

Figure 2.4: A view from Comberow, about one third of the way up the mineral line. Probably taken about 1875, the man, said to be Jack Jewell, stands a little higher upslope than underbridge 14; he carries a can of tallow from lubricating the cable sheaves

we must go. But we stand amazed at what we see: the famous "Incline" — for the engineer, Rice Hopkins, thrust his railway in double track up the mountainside at a steady gradient of one in four for three-quarters of a mile. The difficulties were tremendous - outcrops of rock had to be blasted away and depressions filled in, bridges and culverts had to be built, the strictest alignment had to be maintained - but this was the only practicable solution.

My father would say, "You could lay a row of sovereigns end to end from top to bottom of the incline for what it cost the company to build it". It sounds a hyperbole but is literally true at a cost of 180,000 in good Victorian gold, and though the company may have contemplated their bank balance very ruefully they had good cause to be proud of their creation.

One could travel up, at one's own risk, in an open truck, and from the top of the Incline, thirteen hundred feet above sea level, another engine takes you four miles further, over the undulating moorland, to the end of the journey near the mining village of Gupworthy. But the ingenious working of the Incline must be described. It was operated largely by the cheapest and most basic form of power, that of gravity: the weight of a full truck at the top would pull up an empty truck from the bottom; but the speed had to be controlled, and the five thousand foot steel cable joining the trucks was passed round a steel drum eighteen feet high in an engine-house at the top of the incline, and thence down to the lower truck. The full truck with its five tons of ore would be cased over the lip of the incline, and the engine would initially aid it to pull the empty truck at the top of the cable, then as the descending weight increased and the ascending weight diminished, the engine would control the speed. The system worked well and in thirty years of use only two accidents occurred, both from the couplings giving way. In one, a truck loaded with rails broke away when half-way up the Incline, hurling its load of rails into the next field. The other accident - but this has found a place in our family annals and I must duly locate it there. The coming of the railway to Roadwater threw more than one pebble into the still pond of village life; for a time it brought the "navvies", who no doubt caused some consternation, but it also brought the people of the village into contact with the busy life of Watchet and even - if they could afford it - with the county town of Taunton. Indeed, Roadwater folk were inordinately but understandably proud of having had a railway fifteen years before the pretentious and self-satisfied township of Minehead!

Moreover, the railway came decisively into our family life, for the company built a station at Roadwater, appointed Great-Grandfather Henry as stationmaster and agent, and built him a house. (My maternal grandfather was also a railwayman - a porter, and later inspector, on the Great Western.) Henry was assisted by his younger son William, and William had initiative. When twelve years of age - this must have been in 1859 or 1860 - manning the crossing gates, he heard an unfamiliar noise higher up the valley; moments later, about two hundred yards away, a runaway truck came hurtling round a bend in the track. Without hesitating, young William shut the gates to try to break the speed of the truck, and then ran towards it to escape the flying splinters. The truck of course broke through, and ended its journey in Watchet harbour, but William was commended for his action. In due course the story acquired the embellishment of a puppy, an involuntary traveller in a closed box left on the truck, which bobbed up to one surface and floated in the harbour until the yelping of its occupant attracted attention and the puppy was saved, none the worse. Whether true or not, it deserves to be.

The mines went well for twenty years, and production rose from 4,000 tons in 1855 to 46,000 in 1877; but in the next year a sharp decline began as ore from Spain was brought in more cheaply. Villages were depopulated almost overnight, and the Brendon Hills found their age-old silences again.

The mining company, under the terms of their Act of Parliament, continued to run the railway for nearly twenty years more, but traffic was generally light, though at times excursions were organised, in connection with the Bible Christian and other chapels at Watchet, Roadwater and Brendon Hill or the flourishing Bands of Hope and Good Templars' Lodge. But I must say no more of the mines here, for fear of spoiling the fascinating story told, by Roger Sellick and his collaborators in their "West Somerset Mineral Railway".

For a hundred yards or so the abandoned Mineral Line runs along the bottom of my garden in Washford. There is little visible record of its history: the rails and sleepers were removed more than half a century ago, and bushes and briars have invaded the track. But if you are keen enough of hearing you will detect, on a still, starlit winter's night, the sound, of a going in the tops of the alder trees, and if you close your eyes and keep them close, you will hear a soft hiss of escaping steam as an invisible locomotive emerges from the filled-in bridge and glides over the vanished sleepers on its way to Comberow.

3 Roadwater

Glyn Court

It was in Higher Roadwater, which lies at the geographical centre of the parish, that for more than a hundred years my family made their home. They lived in a spacious William and Mary farmhouse, with a garden and orchard running down to the little stream which form the western boundary of the parish of Nettlecombe. If spaciousness calls up a vision of landed wealth and patrician ease, I must confess, though not without a certain pride, that none of the Courts has ever gained a superfluity of wealth, ease or leisure. Yet their modest means and stationary position have given them interest, for they have been concerned in the life of this parish, in many different capacities, for most of two centuries, and their lives illustrate the movements which have altered or sustained, our society for much of that time, moreover, having been unusually aware of the processes of change, they have consciously tried to preserve the form and spirit of the good traditions of former times, the memory of the worthies of the parish, and also a host of treasure objects which recalled to them the vanished lineaments of those whom they had loved and lost in the golden days of their youth. The associations gathering round these treasures were kept alive and cherished, through several generations, by word of mouth, and it has been my pleasure - though one tinged at times with sorrow - to capture and record many of them in this book.

One who was devoted to the memory of an older time used to dwell lovingly on those haunting lines of Longfellow:

> And the friendships old and the early loves
> Come back with a Sabbath sound as of doves
> In quiet neighbourhoods...
> And the thoughts of youth are long, long thoughts;

and others since his day have looked back longingly to that vanished world and felt the tears rise within them with the yearning for that tranquil land of eternal Sunday which they have never known.

The old homesteads of Roadwater, in the early days of Queen Victoria's reign must have looked very much like those of Acadie so lovingly described in 'Evangeline':

> Strongly built were the houses, with frames of oak and of hemlock,
> Thatched were the roofs, with dormer windows, and gables projecting.
> There in the tranquil evenings of summer, brightly the sunset
> Lighted the village street with mysterious splendour, and roofed each
> Peasant's cottage with golden thatch and. emblazoned its windows.

One suspects, however, that visitors would have appreciated this rustic splendour more keenly than some of the people who dwelt there.

Some of the cottagers in those good old days could, if they had been of the complaining sort, have told you more about the bad side - the grinding poverty, the overcrowding, the infected water, the diphtheria and consumption, the chronic "rheumatics", the workhouse. But for those with the leisure to look around, and the eye to see beauty, the landscape had attained its perfection after long generations of maturing. In the village the speculative builder had not arrived, mean little bungalows and open-plan development had not been dreamed of even in nightmares, and the farmhouses and cottages were still being built with local materials in a living local tradition.

Unfortunately, no artist has left a record of the lineaments of Roadwater in those days, but I should like to try, with the help of family reminiscences

CHAPTER 3. ROADWATER

and the tithe map, to reconstruct its appearance a hundred and more years ago.

We approach it from Washford, along the narrow road past Roughmoor, ankle-deep in mud or dust according to the season. At the entrance to the village, where the side-road comes in from Clitsome - it does not connect directly with Beggearnhuish - the open brook flowing down from Roadwater Farm and past the picturesque cottage on the corner, forms a ford, with a footbridge; but the first substantial building in the village is the prosperous Roadwater Inn, and there is little else, apart from Roadwater Farm and Yea Farm, until we come to Manor Mills. Rounding the corner, we see on the right, where the mission church has since been built, two cottages and a lime kiln; but on the left there is no building until we reach the four Day Mead Cottages, on the site of the Village Hall and close to the corn mill. (Day's Meadow itself stretched considerably further up the valley than the present recreation ground, but even then it was used for the village revels and entertainments.)

The mill leat, which is taken off from the Luxborough stream a good way up and flows through gardens and out by the village shops, here runs open by the right-hand side of the road and then under into the mill.

There is a building up on Knap, the New Inn, kept by Robert Flueilen, a burly man with a determined expression. He gains additional income from tailoring, though in a village community most of his work consists of repairs and alterations, cutting down Stephen's "jackett" to fit Albert and so on.

Behind the village shop is a chandlery, which needs no notice to announce its business: the aroma of tallow is its own advertisement.

Beyond here the road dips slightly to the ford through the river, though on the right a stone footbridge is provided by the dipping place. There are signs of new building, however, and on the left the railway company are putting up a house for their Roadwater agent, and they are also preparing to raise the level of the road, roof over the stream and provide stone steps down to a new dipping place. In the garden of the house stand two gigantic poplar trees, and on the right of the road arc two cottages with lilac trees.

A VILLAGE INHERITANCE

Figure 3.1: Glasses, a seventeenth century farmhouse, Roadwater

Figure 3.2: The Bridge Village Shop, Roadwater

CHAPTER 3. ROADWATER

Here the road to Wood Advent branches off, running alongside an orchard. There are no buildings on the left of Proud Street (soon to be called Station Road, but still taking its name from the Prowsc family) and Oatway House has a fine view down the valley. Beyond the ford at the bottom of Harper's, and over on the right, under the bank below Coachroad, is a blademill, powered by a leat coming down through the fields from Hayne, and run by George Edbrooke, who, in addition to the usual blacksmith's work, had made the iron gates for Old Cleeve Church and also specialises in scythes, billhooks, ploughshare and cutting edges of many kinds. But though the leat comes down from Hayne, there is no road up the valley, and the cottages at Traphole and Hayne are connected with Leighland, not Roadwater.

On the high, rough area known as Scrubbit, the barns are still thatched and in use, and the children play under a fine walnut tree fifteen feet around; while on Hill Close there stands a magnificent oak tree six feet in diameter.

The road up towards Luxborough leads past the Bible Christian chapel, built in 1842 on the only ground available, and set right into the bank of Scrubbit; already suffering from damp, of course, but still in good shape, even if too small for the constantly increasing congregations from the periodic revivals. From here the church path to Leighland and Stamborough leads up over the hill, past the allotments looking down on the Valiant Soldier, past the sawpits and the mounds of charcoal-burners. Nearby the rackfield, where the cloth from the fulling mills down at Vale is laid out to dry. And indeed, the number of mills in this valley is quite extraordinary, for the little stream without even a name, drives no fewer than twelve, from Luxborough and Leigh, through Roadwater and Washford right down to Watchet.

I mentioned earlier the poverty and overcrowding within the picturesque cottages, and social historian such as Ernest Martin, Walter Crotch and F. E. Green have written movingly of the inhuman conditions so patiently endured. But to complete this survey I will describe in some detail the cottage best known to me from childhood, that in which our branch of the family lived for a hundred years:

> A cottage by the Brendon brook
> With many a diamond casement pane
> That looked out on a winding lane:

those lines by one who was born in "Oatway" in 1870 briefly describe the exterior, but they give no idea of the homely charm that greeted you when you stepped over the threshold.

"Cottage" is rather a misnomer. It was spacious, and could have held two families. A yeoman of Nettlecombe, William Oatway, had built it as a dower house for his daughter in 1700, and the date and his initials could clearly be seen worked in the plaster high up on the front wall under the thatched eaves. In front, the vegetable garden ran down to the river, where there were steps for dipping water; behind, a cobbled court led up to a stable and an orchard with beehives, and on to an area of high rough ground known as Scrubbet, where the ruins of a barn witnessed to the former farming history of the property. The house was built to a plan very frequently used in West Somerset; a porch at one front led into a passage which ran right through to the back court, and one door on the right and another on the left gave entrance to two separate dwellings. All visitors come in by the back door, as the front door gave only on to the garden. Once you crossed the threshold and took one step down you found yourself in a very large red-tiled kitchen with a low ceiling and oaken beams. The room was lit by two leaded casements and, at night, by a paraffin lamp placed on a table under a white enamelled dome. The table, which occupied all the centre of the kitchen, was large enough to seat twelve, and at Christmastide it often did. Against one wall stood the massive grandfather clock, which it had been Grandfather's care to recover on restoring the family fortunes: the face was decorated with an inscrutably smiling sun, and marked the seasons, and it proclaimed itself the work of "John How, Watchet". Next to the clock stood a glass-fronted double bookcase which was not locked but kept closed with a late Victorian curiosity: a biscuit-tin shaped like a book and bearing the illuminated words and music of "Good King Wenceslas". The bookcase itself - I am of course speaking of the time of my boyhood, not of Victorian days - was filled with biographies and studies of history, especially of Methodism: Southey's Life of Wesley; "Gladstone; A Popular Biography"; "The King's Son: The Life of Billy Bray"; "The Romance of a Country Circuit"; Lord Roseberry's "Napoleon, the Last Phase"; "The Voyage of the Medusa" - the variety and number were, for the time and place, extraordinary and were reflected in Grandfather's well-furnished mind and his ready command of speech on formal and informal occasions alike.

The kitchen range was, I surmise, a late Victorian improvement, with a high fire box for convenience and a capacious oven on the left, while the right-hand side contained a tank in which water could be heated and drawn off through a brass tap. To the right of the fireplace there always stood Grandfather's hard upright armchair; to the left a high partition had been erected to keep off the draught, and this was provided with a long seat, so that the focal point of the room was, as the word implies, the fireplace. On the walls were various pictures of which I shall speak later.

From the left-hand corner of the kitchen a short flight of stairs, lit by a glazed arrow-slit on the outside wall, led up to the bedrooms - or rather, the bedroom, which had been divided into three by partitions. The floors were, need I say, the bare planking.

From the far side of the kitchen a short passage led to a tiny scullery and larder and also to the parlour, which contained a table covered with a red plush cloth and bearing a stuffed squirrel in a glass case. A side table displayed an elegant mid-Victorian rosewood writing cabinet presented to Grandfather by admirers.

A side-door from this room gave on to the village street, but it was seldom used. The parlour, likewise, was a "best" room, a Sunday room, and it was used just as rarely, even on Christmas or Boxing Days, unless jinks of the younger generations in the kitchen became too elevated for grave and reverend age.

One observation has continually been made to me in conversing with men and women of an earlier generation: in villages such as Roadwater there was no prosperity, but oppressive poverty and privation; yet there was happiness. Having little, they desired little; they had few possessions but held firmly to certain fixed and incontrovertible truths; and they surely have much to tell us for our good, if we will listen, in our modern discontent.

4 My Father

Glyn Court

"If it were permitted to contradict a lady", as said the gallant Mr Elton, I would take issue with my wife's statement that one would be hard put to it to name a date or place having a supreme significance in our particular portion of history. I would identify it as a moment in April 1876, when a baby was born in the village of Roadwater. That baby, after a considerable delay, as is only natural, became my father, and obviously, but for him we should have no story to tell. And as young William George, or "Will" to the family, figures so largely in the following pages, this seems the right time - and I write this on 6th April 1976, the hundredth anniversary of his birth - for me to essay a portrait of him, not only as he is limned in the memory of a son but also as others recollect him. To know the kind of man he was will help to explain the vagaries of the experiences recounted hereafter; but more, he was a countryman of a type now rarely met with, and some such account will help to preserve the savour of a vanished age.

His father, also William, was the village shoemaker or cordwainer, enjoying, in the mid 1870s, a brief spell of modest prosperity. Will, in the heady days of the first Education Act, was sent to the village school on the breezy hillside of Leighland a mile away, and worked his way contentedly up through the standards to the age of eleven, learning the three R's, spelling history and geography and acquiring a beautiful hand. He would say wistfully, "I wish I'd been born with a good memory," but nobody else noticed any deficiency. Still, authority, in its paedagogic Victorian form, fell out with him when he was eleven. "William Court", thundered bearded Authority, "come out to the front". William came out, feeling he had done nothing to deserve a beating and determined not to have one. As the headmaster raised his cane, William also raised his hand, grasped the goatee beard and clung on for dear life; swish and slash as he might, not a single cut landed and William could claim the victory. But not outstaying his welcome he sped through the door and off home. His father, to his amazement, was highly diverted, but that was William's last day at school, and in later years, feeling the loss keenly, he made painstaking and largely successful efforts to acquire the knowledge of which he had been summarily deprived.

It was in his chosen art of carpentry, for which he served his apprenticeship, that he first found the way to excel, being entrusted with the finishing work at sixpence-farthing an hour, a farthing above the normal wage and a substantial advantage with a sixty-hour week. But by a pleasing quirk of nature, even in his best work his consciousness and craftsmanship were enlivened by flashes of the wayward West Countryman - though I will not say plain, downright dilatory. The parish church of Luxborough, in the late 1890s, was undergoing "restoration", and the firm of carpenters in Dunster for whom he worked were asked to provide an oaken pulpit for some weeks later, when with ecclesiastical junketings the church would be re-opened. Will, as the craftsman, had the commission and set to work. The day of the re-opening drew near, but the pulpit did not; the morning came, the pulpit did not; the bishop came, but still no pulpit; and long was the luncheon enjoyed by his grace while a cart trundled over from Dunster and a perspiring team manhandled the pulpit into place. It would be uncharitable to assume that my father meant to keep the bishop cooling his heels, but one may have one's thoughts.

In his middle twenties his health failed and he gave up full-time carpentry and became the postmaster of his native village, combining this with a retail extension of his father's boot end shoe trade. At the same time he fell in love with my mother and should rightly have been able to offer marriage; but my father was not one to hurry things and mother was content to wait; and then came one thing and another - the Great War for one - and Will, such is the power of Family, felt he had to provide for the children of a married sister deserted by her husband; and then a favourite sister cared for him devotedly until she died; and by the time he ventured, into marriage, forty-four years had stolen upon him and, he said, "I'll never get married so young again". But of the ideal happiness of that marriage I will not now speak.

CHAPTER 4. MY FATHER

Figure 4.1: William Court

He had, it almost goes without saying, a strong religious faith, for he was born into that sturdy, democratic tradition of Bible Christian Methodism which originated in North Devon and flourished so astonishingly throughout the West of England and the Channel Isles and even in Canada, Australia and Yunnan. All his childhood memories were linked to the crowded congregations and the plain, foursquare chapels whose beauty, invisible to the casual beholder, is seen in the light of the memories and associations which gather round them. Moreover, the social life of the members centred on the chapels, with their choirs and orchestras, and my father, who had a good, true tenor voice and loved music, found in them the companionship of artistic experience. In his early twenties he offered for the Bible Christian ministry in the footsteps of his brother, but family circumstances held him back, and he settled for the ministry of a local preacher and exercised it for half a century.

With his Methodist faith, inevitably, came his Liberal one, and although the most peaceable soul alive he revelled in political argument, even though he would have acknowledge Goethe's aphorism that "against stupidity the gods themselves fight in vain". He worked hard and long for the cause, canvassing, speaking, chairing meetings, and even in the long years of Liberal eclipse his commitment did not waver. He did not live to see a Liberal revival, but he found a measure of compensation in working for the election of one of the most distinguished Independent Members of Parliament, Vernon Bartlett. But preaching and politics could not fill up the measure of his time, and as his trade achieved a little prosperity - for he was sociability itself, and our progress along the street of a strange town was in the nature of a conversational pilgrimage, with frequent halts to exchange courtesies and comments with complete strangers - he turned to local government and served as chairman and member of the rural district council, as school governor and as Chairman of the parish council for more than a decade. It was in this work that he found his forte, for he was a man to whom most of the village would come for help or advice - with just enough exceptions, such as the following, to remove any likelihood of conceit:

Clerk to the Parish Council: The vote for the office of Chairman is as follows: W.G. Court: For, 53; Against, 0.

Mr Tiler (a determined antagonist): Thik's wrong, Mr Clurk, there's on'y fifty-three o' us yere, an' I didn' vote for 'en!

My father usually had too low an opinion of himself-largely, I think, because he had not acquired the academic and theological learning of his elder brother - but this story he used to tell with relish, and I am glad of it, because he was then responding to other people's consciousness of his worth. Like most of us, he had a few chronic defects, in his case unpunctuality which could sometimes amount to inconsiderateness, and a few foibles: in thirty years of driving he never apprehended that other motorists had discovered our narrow lanes and might indeed wish for a share in them. But as I look back at my father through the mists of twenty years, I know that these flaws count for little or nothing, and I see, above and beyond all else, one who was kind, gentle and good, by conviction a Christian, by nature a gentleman, are one who lived each day for the unending tomorrow.

5 My First Visit

Clare Court

During the first years of our married life we led a rather nomadic existence, living for varying periods in Exeter, Paris, Grenoble, Yorkshire and South Devon, and during this time one tended to regard the home that one had left as a convenient repository for all the possessions, wedding presents and books that one had accumulated over the years. My own family had never been given to hoarding, in fact my father tended to the reverse and was a thrower-away. I could hardly fail to notice therefore the marked contrast in my husband's home in the village of Washford in West Somerset. He was the only child of rather elderly parents with their traditions and customs very firmly rooted in the Victorian era. His mother had been born in 1886 and father in 1876 - quite a generation gap. In the course of their own industrious and even lives, changes had been very slow to occur and possessions were valued, often the result of years of patient labour and saving, and in the sober, industrious, rural society of which they formed a part, it would have been unthinkable to squander uselessly any article that had been either laboriously acquired or reverently handed down from a previous generation.

It was not surprising, therefore, however strange it seemed to me at the time, that my husband's home seemed to be full to overflowing with family possessions. Every room (and there were many, for his father had built the house about twice the size of the average modern home) was crammed with furniture, of which every cupboard, shelf and drawer exuded ornaments, runners, vases, trinkets, hairbrushes and the like. Every floor was generously linoed, carpeted and festooned with runners. In addition to curtains, many of the windows had blinds. Investigation into corners of little-used rooms soon revealed further caches, many consignments of boxes, some cardboard, some wooden, and these too held their store of table linen, crochet mats, unwanted Christmas presents, with quite a few toys which had been lovingly preserved from Glyn's childhood. I suppose that that in itself would not have made the house unique, but in addition to the main structure (which as I have already mentioned was designed and built by my father-in-law) there was a family business comprising a rather unusual blend of village post office and boot and shoe store. There were several outbuildings and sheds, dimly perceived, in which I was vaguely aware that something was being carried on. In the fulness of time I came to realise that the other part of the business comprised a shoe and bicycle repair service, which occupied a large corrugated-iron shed directly to the back of the house and, to my eternal annoyance, directly blocking out the view of the orchard from the living room. However, as I was to come to realise slowly and painfully over a long period of time, village folk with a very demanding post office to run as well as a general business were far too near the breadline throughout the hard years of the thirties to worry too much about such niceties. We have now lived here for eight years and the shed is with us still, together with its partner, an unlovely but commodious tin garage of vast proportions. At one time there was brave talk of a "five year plan" in which we hoped to demolish these ugly sisters but after eight years they are still with us, becoming ever rustier but still defying the attack of westerly gales and the encroachment of rust. It is surprising what the eye can become accustomed to after a period of years - I shall probably be quite put out when they are finally demolished.

There had been a very good market for bicycles throughout the 1920s, and my father-in-law William George, ever willing to expand his very limited trade in the small, not very wealthy community in which he lived, had ventured into the sale of Raleighs and New Hudsons. This had proved popular so that in addition to the great sheets of leather hanging in the workshop, multifarious boxes of tacks and so forth essential to the affixing of new soles and heels, not to mention iron bars not unworthy of a fair-sized horse, there were always supplies of new tyres, wheels and tubes. Presiding over this untidy but homely array of useful objects beamed William, neatly turned out in old fashioned striped shirt, round collar, bow tie and always with a clean white apron. He disliked being dirty. There was usually a young lad or man working away in the shed, generally a country boy (or even two) called by some such name as Bert or Les. By the time that I appeared on the scene, cheap labour was no longer quite so readily available and there was a boy of fifteen named John. Pride of place in the workshop was taken by two enormous wooden benches on which all the work was done, and most important pieces of machinery - the shoe finishing machine, a cast-iron miracle of smooth cogs and wheels, and the splendid Singer sewing machine. This had supplanted the old one made by Grandfather, which in its turn had removed the necessity of doing all the stitching by hand. By the time I first came to Washford in 1949, shoes were no longer being made on the premises, for the factories had long been turning out footwear far more cheaply and easily than they could possibly be made in the village, and besides William's heart had always been in wood as a medium of creative expression and he had never excelled in the art of shoemaking. He could nevertheless make a pair when occasion demanded. We have one still. Rather characteristically they did not turn out quite as they should have done (owing it was said to the poor quality of war time materials) and were never worn.

There was a continual coming and going to this shed, and the door would frequently burst open for John to rush forth and serve petrol to an occasional passing motorist - this latest addition of the pumps providing quite a useful extra source of income but not exactly enhancing the appearance of the front of the house.

I am still trying to given an impression of the house, home and business as it was when I first came to know it and I realise that so far I have said little about the actual house. It is hard to remember much of one's thoughts as a young bride of twenty-two years, as at that age I knew nothing at all about houses and allied subjects and as my experiences had been so very limited, I had very little to go by. All I can remember thinking was that it was large, rather gloomy and terribly old-fashioned, I think it would be true to say that I was completely impervious to the charms of polished oak and copper warming pans. I also thought it very strange that my mother-in-law had to disappear into the post office at frequent intervals in order to carry on strange transactions - all very mysterious, as the phenomenon of the

Working Mother had never come into my ken before. Equally strange was not being able to have meals when one fancied them but according to the stern law of Closing Time or Opening Time. Tea could not be eaten until six o-clock - a complete reversal of the laws of Nature, though as the years went by and business declined, we did coax Granny into softer ways -but only at the price of leaving the door into the shop partly open. With the intolerance of the young I thought it was all terribly boring. It did not occur for a moment to Glyn to explain any of this to me as for him the way of life was as natural as the tide coming up and our popping down for a swim was to me. It is surprising what little bouts of friction can be caused by such a trivial matter as the hour of afternoon tea - especially as they forgot to point out that on Sundays it took place at five o-clock in order to allow plenty of time to get to evening chapel. All very confusing.

The village in which the house is set, though situated in one of the most beautiful parts of the West Country, bears no claim to the title of Prettiest or Best Kept. In fact, considering the beauty of the surrounding countryside, it is of remarkably dull and plain appearance with few buildings of any architectural interest. The exception that proves the rule, of course, is the well-maintained ruin of the Abbey of Cleeve, a Cistercian foundation of the twelfth century. Apart from this attractive pile only a few of the older cottages, thatched and rose-adorned, satisfy the romantic imagination. Most of the older houses are solidly built of stone with no-nonsense slate roofs, reminiscent of Cornish villages. Of recent years the inevitable modern development has taken piece, the worst vandals in this respect being the local authority of about forty years ago. Imagine a sheltered hollow in the gentle green hills of Somerset, generously wooded and watered by a sturdy stream. The name of the river, which once supported twelve mills, was mysteriously lost generations ago, and even in old manuscripts there is never any hint of a name. This is one of the small mysteries of our local history and it would be one of the happiest days of our life if some hitherto undiscovered tablet or parchment could be found with the solution to our topographical mystery. On Ordnance Maps, to be sure, the name is marked as Washford River, and so it has been known for the last few generations, but "Why?" one asks oneself. Why, when all the neighbouring brooks - Pill,

CHAPTER 5. MY FIRST VISIT

Avill, and Swill, Haddeo, Quarme and Oare Water, rejoice in Celtic names, should ours, a respectable full-bodied affair, have none? Admittedly, most of them mean water in some form or another, but oh how much more poetically expressed! The often humblest rivulet barely two foot wide in much more remote areas such as Dartmoor, for example, bears a name; one thinks of Walla Brook and Cherry Brook as lovely examples. Other writers have fancifully called our river the Road Water after the nearest village upstream, but logic and etymology both reject this suggestion. So until folk memory is stirred or a scholar turns something up we shall have to rest content.

The valley, then, is beautiful and fertile, as the monks, who called it Vailis Florida, well knew when they founded their abbey. The position is admirably sheltered, especially from the brisk breezes of the Bristol Channel, and its cosseting warmth is adequately proved by the forwardness of spring flowers in the cottage gardens. As I write, in the first week of May, my own garden is in a particularly lovely phase where flowers of at least two seasons are happily blooming together and will continue to do so for at least a few more weeks. Primroses which started blooming last October, are still putting out more buds. Wallflowers likewise have been flowering almost non-stop throughout the winter and icy spring, while stocks, purple irises and masses of bluebells, pink and white as well as the traditional shade, are making big splashes of colour all over the garden. As if this abundance were not sufficient, broom and forsythia are lighting up yellow torches, while the orchard is a mass of cherry and apple blossom. Nature's bounty is indeed abundant, but in case the reader is beginning to think that he too will come and share this earthly paradise, I should hasten to add that there is a snag. Perhaps to say that "only man is vile" is rather overstating the case, but the hand of man has alas not always enriched the landscape in the same glorious way as those mediaeval builders who first conceived the Abbey. His particular atrocity in the case of our erstwhile peaceful hollow is, not surprisingly in this motor age, the main road running right through the centre of our village. Not so long ago, less than a hundred years, each community lived out its life in splendid isolation. There was a road, to Williton (I wrote "from" and hastily changed it before being executed by the locals) but the route to Watchet over the hill had always been fraught with hazards, but if you wished to proceed to Luxborough you would have had to abandon your vehicle and walked across fields; for the road petered out beyond Roadwater. For better and for worse we are on the main route to Minehead, a heavy burden to bear since the motor car explosion brought the thousands to Butlins. Sadly, our beautiful valley is to be marred by a hideous viaduct when the projected by-pass is constructed [1]. We long for the day when the holiday traffic, amounting to eleven thousand vehicles on a summer Saturday, will be removed from our front doorstep, yet mourn in anticipation the destruction of the environment. But people must live, and there is little doubt that the present situation virtually destroys the social life of the village, rendering as it does, a short journey to the post office a positive hazard to life and limb.

Another small bonus which should not be discounted is the fact that our community is much more representative of a true unit than many of the surrounding villages which, suffering from a surfeit of prettiness, have attracted so many retired couples to live in them. We now live surrounded by elderly neighbours, many of them very pleasant and intelligent people, but many others not sharing at all in our strange tribal ways, harvest fetes and the like. No doubt when the main road is removed from our midst we shall see a new growth of bungalows on the outskirts

In 1950 when I first came to Washford, the train was still running and was still quite an important part of village life[2]. More than one householder set her clock by the 7:50 to Taunton which for nearly one hundred years bore office workers and school children to their day's employment, returning them promptly at 5:45. In fact my first arrival was at the station, which in those days, not so long ago yet very distant in some ways, boasted a full-time station master and, with its well-tended garden, had won the title of "Best-kept Station" on the line. The Great Western Railway (GWR) was

---

[1] In 1970s, there had been plans to by-pass Washford to the South. However, the plans were eventually abandoned after proposed routes uncovered historic sites of interest.

[2] The West Somerset Railway used to operate as part of the national rail network, but was closed in the 1963 as part of the Beeching Review. From 1976, the line was reopened as a heritage railway, which it still operates as to this day.

CHAPTER 5. MY FIRST VISIT

a relative upstart in the history of local transport. The West Somerset Mineral Railway had been established for twenty years when the Great Western appeared on the scene, though they were never serious rivals. The Mineral Line had been constructed in 1855 in order to bring iron ore down from the Brendon Hills to the port at Watchet, about which more will be said in due course. For about two miles from Washford to Watchet the tracks ran parallel and now that both have fallen into disuse, stand as silent, leafy memorials to the coming of the industrial age. Until quite late in the history of the Court family business, much of the stock for the shop had been delivered by rail. Boots and shoes and bicycles from Bristol and Birmingham and Exeter used to arrive in large crates and had to be fetched from the station with a handcart. Proximity to the station was a very important point for a small business whose customers rarely possessed their own transport, and who depended to a very large extent on the choice of stock available at the local store. But already in 1950, dependence on the railway line was much less than it had been and road transport was altering the pattern to a very large extent.

I remember quite well my first arrival at Washford Station, and with typically feminine exactness which brings to mind details quite irrelevant to one's history or the progress of the human race, can even recall what I was wearing on that occasion. It was two days after Christmas, the day we had chosen to announce our engagement to our parents. Although I only had to travel fifty miles from my home in South Devon to the Somerset coast, the journey seemed endless, taking about five hours altogether. I remember taking the first Hart's bus which was running on that Sunday service day, at about ten o-clock and hoping for the best. Transferring to the Devon General at Exmouth I reached Exeter where in the fulness of time a train bore me the thirty miles to Taunton. There was no Minehead train for about two hours, so I ventured into Station Road and for the first time in my life had lunch in a hotel (the only place that was open). I remember thinking that this was very daring. I finally got to Washford at about three o-clock where Glyn met me at the station. My overriding feeling at the time (apart from the thrill of being officially engaged) was the innocent desire to please my future parents-in-law. I had nothing to fear, they welcomed me with open arms, called me "dear" and seemed to accept me without further fuss as one of the family. Easily the hardest problem to overcome was how to eat the meal which they had kindly saved for me. I wished in later years when I came to know her better, that I had asked Mum whether she was nervous about meeting me - alas one does not think of these things until it is too late.

6 Times Remembered

Clare Court

In the course of writing any part of this account, which originally began as a straightforward description of our experiences on taking over the family business, I became more and more involved in the early history of our home and the people who built it. Gradually the story moved as it were out of my own hands and I found the subject matter leading backwards in time of its own volition, through the forties to the years before my birth. I must confess unashamedly, that if anyone had asked me when we first conceived the idea of writing this book who were to be the most important characters in it, I would have said Glyn and myself. As the tale progressed however, it became increasingly obvious that the real hero and heroine were not ourselves but Glyn's parents, William and Ada. Little by little and bit by bit, I started to put together all the many pieces of information which I had unwittingly collected over the years - the oft-repeated tales to which one listened oh so reluctantly, twenty or so years ago.

One has mixed memories of the time when all this information was so unwillingly received. When I first came to Washford and though older members of the family were still alive, the traditional time for getting together around the fire, in fact almost the only time free from other interruptions, was Sunday evening after service at the chapel - a sore deprivation to us, the pampered, over-educated and intolerant young, who would have much preferred to listen to a nice concert on the radio or read our books.

William and Ada always attended evening service at the home chapel of Roadwater, and this was generally the highlight of the week for them as it was the only time they were able to spend with his sister and any other members of the family who happened to be visiting. The meeting place was in one of the cottages, which adjoined the widest part of the road through the village - the Bridge, as it is always known. This area, though hardly meriting the description of "square", served very well in the past as the hub and focal point of village life. Roadwater straggles along the cleft of a steep and narrow valley which is overhung by dark trees, so whichever house was chosen it was certain that very little daylight would illumine the proceedings. There was no escape as we dutifully filed into the tiny cramped, room smelling of mothballs and paraffin lamps - except for Glyn who would delay his appearance round the tea pot for a considerable time by lingering at the keyboard of the organ. His parents were very proud of his playing and never protested if the practice went on for a goodish spell. There is a certain finesse in doing what one wants to do without upsetting the older generation, and as an adolescent he had perfected, the art of disappearing when unpleasant or boring tasks seemed imminent. He tells me that he used frequently to retreat to the small copse which stands up the hill at the top of our garden, and there, safely out of earshot of the house and away from the continual annoyance of telegrams, he would, truthfully claim that he had not heard his parents when they called him. In this quiet spot he read his way through a good many books, including most of the plays of Racine. The copse, though less secluded now than at the time of which I am writing, is an embowered, spot overlooking the Abbey, though perhaps more suited, to the reading of romantic poetry than of seventeenth century tragedy. There is a piquancy, though, in the contrast between our homely scene and the stately characters of those long dead kings and queens fighting out their battles of love and hate in beautifully measured Alexandrines, which I find, particularly appealing!

I, however, had no excuse to linger, and not being a rebel by nature would have found it difficult to hurt the feelings of my kindly parents-in-law. For I had so much to learn, and the code of behaviour which was expected from me was not one of which I had any previous experience and demanded my full attention. Their way of life, based on Methodism, was ruled by what seemed to me strange habits and taboos, as alien to me as the customs of some foreign tribe. For example, when I was first welcomed into the family I found it difficult to understand why I must never mention alcoholic

CHAPTER 6. TIMES REMEMBERED

drink of any sort, let alone disclose the terrible fact that my family regularly brewed home-made wine. Playing cards (the "devil's pictures" to an older generation) were also a forbidden subject, and I had to remember not to mention that we often played bridge and whist at home - for buttons never money, as there were some taboos even in my family. The vocabulary too puzzled me. Temperance, a word which was constantly on their lips, did not seem to mean what I thought it meant but it was not long before I came to realise that its true meaning was Total Abstinence in the particular context of the flourishing local nineteenth century Temperance Movement. All the men of the family had signed the Pledge and this too was frequently spoken of, but no one seemed to think it necessary to explain to me what was meant.

So there we sat, eating our bread and butter and drinking our tea from the carefully preserved china tea service with pink handles that was brought out on these occasions. And then the reminiscences would begin. Stories, incidents, biographies of long-dead friends, memories of childhood recalled in all the circumstantial detail - all these and more were repeated time and time again on those Sunday evenings. The tale would unfold like a symphony, beginning generally with a theme by William, the conductor of the orchestra. As he developed it the other members of the gathering would offer their contributions or develop a theme of their own at a given signal from the leader, and gradually the exposition would come, rise to its climax and finally subside to its logical and expected conclusion. As the years passed and I became familiar with certain stories I came to know the effect that certain words and phrases would have, for the same situations would provoke the same reminiscences. For example, whenever any ironing was being done, Ada would very easily launch into a little tale about her sister Florrie who once kept house for a lady who did not believe in ironing her underclothes. With experience, I came to learn how to steer the conversation gently away from this not particularly interesting subject. Garden herbs and sage in particular always reminded Ada of her childhood, so that if stuffing was being made I came to expect an oft repeated account of the making of faggots from the freshly killed pig at her cottage home in

Lydney. The faggots probably tasted delicious - though I fancy they used to put in too much sage for my taste.

I realise now, though at the time I did not, as I listened to all these tales and shared the simple refreshment with my husband's family that I was hearing the swansong of the last generation in modern times who relied to a very large extent on the spoken oral tradition word to transmit their history from one generation to the next.

I can see now that the continual repetition of the same information was an essential part of the tradition, for only in this way would the proper continuance of the story be ensured. Besides, the oldest stories were the ones that were loved the best, and every repeat performance evoked happy memories of the past. It is not in my province to say whether the older stories changed much as they came down through the years. All the evidence that we have of such matters would point to the fact that they did. As none of us was present at the original events it is obviously impossible no to prove or disprove anything - but it is quite beyond dispute that however much variation there might be in detail the facts were based on true happenings. Some of these tales, which Glyn will be recounting in another place, originated in a most astonishing assortment of subjects. Birth, death, childhood reminiscences, the soil, a liberal sprinkling of humour, some coarse (though these versions were never considered fit for my ears), religious experiences - and always lurking round the corner, his forked tail visibly twitching - the devil. There is one of these tales which even now after I have heard it so many times, chills my spine to the marrow.

Dear William, Ada, Selina, Lily, Lewis and Walter! It would be easy to scoff at the regularity of your lives, and the satisfaction and contentment which such a simple evening's entertainment gave you, but like so many things which exist no longer, it is only quite recently that we have come to learn the value of what you said. Believe it if you can - but I find myself trying, often unsuccessfully, to remember some of those conversations. Perhaps you will forgive me though if I tell you that I am not the only person who did not listen properly to what you used to say. Even Kathie, who is over 70, tells me that she too paid little attention to your stories, Selina, and it

CHAPTER 6. TIMES REMEMBERED

Figure 6.1: Kathie, Selina, Lewis and Walter

was only with some perseverance that I was able to find out a few details of your life. And even Glyn does not remember many of the sayings that I seem to have retained. He admits that he used to switch off whenever the "old days" were being discussed.

To return to the subject of William and Ada unconsciously taking over the book. If they were alive today they would be very surprised indeed to learn that anyone could possibly be interested in their lives and work.

Poor William struggled with an inferiority complex all his life, convinced as he was of the superior ability and success of his elder brother Lewis. True, Lewis had done well for after educating himself he had become an ordained minister in the Methodist church, William too had longed to enter the ministry but there were obstacles in the way of achieving his heart's desire. For one thing his health as a young man was not good, and even when this improved he had taken on the further burden of bringing up his sister's children. Then there was the necessity of learning Greek, Not surprisingly classical languages had not been included in the curriculum at the tiny Leighland school and even if they had, William would have had little time to learn them, leaving as he did at the tender age of twelve. Frustrated but not totally daunted by his lack of education, he did his best to make up for it in later years. The whole of his creative talent, which was considerable, was poured into his life. The great loves of his life, apart from the chapel and all its activities were music, woodcarving, the countryside and its history. The high point of his achievement, were the building of his own house and the creation of the garden, and I now propose to set down as accurately as I am able, the history of its construction.

The Building of the House

7

Glyn Court

First, one must try to imagine the village as it was early In 1914 (Figure 7.1) - a road curving past the station, down to the stream, and up the ramp the other side, much as today. The coming of the mineral railway had made very noticeable alterations in the landscape of this little corner, for the line ran straight down the side of the property and virtually under the window of the cottage. Its construction posed quite a problem, for the road had always run across the flat water meadow by the stream and then made a short sharp curving ascent to the cottages and chapel. In order to gain the necessary height a long sloping ramp had to be built over the top of the old road. The edge of this road can still be seen protruding from beneath the ramp - the tunnel has not yet been filled in. Traffic consists of an occasional horse and cart. The only car in the neighbourhood is owned by Count Hochberg of Croydon Hall, but as he has just gone back to Germany it is unlikely that we shall see it. The cottages in the village are rather shabby and the inhabitants do not look very prosperous. At the top of the ramp, we pass a little group of three cottages. These are occupied by two old ladies, Rhoda and Annie. Although the cottages appear low from the road which has been raised a few years earlier the interior is even lower, for it is necessary to descend three steps to the room from the front door. The lowest cottage, the one at the end which still survives, has suffered similarly from the raising of the road, and light in the main living room window has been completely blocked out by the bridge. To make matters worse, it has been damaged by fire. Instead of demolishing the remains, William is rebuilding the cottage on the foundations of the old one, the former living room now becoming a cellar. This no doubt accounts for the extraordinary shape of the place - a section from a large wedge with not a single right angle anywhere in it. As far as can be surmised the foundations date from the seventeenth century. Next to the cottages and on a higher level, there is a large field hedge running up at right angles to the road, shielding the "drang" - a narrow path leading out at the side of the two tiny cottages.

Then there is a high wall with an orchard visible above it. The front of the orchard, facing the road which is not made up, is bounded by a sturdy wall, the top of which is finished off with those alternate standing up and flat stones so typical of this part of Somerset, and known as cap and gap. It is not a particularly attractive finish but is utilitarian, and has a certain unity in that it continues, more or less right through the village on both sides of the road. We must stop at the gate of the orchard for we have arrived at Mr Bellamy's. The orchard belongs to him, as do the cottages, a well built stable, wash-house and a couple of stone privies and pigsty. Mr Bellamy carries on his business in the bakehouse, turning out batches of sweet-smelling bread from his crude but effective oven. This is heated by the laborious method of burning bundles of sticks (faggots) inside it and then raking out the ash. In the house, his daughter, Mary, and Ada are busily occupied in running the Post and Telegraph office - a very important place in the village, patronised by everyone, including the gentry.

James Bellamy is getting on in years and is handing over his business to Henry Chilcott. He has sold part of his land to William Court who intends to marry and build himself a house. The damaged cottage is to be rebuilt to house the baker and his family who will pay rent of 5/- per week to William - an arrangement which will continue for nearly 60 years. One threatening cloud on the horizon is to grow increasingly larger and cast its shadow over at least one of these projects. Unknown to James Bellamy, William and Ada and the other personages we see moving about in this little scene, the Kaiser's war is to cause considerable deferment of their plans. When the war does break out in August of the same year, everything has to wait and Ada patiently puts off her wedding plans with William until it is over. Even then it is another two years before William, who is now 44, and spurred on by the loss of his favourite sister, Tilly, finally makes up his mind to marry.

CHAPTER 7. THE BUILDING OF THE HOUSE

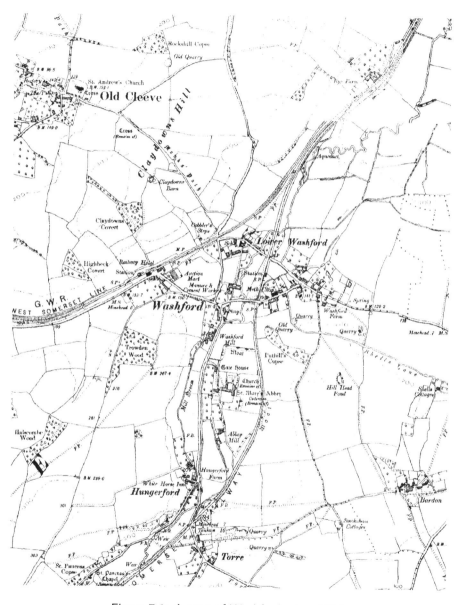

Figure 7.1: A map of Washford, circa 1910

Figure 7.2: View of Washford from Trowden Copse, circa 1900. The West Somerset Mineral Railway can clearly be seen in the centre of the photo.

Figure 7.3: View of Washford, taken from the field to the rear of Hill Head House, circa 1920

CHAPTER 7. THE BUILDING OF THE HOUSE

The burning question for William and Ada was how to raise enough money to start actually building the house. In 1920 it was a fairly unusual situation for folk of their social class to attempt such a project and 95% mortgages were a concept which had not yet been imagined. Also, both had a very deep dislike almost amounting to fear, of borrowing money. However, borrowing it had to be, from the bank and not from a building society. The money borrowed, amounting to £800 in all, would mainly be used to pay for materials as William would do a large part of the construction work himself; stone was cheap and not far to bring - while slate could be obtained from the ancient quarry of Treborough, a few miles up the valley. Transport costs were minimal, and the stone came virtually free of charge, the only payment exacted being 1/- duty on each cartload that was removed from the quarry opposite the farm. Timber also could be had locally, and William never lost an opportunity of acquiring pieces of wood which others had thrown away, or purchasing second-hand bargains. Of course, the sheer manual labour of dressing the stone, carting it and unloading and so forth could not possibly be undertaken by one man working alone, and William did enlist the assistance of at least one mason, now an old man in his eighties still living in the village.

Building a house was an operation which even in 1920 was not to be accomplished without a modicum of official approval. Before commencing any new "development" as we have learnt to call it, a plan had to be drawn and submitted to the council, for though prosperity as we have come to know it had not arrived with its wholesale consumption of open fields, there was a sufficient amount of new building going on to warrant some sort of control. We still have this drawing and very interesting it is William must have spent a good deal of time planning his house, for the finished version correspond remarkably well with the original design (Figure 7.4) . The one major difference is that the shop was originally intended to be a single storey structure joined to the house on one side. When he came to build, this part, however, William decided to continue the walls upward over the shop end square off the total design of the house. Perhaps he felt dissatisfied with the rather lop-sided effect that the shop gave to the building -in any case the materials cost so little that it was not so very much more expensive

A VILLAGE INHERITANCE

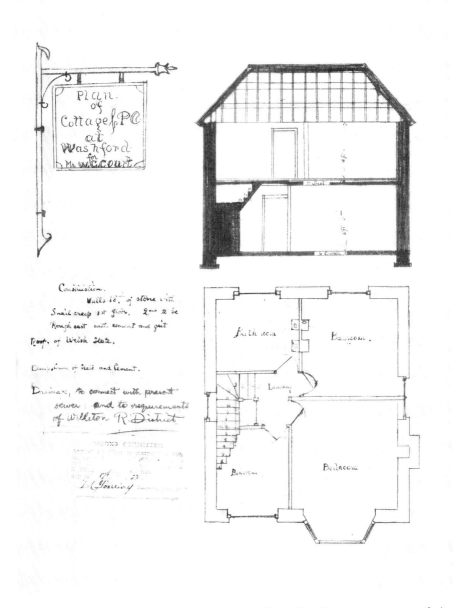

Figure 7.4: Original drawings of the house (Part 1). Produced as part of the planning application submitted by William Court in 1922.

CHAPTER 7. THE BUILDING OF THE HOUSE

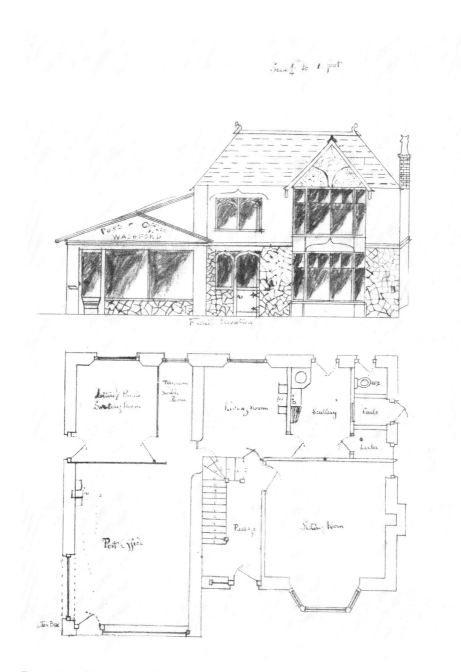

Figure 7.5: Original drawings of the house (Part 2). The original planned footprint can be seen for the house, highlighting the single-storey shop.

to build on up and construct a gable to correspond with the one on the either side of the house. Problems inevitably arose, however, and he must soon have found the additional cost of all the extra materials heavier than planned. This probably explains why for fifty years the windows at the back of this side of the house were glazed with odd panes of glass, some clear, some opaque, some reeded. The frames too were odd sizes and presumably oddments acquired from junk heaps. One unexpected benefit of the fire in 1971 (Chapter 18) was that the firemen smashed the glass panes most decisively so that at last I was able to, get rid of these ugly windows. No one shed any tears over that loss.

The plan was drawn, approved, and the next step was simple - William pegged out the site himself and started to dig the foundations. When they rose a suitable distance above ground level the damp course was laid - a course of Treborough slate, clearly visible against the warm red sandstone.

Drains were presumably connected, up at an early stage, but as the building regulations of 1920 did not insist on plans of drainage, there is no record of the exact location of our sewer outfall. The only clue we have is a, distinct diagonal mark which appears on our lawn in time of drought as a set of tramlines. Where the pipes go after they leave the lawn is a mystery that will probably never be solved, except by an unusually intelligent mole.

As soon as the house was habitable, William and Ada moved into it, some time in 1922. The removal must have been a major operation, as not only did they have to establish themselves and get the feel of a new home, but the post office and business had to be installed as well. Miss Bellamy relinquished her superintendency of the Washford Post Office and after fifteen years of apprenticeship Ada now became the postmistress. This was a serious responsibility and one which I think gave her great satisfaction. The hours were long but the pace of life relatively calm and quiet, and it was pleasant talking to the villagers, and helping them to sort out their problems. At about the same time William had formally relinquished the situation of Postmaster at Roadwater and handed it over to his sister Selina - a transaction which was suitably blessed by the Head Postmaster. Selina would not be able to deal with the full scale boot and shoe store and repair

CHAPTER 7. THE BUILDING OF THE HOUSE

service on her own, so William was faced with the not inconsiderable task of transferring all the paraphernalia and much of the stock to the new premises at Washford. I am heartily convinced that he thoroughly disliked the having to change everything, and can easily imagine him affirming that this would be the first and last time that he would ever move house. Some of the items were heavy, and no doubt it took numerous journeys to Roadwater to fetch everything. The "James" motorcycle was now obsolete and he soon progressed to a motor car - one of the few in the village - a Calcott tourer with collapsible hood.

Not the least of the problems connected with the removal of the business was where to have the workshop. Shoe repairing is a trade requiring plenty of space for the sheets of leather, work bench, sewing machine, stock of tacks, nails, heels, and so forth. The only suitable building was the wash house. It was not really large enough for the purpose and in order to get to it customers would have to walk right across the back of the house and round the corner into the garden, but it would serve for the time being.

The shop was a large and commodious space, but as to begin with there was no equipment to go in it, William had to make everything that was necessary, knocking up shelves and a counter out of odd pieces of wood. This part of the building was never really finished off properly, partly because of the lack of money, and partly because it was in such constant use once the post office and store began to operate from there, that there was little opportunity for doing anything more to it. The walls were plastered, received a hasty coat of whitewash and after that were never again painted. The shortage of money led to the ceiling being finished off with laths of thin plywood, a cheaper and quicker finish than plastering. The unexpected effect of this was that the wood had the effect of creating a sound box over the post office area so that every sound made above was heard and magnified through the thin floorboards. This used to cause quite a few problems when some years later my children used to take it into their heads to have noisy games in the room above, jumping from the high box spring bed on to the floor with devastating effect. Poor Granny used to get very upset at this, I think she expected the "customers" to complain. Unfortunately, as I had not grown up in the environment, I was never able to induce in myself the state of quasi-religious veneration for the Post Office and in any case it gave the pensioners something to talk about!

During the building of the house William and Ada had been living with Miss Bellamy at the Post Office over the road (Figure 7.7). It was not a very happy arrangement and understandably enough, they were longing to get into their own home at the very earliest opportunity. Ada often used to say how she never missed going across to the house one single day all the time it was being built. As soon as one or two rooms were habitable, they moved in, surrounded by bricks, plaster, cement, tools and all the appurtenances of an unfinished building operation. Many doors and windows had not yet been made, and the fireplace in the big room was not to be completed for another eight years. However, it was four walls, and although we have no record of their feelings it must have been a very happy day when they began to camp out in the newly plastered rooms. The empty unfinished spaces must have seemed rather eerie and hollow and the focal point of the house very quickly became the sheltered, sunny living room at the back, with the adjoining scullery, or back kitchen. The fire in the living room, always known as the kitchen, heated the water, a rare luxury for them, who had never enjoyed more than a cold tap. It was one of those rather fearsome black stoves, with two ovens and hobs for boiling over the fire - a very functional arrangement which one still finds as a standard fitting in many houses in the North where coal is cheap. The stove was not particularly economical, but for a long time it was the only cooking or heating facility in the house. Also, it must have been well made as it lasted for nearly forty years.

All the woodwork in the house was made by William - that is to say, all skirting boards, doors, window frames, and ornamental exterior woodwork. Altogether, the house has nineteen doors and about twenty windows, some of which are large bays with up to fourteen lights in them, so you will see that he had a good, excuse for not doing the gardening as well. The "best" part of the house - i.e. the front, North side, was destined to receive the cherished oak that he prized so much. Many of the pieces had been saved from old buildings or even rubbish heaps, and every panel, every door frame, every carved knob (and there are many) was worked by hand. As any

CHAPTER 7. THE BUILDING OF THE HOUSE

Figure 7.6: A photo of Ada, Glyn and William outside the newly constructed house. The shop can be seen to the left part of the property.

Figure 7.7: A photo of the Old Post Office in Washford, before being relocated to Hill Head House

A VILLAGE INHERITANCE

Figure 7.8: A view of the cottages previously built on the land. The two smaller cottages were demolished in the 1920s, and were located where the driveway is now. The photo was taken around 1925, as the eaves of Hill Head House can be seen in the top right of the photo.

CHAPTER 7. THE BUILDING OF THE HOUSE

amateur handyman will know, oak is hard as iron, and consequently driving in screws or fixing hinges becomes a major task. An amusing discovery that we made when trying to cure a door that persisted in lurching at an undignified angle, was that it was held on by only two screws, one at the top and one at the bottom. Fortunately the electric drill has arrived on the scene to take the backache out of this sort of work, and the door now boasts far more screws than it ever knew before, Similarly, several of the windows had never been opened, which annoyed me as I like fresh air, and the reason soon became apparent - some had no stays or catches on, others had not even any hinges. One day we will catch up with all these little jobs but it takes persistence and is also very expensive.

I have mentioned my father-in-law's love of oak - this had no doubt been impressed on him as a young man when, abandoning the family tradition of bootmaking, he went to train as a carpenter's apprentice. His wages soon rose from 6d to 6 pence and one farthing per hour, 1/4 d more than the ordinary carpenters, as he had a natural flair for the work and soon became skilled. To the end of his life he could not bear to throw away a piece of wood, and we have had ample cause to bless his forethought. Looking round for gateposts in our enormous garage where most of the old wood was stored we found two long beams- resting across the traverses which support the tin roof. They were of oak and we had been looking at them for years without realising what they were. Much of the old wood was virtually useless of course, and only fit for the bonfire. As my old gardener remarked "Tis old as Adam, Madam!"

We have now been living here for seven years and I think that we have reduced the wood to manageable proportions - although we shall not have to look very far for kindling sticks for ten years at least.

People often ask us why the corrugated iron monstrosity, known as "the Garage" is so enormous. The reason is that when delivery of the mail by motor vans first started, space had to be found to keep the two vehicles which were based at Washford. These vans were very high and much larger than the modern ones. One was a Morris Cowley, one an Oxford. They had calor meters on the front of the bonnet and regularly used to boil when going up steep hills. William had to build a garage for the vehicles as cheaply as possible, and threw this enormous lean-to roof up against the wall of Butcher Shepherd's slaughterhouse next door. Relations were quite strained for a while, as the building operation blocked out the light from one of the butcher's windows. Nor was it a straightforward task, as the ground sloped away at an inconvenient angle, so literally tons of soil had to be dug out to create the necessary level space. We have never quite made out what happened to all this soil. As a finishing touch to this unlovely but useful creation, the Garage, William constructed a sliding door. It still slides perfectly after forty-three years, but is so heavy that we rarely bother to close it. On the front of the door, still faintly visible, is the legend:

W, G. Court
Garage

Glyn remembers his father painting it on and the pleasure that he derived from making the letters appear to lie flat on the corrugated material. Frequent interruptions to the work had to be made before William was satisfied with the perspective.

In one corner of this edifice, (which when tidy will comfortably hold four cars) stands the 1932 Austin 10 in which my parents-in-law drove around until William's death in 1953. The car then passed to us and we drove it really hard for another five years. We were living in Yorkshire at the time so the 200 mile journey must have taxed the engine considerably. She never broke down however. The previous car, a Calcott, was not preserved, I cannot think why not. It would have been valuable if it had. Black mark.

Above the Austin, there is a further cobwebby extension, looking more than a little improbable perched high up seemingly in the heavens, like a strange attic, full of mysterious pieces of twisted metal. The illusion of height is given by the steep rise in the ground level at the back of the garage, and a close examination reveals a heap of very old bicycles. The one at the bottom looks as if it might be pre 1914 vintage. We are putting off

CHAPTER 7. THE BUILDING OF THE HOUSE

taking the bicycles out until we have the time and money to deal with them properly. Meanwhile they will probably not deteriorate much more in a mere ten years or so than they have in the last thirty, forty or even sixty. Ten years at Washford, as I have come to learn, is a very short space of time indeed.

The rest of the garage proved a fruitful quarry when we were having one of our first turn-outs. Several advertising signs from the 1920s and '30s turned up - the metalled enamel variety. The rest of the space tends to get filled up with unwanted pieces of furniture, and boxes of burnt books left over from the fire.

The days of the Garage are numbered now as rust is making progress and quite a lot of rain finds its way through the roof, but let it not be said that its life and work have not been recorded for posterity!

8 Of Oaken Things

Clare Court

Having built the house William's first and most pressing task was to finish off the floors - a not inconsiderable labour considering the area to be covered. A quick examination of our floors will soon reveal that the entire ground surface of the downstairs rooms is paved with wooden blocks. The shop, sorting office and living room floors were made of deal, for the precious oak would not run to covering the whole of the ground floor. William made every single oak block himself, planing the wood by hand, sawing the planks up into the required sizes and then laying them in herringbone pattern. The blocks measure approximately 8" by 2" by 1" thick though very few conform exactly to these measurements. Some are of irregular size and shape, such as the curved ones at the bottom of the stairs. In the course of writing about the floors it occurred to me that it would be an interesting calculation to work out just how many blocks were needed to cover the entire floor space. We did a few multiplication sums and came up with the grand total of 1,600 oak and 3,000 deal blocks.

There is one rectangular patch in the former shop which was not so paved. It was under the counter and William evidently did not consider it worth his while to waste labour and wood on it. Another corner which was never finished is under the stairs - an irregular triangular which still patiently awaits the day of fulfilment and completion. I wonder why my father-in-law never finished it? Perhaps a customer called to collect a pair of boots while he was on his hands and knees under the stairs. Perhaps, as I have often done, he hit his head on the massy oak as he got up with stunning effect. Be that as it may he never returned to finish off the corner. It was not because of the shortage of blocks either – there are still some out in the shed waiting, patiently waiting.

Over the years this oak parquet has been lovingly polished to a rich and mellow golden brown which warmly welcomes the rays of sunlight as they filter through the stained glass in the hall door. Unfortunately the wood has shrunk slightly over the years leaving narrow cracks between each block. In the main traffic areas the pitch with which they were stuck down has also worn away so that it is possible to prise out the blocks if one wishes to remove small objects that have disappeared into the cracks. This, needless to say, was a great attraction to the children in their younger days and our eldest daughter at a tender age spent many happy times removing as much of the hall floor as her little hands could lift up - and a surprising amount it was for a two year old! The game was so fascinating that she became quite cunning over it and learnt how to lure her Granny into the other room, shut the door quickly and dash back to continue her task unaided. Fortunately we usually managed to rescue the blocks before they travelled too far away from their proper resting place.

Every house has its own noises, its own particular creaks, bumps and gurgles and another rather endearing feature of the floor blocks is the faint rocking sound made by the cats as their soft feet tread over the floor. It is a friendly little noise, something between a tap and a touch, which has become one of the idiosyncratic features of our home's individuality. When the day comes, if it ever does, that we have the floor relaid and all made perfect and whole, we shall miss the sound very much. The same could be said of the unfinished corner under the stairs. For years, this annoyed me intensely but long habit has made me grow used to it. After all - one wonders - is perfection necessary to our happiness? I think not. As long as some things remain in their unfinished state, there is always a stimulus - firstly to one's creative and orderly instincts, which command that one day the task shall be completed. Secondly, and by no means of lesser importance, there are the human associations (in the case of the floor I might be tempted to say human and feline) which breathe life into otherwise uninteresting and inanimate objects.

I think perhaps that this is why some stately homes and museums seem so soulless and deficient in human interest. They have been polished, tidied and set in order beyond the normal imagining of those who once lived in

CHAPTER 8.   OF OAKEN THINGS

the rooms or used the objects which are displayed. This is one reason why I feel that our own home and little museum with all their imperfections, possess a quality which is so frequently lacking in those which suffer from "la manie de la propreté". They show man as he really is and not as an ideal in all the vigour of his creative talent, which however great, is not entirely immune from attack by occasional bouts of lethargy, laziness or boredom. They also show him as a very busy person who simply does not have the time to finish all the tasks that he has begun.

An interesting feature of our hall, which is entirely panelled, floored and furnished with oak, is the staircase. My father-in-law had at some time rescued an unwanted mill-wheel from one of the ten or so disused mills on the stream - probably New Mills at Luxborough. What condition the wheel was in when he transported it from the site we shall never know, but the sight of so much good timber going to waste was obviously too much for William to bear, and he conceived the idea of using the paddles to make the stairs in his house. Years of use and submersion in water must have made this a laborious and difficult task, but eventually the stairs arose as it were from the mill pond, ascending in a pleasing though somewhat dangerous curve to the landing. Despite William's efforts he was unable to remove the mark of a giant iron bolt which had burnt itself into the timber. The bolt has left a geometrical black stain on one of the stairs. We had often wondered about the origin of this strange black mark, but it was not until a few years ago that a visitor to our house told us the story about the mill wheel which Glyn had forgotten literally for decades. The explanation of the mark suddenly became very obvious.

The newel posts and banisters were also hand-carved though they too did not take kindly to the introduction of central heating into the hall. Rather characteristically, William's concentration was distracted from finishing the banister off with uprights and this left rather a large open space which must have a strong feeling of insecurity to anyone standing on the landing. Time went on however and still the banisters were not completed - until suddenly the arrival of a baby, which quickly developed into a toddler, demanded urgently that something be done to fill the gaping void. William solved the problem - quickly and effectively - he brought into the house the side of a bicycle crate which he proceeded to rope to the banisters! This crude contrast apparently did not upset his aesthetic sense, for the crate remained there for years, in fact, until Glyn came back from the army in Burma in 1947. At this point William evidently considered the time had come to replace the crate with something better, and the top part of the landing was fitted out with slats. On close examination they do not quite come up to the standard of the rest, but fortunately the light is not too good at the top of the stairs. On the opposite side, however, the slats are of very rough wood hastily nailed in, I imagine, to stop Glyn as a baby falling through. Perhaps one day we shall find a carpenter who will make it a labour of love to match the craftsmanship of the hall entrance, and finish off the banisters in fitting harmony with the rest. Until that day comes, the four-footed members of the household know that here is one place in the house where sharpening of claws is not forbidden.

Not content with making all the woodwork which was needed for the house, skirting boards, windows, doors, panelling, flooring and more, William also turned his hand on more than one occasion to making furniture. By trade he was a carpenter and not a cabinet maker, and although, when necessity urged, he would produce a polished piece of work, furniture making was a secondary interest for him. When we first had a home of our own we had no furniture so Glyn's mother gave us one of the home made beds. We slept on it for years. These beds were, of course, of oak and consequently though their qualities of endurance were truly British they were hardly calculated to fill the heart of any housewife with delight. For one thing, they weighed a ton, or so it seemed if ever one desired to move them from one side of the room to the other, and for another, they were almost a danger to life and limb, as William had not realised that sharp carved knobs on bed posts were hardly practical - in fact downright dangerous. Both head and foot rails were chest high, and the slats across the base of the bed were pieces of solid timber. When we took the beds to pieces we noticed for the first time that each piece was inscribed with Roman numerals I II III IV. The sides were united to the base by means of iron bolts ten inches long! On top of the slats reposed heavy box springs, also with wooden sides to add to the already considerable weight of the frame of the bed. The crowning

CHAPTER 8. OF OAKEN THINGS

glory of the structure was a feather bed and over all reposed a white linen bedspread.

There were two such beds, and such was their gravity and seriousness that it would have been quite easy to imagine Matthew, Mark, Luke and John standing vigil at the corners. The best bed on which William and Ada slept boasted, in addition to its solidity, twin panels of carving at head and foot. Unfortunately one section of a foliage capital had broken off along the grain of the wood, rather spoiling the symmetry of the design, and as long as I can remember seeing it, this part was always tied on with a piece of post office string. Both these beds now repose in the bakehouse awaiting their call to a further life but the trump has not yet sounded for them. They are too good to be thrown out, but far too cumbersome to use. My plan is to work them into the banisters for in this way the carving will not be lost.

Apart from a chair of no great distinction, William's best piece of furniture is undoubtedly the three-cornered cupboard which stands in the corner of our front room. Ada was very fond of this cupboard as William had made it for her as her birthday present in the first year of their marriage. It is in the late Victorian style and is opened by one of those fascinating wooden rings carved from a single block of wood. It is a pity that the lower half (in which George Hoyle's model of the steam engine was always kept) never got finished, but William was skilled at disguising his little incompletions and it is only on close examination that you will notice that the wood is a panel from a tea chest, cleverly varnished.

9 An Artist at Home

Glyn Court

Whatever its imperfections, our house is unquestionably individual, and (as my wife has hinted) this is because it was planned and, for the most part, actually built by one man, my father. As he saw it, the ideal house had little to do with architectural fashion or modernity but everything to do with the old values of village society and its craftsmen; and as so much of the old life was passing away, and he treasured the memories of the friends of his youth, he determined to preserve what he could by that workmanship of his which sprang from the soil of Somerset.

The old craftsmen had been compelled by poverty to use their materials with the most rigid economy; my father's generation, though they were beginning to live more amply, would never throw away a good nail or screw, never cut a knot in a length of string, never discard a length of timber; a cobbler - as I can remember from the war years - would juggle for long periods with a bend ox leather to find an extra sole or even an infilling for a cue. "Wicked waste" was a phrase often heard on their lips. Yet not only economy was at the root of this behaviour, but something deeper, a respect amounting to reverence - though they would not have consciously named it so - for the materials of their craft and love and intimate understanding of their qualities. It is traditionally in carpenters and wheelwrights, working with living individual material, that this attitude has always been most highly developed, and in this also my father ran true to the type, He loved all timber, I believe, but not uncritically, and he had his favourites. Nothing could arouse his enthusiasm like good honest English oak: he loved its hardy, workable close grain, its mellowness and dignity; he would caress it and lovingly feel its texture, but he would shake his head sadly over the Austrian oak of which more and more came in after 1900, easier to work, maybe, but it had not the character, the staying-power, the hardy grain of the true, well-seasoned native. Perhaps he saw a parable in it too. Besides, as he saw it, the true carpenter, if not the joiner, should in some measure make the dead tree live again, and to all the flat surfaces of the heavy oak in his house he gave a natural finish with saw and plane alone, and on the curves he left the marks of chisel and gouge, only slightly evened by sanding. "Here is good timber", he seemed to say, "let it be".

By the time he came to build his own house, however, the good timber of his youth was hardly to be found. During the Great War the hardwood forests had been mercilessly felled, the stocks of matured timber so carefully laid down over the years were exhausted, and were not being replaced.

In this dilemma the ingrained habits of economy came to his aid. As my wife has written elsewhere, he rescued beams and panels of oak from a rubbish heap, worked on them, and pieced them together to make doors; from a mill in his village which had just ceased to work he salvaged the mill wheel; out of the cross-pieces of this he fashioned the surround of his sitting room fireplace, in which the bolt holes are still visible; and he made his staircase, both treads and risers, out of the vanes.

It was, I believe, a matter of pride with him, not merely a result of straitened circumstances in the 1920s, that he should use local materials throughout his home. Very remarkably, using local resources, and working in a local tradition, he nevertheless built a house peculiar to himself and in some of its components, at least, quite unique.

Certainly his slate fireplace is unique. Slate seems an unlikely material, but my father had two good reasons: availability, and - better still - sentiment. The latter argument he never could resist.

Near Treborough, on the steep hillside two miles above Roadwater, is an abandoned slate quarry. It has long been deserted; the last two regular workmen, Eli Vickery and his son, ceased in the late 1930s; but in my father's youth it provided employment for thirty men. Father was determined to have a capacious fireplace in his best room, and one built naturally of local materials; and since sandstone was unsuitable, slate was the answer, if it could be used satisfactorily. In these parts, of course, it

CHAPTER 9. AN ARTIST AT HOME

Figure 9.1: The fireplace, constructed by William Court using locally sourced timber and slate.

was employed not only for roofing but also, in its shillet form, for the fabric of the houses. The fireplace is, in fact, the only part of the house that I can remember being built, for the rest was pretty well complete before I began to sit up in the cot and look around: but I was allowed when two years old to lend a willing and no doubt useless hand at mixing the mortar.

Father bought a couple of hundred quarter-inch slate off-cuts and as many slate slabs, and set to work grading and shaping and cutting them to form the pattern he saw in his mind's bye. The fourteen three-inch slabs forming the fire-back were soon fixed and then came the huge fire-bricks at the side, with holes which he bored four inches deep to take the ornamental kettle-crooks he was to get the village blacksmith, Tom Kerslake, to forge. His plan for the front was, I think, completely original, unless he received a hint from a fireplace In Cleeve Abbey; certainly I have not seen its fellow. He conceived it as an arch of laminated slates resting against, rather than supported by, buttresses - also of laminated slate - in such a way that the underside of the arch and the inside edge of the buttresses formed one continuous curve; while that inside edge again, when viewed obliquely, formed a double curve. To make the buttresses, he laid slate upon slate, with a layer of mortar between each, to a height of two feet; and no one slate was of exactly the same size or shape as the next, and this is how he obtained his curves. At two feet he inserted a template and built his arch, achieving a curve on a curve, though he afterwards always felt slightly guilty that the great weight of the slates had forced him to use a few inches of copper wire to keep them firmly in place. With this complete, he laid his hearth - a hundred slabs of solid slate set in a semicircle so that the lines of the mortar drew your gaze toward what was literally the focal point of the room and the home. Semi-circular pieces of slate rounded off the inside of the fireplace, and in due time he added an overmantle and a surround and mantlepiece in four-inch oak of immemorial antiquity.

I have of course known this fireplace practically all my life, but only recently have considered it closely, and now I marvel more than a little that my father, with no mathematical knowledge, and little training in constructional design, should have produced a work in which the abundant curves are so perfectly balanced and held in check by the perfectly horizontal or

CHAPTER 9. AN ARTIST AT HOME

vertical structural lines of the material itself; and yet on further reflection I wonder less, for the curves, I should say, could not be described in terms of mathematics, any more than - if the comparison does not cause too broad a smile - the curve of the dome of St Peter's can be found in geometry. I cannot imagine that my father, who had no love for straight lines and often said "You'll never find a straight line in nature", would have used any more complicated instruments than a foot rule, a length of post office string and a pair of compasses; probably he thought of the slate very much as he thought of his timber and tried to shape it as he would shape timber with an adze, tried to construct with it so that a grain was created. If he did work by old English rule-of-thumb, it carried him a long, long way.

10 The Garden

Clare Court

Almost as soon as William and Ada had got themselves into the gaunt, bare shell of a house and installed their belongings, they began the task of making a piece of garden near the house - mainly a patch of orchard grass, which soon responded to cutting and became a very pleasant lawn. Garden making was quite a new experience for Ada, and as they began the tasks of making paths, and establishing beds of flowers, she very soon found herself in her element. For years she had been tied to the house across the road for all of her waking hours - counter work during the day while after hours she coped with all the whims and fancies of a domineering and not very sweet-tempered taskmistress. Suddenly she found herself in her element, and as the busy years slipped by she spent more and more time in the garden. It became a hobby and an amusing challenge to collect stones for rockeries and ornaments. Often on an evening walk she and William would see a stone which caught their fancy and laboriously carry it home between them. The cliffs at Watchet are veined with seams of alabaster which was an important factor in the establishment of the paper mill over two hundred years ago, alabaster being an important whitening agent in the manufacture of paper. The colours are many and varied, from rose and white to creamy yellow and green, and many pieces of alabaster found their way into the garden. Unfortunately, once it has been cut away from the cliff and left for a while in the open air, the delicate shades and sparkling crystals of the stone become quickly misted over and after a few years it becomes badly discoloured.

As the years went by and their business became established and relatively prosperous, William and Ada were able to afford more help with the shop and post office and this enabled them to spend more time in the garden.

At its heyday during the 1930s, our modest domain at Washford was a veritable little empire, with constant coming and going of postmen and customers throughout the day. William always employed at least one "boy" to help with the repairs - sometimes he had grown to be a man while in the service but had usually started his employment with William on leaving school. Ada always had a girl in the office and one or two telephonists. One of William's dislikes was vegetable gardening, and he was only too happy to delegate entire charge of this part of the garden to Bert or Graham or Stan. Country boys all, they were usually wonderful gardeners, and never happier than when "spitting" or burying the dung. William could occasionally be seen, in waistcoat and hat and bow tie, tastefully clipping the ornamental hedges into fanciful shapes. A great lover of the curved line, he did not care for his hedges to be straight along the top, and the nitida sported many simulated pillars surmounted by knobs and joined by graceful curved spans that would not have disgraced a gentleman's residence. Alas! In these utilitarian days, they are not a faint shadow of their former selves, but here and there an obstinate downward curve and drunken pillar leaning precariously to one side, wryly remind us of their departed elegance.

Ada on the contrary adored flower gardening, and this was her main relaxation, affording the principal outlet for her creative talent, not forgetting the crochet work of course. Unfortunately I never saw the garden at its peak. When I first came to Washford, old age and ill health were beginning to take their toll, and the ornamental rockeries had quite a few weeds in them. Out of self-preservation we have had to eliminate many of the smaller beds as it was quite impossible to keep them all tidy. One day when everything else is finished I hope to get the part that remains back to something approaching its former charm. One is speechless at William and Ada's industry as, at the same time that they were creating the garden, they were also running the business and Post Office, finishing the building of the house, bringing up a child and taking an active part in church and council work. It is perhaps hardly surprising that some things were never completed.

CHAPTER 10. THE GARDEN

I have already mentioned Ada's rather naughty habit of acquiring stones for her garden. She need not have carried so many; ten years after the house was built they were to have far more than they could use when William demolished the two old cottages. An astonishing assortment emerged from the rubble - fragments of capitals, octagonal sections which must surely have been the vertebrae of columns, curved stones, square stones, rectangular stones - all these and more emerged from the masonry as the walls collapsed and the dust began to clear. The largest pieces were enormous and could only just be lifted by one man on his own. They stand around the garden at various points, silent memorials to the mediaeval masons who first quarried and sculpted them. I sometimes wonder what they were called, those masons of long ago. Were they Cridlands or Burnetts, Goodings, and Locks in the village In the Middle Ages? What did they talk about while they were shaping the soft red sandstone into those gently rounded curves or geometrical shapes? The success of the harvest, the monks at the new Abbey, and did they grumble about the taxes - or simply talk about the weather? The air is silent and there are some questions to which we shall never know the answer but six hundred years after the Abbey was first founded the stones continue to bear silent testimony to those long-dead craftsmen. Then again, the imagination flits over another period of time, to the 1560s, when the Abbey Church was pillaged after the Dissolution of the Monasteries. Were they descendants of those masons, who came along with their oxen and took away free cart loads of stone? It seems a miracle that the actual Abbey buildings still survive, but this part of the Abbey continued to be used as a farm and perhaps even as a place of residence and that is presumably why it was never allowed to fall into too bad a state of repair. Of the church, however, not one single stone remains. Patient excavation has revealed the shape and size of it, and the bases of the pillars are clearly to be seen. It must have been a magnificent sight in its prime - such a splendid building with its soaring nave and tower amidst the lush greenery of the valley. Monks always seem to have had a wonderful knack of finding the most sheltered and fertile spot in which to build their Abbeys. This well-watered vale, so effectively shielded from cold winds by its surrounding ring of hills, must surely be one of the gentlest nurseries for cultivating tender plants. One can easily imagine vineyards growing here in mediaeval times for it is known that the vine was cultivated in this area.

Before the supply of stones became so abundant the first paths and steps in the garden were made of the most readily available materials. Treborough slate, which figures prominently, was used to pave the principal paths. Slate has its disadvantages among which a tendency to become slippery in wet weather is the worst. However, we know our paths well and rarely slip on them ourselves. Some of the slabs are very large and thick, and the labour of moving them and putting them into place must have been enormous. One particularly splendid square piece which we have served for forty years or so as a base for the stamping pad in the post office. It is about two foot square and two inches thick - they evidently anticipated heavy use! It would not have been out of place as a chopping block. I have not yet found a use for it but no doubt the day will come. I am beginning to see the wisdom of the old country adage "keep a thing for seven years and you'll find a use for it"!

To start the garden off then, they had a good piece of grass at the side and front of the house, and a few paths. Shortly afterwards they made some steps leading up from the lawn towards the wash house, and these have always been very successful as a background for family photographs. The paving was of red sandstone and finding it difficult no doubt to finish off the steps in the desired curve with such an awkward material, William cast the ends of the steps himself in concrete which has mellowed over the years to blend with the natural stone. He was talented too at designing his garden ornaments and casting them in cement, and Benvenuto Cellini can hardly have had greater satisfaction at the unmoulding of Perseus than William at the production of his plant pots and ornamental plasters. The moulds for these lie around somewhere still. The cement he used must have been different from our modern variety as it has weathered to a pleasant greyish shade. Some of the steps have an almost glass-like smoothness - I am told that the materials for achieving this type of finish are not obtainable nowadays. When desiring to create a variation in the finished product he would set small pieces of alabaster broken up into the moulds, or occasionally pieces of sandstone in different shades. I enjoy putting plants

CHAPTER 10. THE GARDEN

Figure 10.1: Cleeve Abbey, Gateway

Figure 10.2: A sketch of Cleeve Abbey Chapter House made in 1907

in these pots but alas! I lead a busy life and am frequently prone to forget them, upon which the unfortunate occupants languish and die. One thing is certain - I could never introduce factory made ornaments into our garden to stand beside those that we have - although quite pleasant in appearance, the contrast would be hopelessly incongruous.

Besides the steps there are two hollow pillars made by the broken alabaster mould method surmounted by two more pots. He also constructed two steps to the lower level of the garden which was later to contain the pond. The pillars beside these were made of old bricks in order to achieve a more attractive appearance, and William painstakingly chipped the edges from each individual brick. These pillars are hollow, which tempts garden birds to build their nests inside. Unfortunately our two cats are only too aware of their presence and despite our efforts to protect the squatting family of baby sparrows this spring, the mother abandoned the nest in the face of such energetic feline interest. Even when there is nothing inside the pillar, it is not an uncommon sight to see a cat's tail protruding from the top - our adventurous and agile cat likes to know what is at the bottom and we often wonder if she will succeed in getting herself out again. Rather to our surprise she generally manages the feat unaided.

All the lower part of the garden would have been made during the 1930s after the two old cottages had been knocked down, and one is continually amazed at the achievement considering the nature of the times. From about 1930 onwards the villages were hit very hard by the depression. The majority of the village population was living on a very low income, and many on the five shilling per week unemployment benefit. Takings in the shop dropped to a pathetically low level, just sufficient to live on with little or nothing left over to pay back the heavy interest charges to the bank. For years money was in such short supply that every possible expedient was resorted to in order to manage without it. And yet throughout this time, William and Ada never stopped working in the garden, creating charm and even beauty from materials that were readily to hand and which cost little or nothing. As far as the actual plants were concerned stocking the garden was very much a family affair. Flora Thompson in "Lark Rise" describes how cottagers in the 1880s lovingly tended their plots and filled their tiny gardens with

CHAPTER 10. THE GARDEN

clumps of cottage flowers, which they acquired by exchanging with each other. Country folk of the labouring class rarely had pence to spare from their low wages to buy seeds, and so it was, indeed still is, common friendly practice to give a neighbour a slip of an admired plant. Ada continued the tradition and nothing gave her greater delight than to acquire a new cutting or give a home to a languishing plant. Her favourite birthday or Christmas gift would be a rose tree to augment her collection. Unfortunately I do not know the origin of those that survive of the eighty bushes which she once counted in her garden. Some of them are very old to judge by their stems, and of varieties rarely seen nowadays, so perhaps they are a legacy from the pre-1914 cottage garden. The blooms are smaller and nearer to hedge roses in style and colour than the enormous waxy monsters to which we have become accustomed. One in particular which I estimate to be at least forty years old is of a very unusual pinky mauve shade. Sad to relate, during the fifties and sixties when the upkeep of the garden was becoming increasingly difficult, Ada discovered chemical weed killers, and not understanding the danger in using them poured large quantities of sodium chlorate solution over the paths. The inevitable result which never failed to surprise her was that many plants disappeared, never to be seen again. Several ornamental trees were also severely affected and branches died on the almond and cherry trees. It has taken several years for the garden to recover from this chemical assault and we have partly nursed the sick trees back to health. Although their shape is ruined, it is nice to keep some trees from the original garden, however imperfect they may be - especially when one remembers the loving care and devotion with which they were raised, sometimes from a pip or stone.

Ada was in a more fortunate position than her labouring ancestors when it came to obtaining flower and vegetable seed as William held the agency in the village for Webbs seeds. In those days when there was still a strict code of honour prevailing among wholesalers and their customers in the villages, the agency to such a firm was a valuable asset not to be lightly dismissed. If you were the sole agent then you knew that you really were the only shop to be selling that particular brand of goods and would never suffer the annoyance which we had to endure when we tried to run the shop for a while of seeing another shop in the village selling goods which were traditionally our preserve. That sort of integrity is hard to maintain in these competitive days, but its loss was a sad day and drove one more nail into the coffin of the spirit of mutual trust and confidence which used to prevail between traders in the same community. In the early days the seeds used to arrive by train in strong, pleasant looking wooden boxes - we have two or three of them still, and the one in which I keep my spare cutlery does not look out of place near the polished oak under the hall stairs. Ada was as proud of Webbs seeds as if she had ripened and harvested them herself and many a bed of cornflowers, stocks, nasturtiums and candytuft flourished under her care. She was not a very methodical gardener and I never remember her raising seedlings and transplanting them into pots when they showed two leaves and all that sort of thing. She just had green fingers and her constant vigilance - for she thought nothing of going out in the garden after sorting the morning mail for a couple of hours before breakfast, which she herself did not eat and in the long summer days was quite likely to be still out until darkness came in at around ten o' clock - ensured that the seedlings were not eaten by slugs or smothered by weeds. As already mentioned she was an inveterate pip planter and as she grew older the pots on the window sill became one of her principal interests. After her death there was a fine little orange tree and several budding date palms on the sill of the larder window, but I am afraid in the chaos that prevailed for the first year of running two homes and shuttling to and fro between them, the plants were neglected and suffered an untimely death.

The tradition of window sill gardening seems to be very old among country people and it is one of the most delightful characteristics of the English village scene. To me it seems a small miracle that when the production of food occupied such a large and important part of their lives, cottagers always managed to find a corner for a clump of phlox, sweet rocket and a briar rose as well as the sweet smelling and decorative herbs, rosemary, thyme and sage. The window sills (or sill) were a valuable extension of the often tiny garden as contrary to general belief many cottagers have virtually no garden at all. Fashions in window sill gardening do not change very rapidly and it still a fairly common sight in these country parts to

CHAPTER 10. THE GARDEN

see a maidenhair fern or Mind-your-own business overflowing a Victorian plant pot decorated in those rather vivid shades of green and pink so beloved of our grandparents. It was pleasant too to see, when a group of modern bungalows was built in our village for older residents, that it was literally no time at all before the windows, much larger than any most of the occupants had ever owned before, boasted a delightful display of Busy Lizzies, Christmas Cactus, scented geranium, and other traditional cottage flowers, as well as the more modern varieties of gloxinias, begonia and primulas. The only nation to outdo the English cottager in this respect must surely be the Dutch - to drive along a street of tiny bungalows almost anywhere in Holland is like visiting a florist's display, so crammed is every available inch with a wealth of leaf and bloom, climbing vine and trailing fern.

Gradually then, the garden took shape, with a stone added here, a cutting there, a seedling oak tree raised from an acorn in the hedge, and tell it not in Gath, more than one mysterious stranger which somehow accidentally found its way there by way of Ada's handbag after a visit to a park or garden. What a strange malady it is which seems to afflict many gardeners who are scrupulously honest in every other way - the burning desire to break off a small piece of a plant which catches their fancy! It is a disease which cuts right across class and social status and I confess that I myself am not totally immune from it. There seems to be a rough moral justice being meted out from above as somehow or other these "acquired" cuttings rarely seem to grow.

After the demolition of the cottages there was such a large quantity of stones to dispose of that it took years to "find a use" for all of them and it must be confessed that the main use for a large quantity of them was to provide a convenient home for snails and weeds. Over the years we have gradually put together the evidence together with what Glyn can remember, and the analysis makes an interesting study of the old country philosophy that nothing must ever be thrown away. Take the stones to start with - I have already described the uses to which the best ones were put, steps, building walls, ornamental pillars and a simulated well, incorporating the curved stones from the pillars of the former church. Selecting some of the square blocks, William even took the trouble to make a mounting block, chipping out a date and incorporating it into the stonework. I am sorry to say that most of the block has been submerged by the car park and only the top slab is now visible. It would not be too difficult to dig out the stones and reconstruct it somewhere else and perhaps one day the money will be found to have this done. Needless to say, it was never used as a mounting block- I doubt whether Ada got on horseback in her life. Grandfather William had always kept a pony and was a well-known sight riding to services and meetings, so William had learned to ride. But he discovered the internal combustion engine at an early stage and bought one of the first motor cycles to be seen in the district - a 1913 "James" (Figure 10.3). We still have it.

Of the vast surplus of stones remaining, many little rockeries and walls with little paths intertwining were constructed. Quite a large number were used to raise the level of the path leading out to the road - since the raising of the main thoroughfare all the paths and gates had had to be altered and there were steps up to the road. We discovered masses of these buried stones when digging a trench for a new drain - it certainly did not make for very rapid progress as each one had to be prised out individually and lifted out by hand. These were the very rough stones in their natural state as they would have left the quarry in the thirteenth century - the infilling of the massive walls of the Abbey Church.

One cannot help thinking that by far the best solution would have been to get rid of the rubble in some way - invite farmers to take the stones to tip in gateways and that sort of thing. It would certainly have saved a great many headaches and backaches in later years. However, these were not William's methods! The very idea of actually getting rid of something that was not only necessary, but actually an encumbrance, was utterly foreign to their philosophy. Having left behind them the century when working folk had few, if any possessions apart from the bare necessities of life, they had not re-adjusted to the dawning of our disposable, pre-packaged, throwaway age. There is little doubt that already the problem of refuse disposal was beginning to be felt for there were no regular rubbish collections in those days. Many of the items which had to be buried in the garden were symbolic

CHAPTER 10. THE GARDEN

of the motor age which was getting well under way and leaving its mark even in rural corners such as ours. A neighbour tells us that the top of the garden has had just about everything imaginable thrown on to it, including a large quantity of old car oil, acid from batteries, not to mention the batteries themselves, all of which we now know finds its way into the water supply and pollutes our rivers. Pollution was a word unknown to them - William and Ada would have been quite put out if anyone had pointed out to them that they were harming the environment by these and similar activities such as the lavish use of weedkiller. It has taken writers such as Rachel Carson to awaken us to the true horror of these problems - yet still one can walk into a hardware store and buy enough deadly poison (disguised as sodium chlorite or paraquat) to kill off the entire population of Washford.

Sometime in the early 1930s William and Ada had been to a sale at Wedmore and acquired very cheaply a large quantity of second hand materials. This sale was often mentioned and I think: that it must have been a big event in William's life. I used to wonder why they spoke of it so often, but as Wedmore is at the other end of Somerset and they never went away on holiday until well into the 30s it is not difficult to see that a journey to a completely unknown town was quite an exciting excursion. Having got to Wedmore he evidently considered that the greatest possible value should be extracted from the visit and bought a large quantity of stained glass. Several of the doors and windows in the house were subsequently made to fit round the glass and some of it was even used to beautify the door of the Toe H. Other panels never found a use and lay around in the corners of outbuildings along -with the oak Grandfather's sewing machine, the globes and (mostly; old crates and rubbish. One pair of glass panels in particular must have caught Ada's fancy as she kept them in her bedroom. They depict knights in armour apparently keeping vigil, and at a casual glance one might think that they are old, but the expression on the faces of the knights is so righteous as to be comical. I can only guess that they were panels in the door of some large Pugin-type Victorian residence which was being demolished.

What else have we which was created from all this spare material? Stones, bricks - gradually, laboriously and with an infinite amount of heavy physical labour these were dispersed. Then there were the red quarry tiles from the cottage floors, of a thickness undreamt of nowadays! How surprised our grandfathers would have been to see us bring home a few cardboard boxes from the hardware shop and stick down a whole floorful of tiles in a mere matter of hours. These quarry tiles measure eight and a half inches square and are an inch and a half thick. They are of a pleasant mellow brick-red shade and have lain now fully exposed to the elements for forty years or so without suffering any apparent deterioration. They make a pleasing path around the summer house and also finish off the top of one or two of the ornamental pillars. They must be strong; as only last evening, one of our cats jumped up rather suddenly and to her great surprise knocked one of them sharply to the ground. The cat was very surprised at the sudden disappearance of her perch but despite the sharp bump the tile did not break.

Surely I must have nearly finished the catalogue of re-usable materials from this pair of apparently very ordinary and humble two-room cottages but not quite. Right at the back of our cavernous tin garage one day, Glyn discovered a quantity of old oak, apparently roof beams, from the cottages. In true cottage style they had been hewn from the native tree at a point where a branch curved at a suitable angle for holding up the roof. Suddenly light dawned as we compared them with a little sitting-out place which we call the Sanctuary - the two old pieces of rather wormy oak which form the arch of the doorway were identical with those in the shed and were obviously obtained from the same source. How clear becomes the meaning of the expression "roof tree" when we look at these old beams, hacked out of the living oak when England's wooden walls still encircled the land. The oak is by no means such a common tree in these parts as once it was, though the village can still boast one or two splendid specimens in the precincts of ancient Abbey Farm. The ancestor of these trees is recorded in old records pertaining to the Abbey. Oak seedlings have an attractive habit of appearing in the garden and I always try to nurture them, with varying degrees of success. The only oak tree that we possess is a good specimen about forty to fifty years old, growing in the hedge at the top of

CHAPTER 10. THE GARDEN

our garden. Ada and William planted the seedling there and it seems to like the situation.

Another enormous beam which must surely have come from the cottages forms the traverse of the ornamental gateway which William built on the site of the old front entrance of one of the cottages. The uprights of this gateway are also massive - presumably they were once beams as well. One curious fact is that even after standing outside fully exposed to the westerly gales for over forty years there are still patches of yellow distemper adhering to the wood in some places. This attractive portico was finished off with a home-made double gate, and here again the top of the gate was designed as a curve and not a straight line. Unfortunately in this modern motor car age the necessity for more parking space became pressing and we were obliged to raise the level inside the gate to bring it up to the road. The contractor did not like to interfere with the gate posts in case the whole structure collapsed so the proportions are no longer very satisfactory. Fortunately for our little piece of history, however, one of one local photographers went around taking shots of the village in about 1936 and incredible though it may sound, the village post office is still selling one of these - a rather charming view of the cottage and gateway, complete with a flagpole which William erected for the Silver Jubilee in 1935 (Figure 10.4).

That must surely be all the re-usable material which as far as we can deduce found its way into various parts of the garden - but perhaps not quite all even now. Right at the back of the garage we found a heap of old tiles from Victorian fireplaces - of various designs and in lowering degrees of crudity as far as colour was concerned. The best ones were a deep olive green or burgundy red. The worst had bouquets of orange and purple flowers - William Morris gone wrong. The tiles are well over a quarter of an inch thick and the glaze nearly as thick as a sheet of glass. It seems very likely that some of them came from the cottages. We found a use for some of them when converting the wash house into a holiday chalet -they fitted the window ledge perfectly and it gave us great satisfaction to fit them into place and finish off the window so pleasantly and usefully.

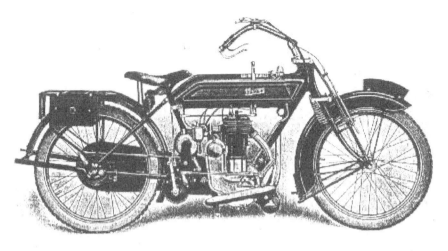

Figure 10.3: Advertisement for the 1913 James motorcycle

Figure 10.4: The front entrance to Hill Head House and the neighbouring cottage, 1935

CHAPTER 10. THE GARDEN

In fact one of the most enjoyable aspects of living in a place like ours, now that after eight years the worst of the confusion has been sorted out, is to re-use some of the things that have been lying about for so long. I have been fortunate in finding a handyman who also enjoys this sort of thing and it becomes quite a game to find what we need somewhere on the premises. For example, we needed a brass door knob when tidying up; the door of the outside toilet - we knew we had seen one lying about somewhere, and on duly searching for it two were found! Pieces of wire and odd lengths of wood of course are always to be had. A year or two ago gypsies called one day and persuaded us to part with a lot of old telephone wires and scrap metal. I was glad to see it go but could not help wondering how much the lead in the wire was worth. Our neighbours know that they can always come and ask us if they need a few pieces of wood for knocking up a rabbit hutch or fruit cage.

Last but not least I must not forget the window frames. They were rather small and old, so that even William found it difficult to find a use for them. They are still with us and it seems unlikely that they will ever be used. Some of them found their way into the back wall of the garage where a student of the subject will readily observe a veritable patchwork of lights serving the dual purpose of usefulness and economy: useful, as they let light in for seeing into the back of the garage, and economical, as they presumably proved to be a cheaper way of constructing a wall than purchasing yet more corrugated iron!

11 An Artist Abroad

Glyn Court

My mother had always promised herself that when she had a garden of her own there would be a little stream purling through and adding its liquid music to the scents and colours of the flowers; but my father thought differently: he had too keen a recollection of the floods which time and again had swept down the valley and inundated his boyhood home; so when, on his marriage, he moved from Roadwater to Washford he chose the site for his new house on the hillside.

His land was a quarter of an acre of orchard, with various buildings, and half an acre of vegetable gardens attached to three ancient cottages. This garden sloped down on the west to a cutting of the abandoned West Somerset Mineral Railway, while along the northern boundary ran the main road from Minehead to Taunton, which had been raised sixty years before to cross the railway by a ramp and now ran level with the eaves of the cottages. Mother soon had a garden and cultivated it happily, but it was not everything she desired, for so much of the land was cultivated by others, and her flowers and shrubs needed room to grow and blossom freely. She had to wait - fifteen years, I guess, for even if room had opened up, times were difficult, hours were long, leisure was short, and living was hard.

Father was distressed that she could not have the garden of her heart, and that he could not provide one of the few things that she, undemanding soul, would have loved to have; but within the limitations of space and time he would do all that imagination and hard work could achieve.

Gardeners, like poets, are born, not made, and the poetry of his sensitive nature went into his strong, stubby craftsman's hands. When the desire to create came upon him - and it frequently did - he expressed it not in words but in the works of those hands; and they took an astonishing variety of

A VILLAGE INHERITANCE

forms. Moreover, his own taste in gardening, like my mother's, ran toward the beautiful and decorative rather than the utilitarian: he would rather build ten flower gardens than dig one vegetable plot.

I hardly need say that this was not indolence on his part. Hard work and he had never fallen out. They were lifelong acquaintances and the best of friends; but after a few early struggles with a spade and a bizgy in his father's garden he had decided that, inscrutable though most of the decrees of Providence might be, one of them was clear as crystal: that he was not meant to be a gardener and he held firmly to this article of faith.

During the war years, when the broadcasts of those hortatory horticulturalists the Radio Doctor and Mr Middleton made us acutely conscious of the need to grow more food, the vegetable garden was painstakingly mapped out and seeded and raked and hoed and scuffled, but it was generally the current Bob or Graham or other lad of pre-military age who performed the surgery.

I will not say that my father never gardened, but his distaste for it was made strikingly evident when that health-giving exercise known in the classic tongue as "spittin' up a rap for the teddies" was entrusted to the proven and many-sided incompetence of his sixteen-year old son. But to make a garden, to create an outdoor home, to see those lawns, paths, flower-beds and ponds conceived in the imagination, gradually being clothed in the garments of colour and shapeliness and liquid light, there was work for the artist that he was and would never have claimed to be. And another incentive, perhaps even stronger for him, was the delight in the garden my mother found as soon as she had one of her own and as soon as the opportunity came he set to work with all his vigour to build her an ornamental garden to complete the home he thought she deserved. But eventually, and suddenly, the opportunity came. The old couple in one of the cottages died and their daughter moved away; and another cottage was made uninhabitable by fire. So my father, much as he loved old for old's sake, demolished them, and the stones and cob of which they were made went, some of them, back into the earth, but far more - and here Father seized his opportunity - went to make mother's garden.

CHAPTER 11. AN ARTIST ABROAD

I have spoken of the old country virtue of thrift, economy, making do, never throwing away, using thrice over, but it comes as a surprise - and raises a chuckle - to find the creative gardener just as ardent an economist as the carpenter or the shoemaker. After all, his raw material is reasonably cheap.

The cottages had stood in a hollow, pitched with cobbles, between the embanked vegetable garden and the raised level of the road, but the rough debris raised the ground by three feet and on the site of the cottages he laid out a triangle of lawn with a sunken rose garden. But after all that, an incredible quantity of building materials remained over, and every item bore the marks of its history: roof trees hewn with the adze and notched and numbered to take the roughly sawn rafters; wall-plates and joists studded with nails and brads forged by a sixteenth-century blacksmith; heavy doors with massive locks nearly a foot square; oak floorboards from the bedrooms, hand sawn three centuries before, not squared off but left in the shape of the trunk of the tree; red chimney bricks of more modern date; quarry tiles which had, as a luxury, replaced the beaten earth floor downstairs; incongruously, a few bright glossy red tiles from the Victorian fireplace; and stones ... ah! The stones, of every weight from a pound to a hundredweight, red sandstone, yellow sandstone, blue lias boulders, Doulting stone ... there seemed no end to their variety. A curious philosopher might have wondered why a Jacobean builder, forced to fetch and carry by pack-horse over ways that were quagmires, should have gone to seven or eight widely separated quarries for stones for three small cottages but on looking more closely he would have seen what soon became apparent to us as well: that one huge quarry provided these stones, the Cistercian monastery two fields away, for we could see that many of them had been shaped by the mason's chisel; there were sandstone segments which had gone to form the massive pillars of the church; quoins and chamferings of Doulting stone; stone from mullions; and it all taught a piquant lesson in social history: that whereas many of the leading families of the realm owed their prosperity to an unscrupulous pillager of the Church, honest Hodge was not slow to follow where Marprelate led.

The stones served a multitude of uses: paving, edging to new flower beds, building retaining walls, rockeries, ornamental steps: some of the

A VILLAGE INHERITANCE

best square-cut stones went to make a fine upping-block, though by that time father was unlikely to acquire anything much more equine than a new Hudson or a hobby horse.

From the oaken king-posts and cross beams he made a gateway, capped with the coping tiles, and, in the garden, a little shingle-roofed summerhouse in which they would sit on Sunday evenings in summer looking down over the fields to the stream and the hills beyond.

But the most distinctive creations were from the most unpromising material, the red brick of the cottage chimneys. He thought that, even if Ada could not have a stream in the garden, he would give her the next best thing, and just over the hedge of the house lawn, in the cottage garden where the rows of kidney beans had stood, he constructed an ornamental pond, roughly in the shape of a harp, with arms curving round the foot of an old apple tree - a Tom Putt, I think. He took great pains to seal the floor, and - again economically! - set the concrete of the sides to harden behind shields of flattened oil drums ... And to this day, if you look hard, you may see imprinted the cabalistic sign.

Over the lower end of the pond he constructed a little bridge of bricks set alternately flat and on end in a cap and gap pattern, with a mosaic foot-way, and although worn away here and there it is as strong as on the day he made it. Typically, though, he would not use a sharp-edged brick anywhere, but very carefully and laboriously chipped off every edge of every brick before he set it in place.

But his triumph of improvisation was the summerhouse. Father had always loved the picturesqueness of our unspoilt villages, of which the epitome, in many ways, was Dunster; and the jewel of Dunster village is the seventeenth century yarn market. Father took it as his model, but it was not in him to copy anything slavishly, and the construction was uniquely his own.

The ground-plan of the yarn market is a hexagon, a geometrical figure which is both easy to construct and pleasant to contemplate; the one which best combines the qualities of the strength of the rectangle with the grace of the circle. This regularity would not do for Father. It was easy to achieve,

CHAPTER 11. AN ARTIST ABROAD

Figure 11.1: The Summerhouse. Built in a similar pentagonal design to that of Dunster Market

and therefore probably meretricious and suspect. So in a cement base he laid down the foundations of a five sided summerhouse.

This is a simple enough calculation for a geometrician, but Father knew nothing of interior angles, and sums of right angles and suchlike arcana and his projector and theodolite were a spirit level and a two foot rule or a length of string, and several pounds' weight of patience; so that the plotting of the summerhouse seems to me worth recording.

Having said that, I must go further and confess that it is only since beginning this chapter that I have looked at the summerhouse closely, and only now that I have realised the reason for its proportions. Everything was built round the windows! Some time before this, from a journey to Wedmore - unforgettable to them because the apple orchards were seas of blossom - he and mother had brought back a miscellaneous collection of stained glass windows, diamond panes and leaded lights, and at last he had found a proper use for them. So the lights flanked by diamond panes, determined the length of the sides.

At his five corners he dug holes three feet deep and planted sleepers from the local branch line of the G.W.R. Four of the sides he then filled in nearly up to waist-level with his hewn-edged bricks, but even here he aimed for unobtrusive variety: two of the sides, the three lowest courses and below the three topmost, are set in a pattern of blocks of three, alternately vertical and horizontal, with a clay tile from the cottage floor inserted centrally rather as a bas relief: those seen from the garden are set in his beloved herringbone pattern, and the square tile has become a diamond.

On each of the top courses he placed a sill, curved on the inside to form a simple decorative ledge, and on these he set the lights, which filled in the whole space to the top of the posts. The fifth side took the door of his favourite double or stable door type, the lower half made of light oaken boards of irregular shapes cunningly tongued and grooved, the upper half a partly coloured leaded light set in an oaken frame.

With joists and boards from the cottages he made the pentagonal roof, and he clad it with shingles, out over one window he constructed a gable with a light shaped like a formalized ivy leaf. On the summit he placed a cone of cement, like a visual echo of the ivy leaf, and he crowned the whole structure with a weathercock, a confident, challenging bird. He was most carefully drawn for balance and cut out by hand from a sheet of copper and he has stood up to the storms of more than thirty winters. In my heady youth, an occasional apple core was hurled to see how fast the fickle fowl would revolve, but he has borne up bravely, gyrating on bicycle ball-bearings, and he is still pert and lively enough to have served as a model for Milton's roystering rooster who

... with lively din
Scatters the rear of darkness thin.

All round and within the summerhouse Father laid in a pattern the red tiles which perfectly complement the brick, and as a finishing touch he fixed swivel seats - post office sorters' seats - to the uprights, and the little pleasure-dome was ready for every modest festivity to which the soft summer days would invite.

Of course, much as he loved plain wood, he bowed to the necessity of paint for outdoor work; but at least five years before, he had bought a two-gallon tin of orange chrome paint and only used a pint on the garage door; so it was brought out of retirement, put into service for the window sills - and it is as cheerful a colour as heart could desire - and then it was laid back into store in the Aladdin's cave of a workshop. There it matured and increased in virtue and strength, until, thirty-five years later, I gave the window sills a second coat, and by that time the orange chrome would not have disgraced the palette of Veronese himself.

12 The Business as I remember it

Glyn Court

The most subtle anatomist in the kingdom would be hard put to it to find any quantity of blue blood in my veins, and I summise that the somewhat sluggish liquid is rather a compound of red and white corpuscles, shoemaker's dye, machine oil and Post Office ink. At least, if one or the other of the last three is not traceable, then all talk of "environmental conditioning" is mere psychiatrese.

The village post office of Washford, in which I grew up, was very exceptional. There is a strange fascination in the thought of one particular human activity being carried on in one unchanging spot as the generations come and go, and a few years ago I was enthralled to learn from a North Devon schoolboy that his family had been occupying their farm, of their own name, ever since the fifteenth century. The post office at Washford could not claim such a history, but for at least a century and a quarter, and probably for two centuries, the postal business of the community was carried on in two houses which faced each other across the village street - our house and the old office.

When my mother became the postmistress in 1921 and moved from the old place to her new home, no one knew how long the service had been operating: apparently it was for longer than that term within which, in the legal phrase, the memory of man runneth not to the contrary. Fifty years later this was confirmed to us, and in a surprising way, for our neighbour, who had bought the old post office cottage on the death of the former postmaster's daughter, set about remodelling the interior. He removed the entrance lobby which had been the telegraph room, and demolished a partition, and in behind this he found papers which had lain undisturbed for nearly 120 years: light green registered letter forms dated 1853 and showing - which tickled our vanity - Washford as the head office and Minehead as the humble sub-office. Even more surprising, another neighbour brought us in a brass button from the garden which, from its condition, had evidently lain in the earth for many, many years. It showed a head of an eighteenth-century type - we were tempted to assign it to George I since it faced to the right - and the letters P.D, which we took as indicating "Postal Department". The British Museum could not enlighten us as to the origin, so "Postal Department" it remains, and we are convinced that this activity, in one way or another, has gone on here for at least two centuries.

Nevertheless, the business activity as a whole was much more varied. As my wife has explained, when my father was building the house, he added a single storey wing in sandstone and snail-creep to carry on the cycle and footwear trade; then, having an eye for symmetry, he continued the outside wall - only in brick and rough-cast, because of the expense - to make a second storey and roofed over the whole area. All the woodwork in the house came from his plane, and all the fittings in the shop were his work, too - not that any village store, in those innocent days, would have been fitted up by an outside agency: such a fall from grace was mercifully hidden in the future.

The post office and shop as I remember them from my boyhood were pretty constantly busy, as we catered for at least three sets of customers. In the 1920 we were still in the throes of the first Vehicular Revolution, and working men were buying Hercules and Raleigh cycles as eagerly as their sons and grandsons buy Rover 3000s, only less frequently and, comparatively speaking, at much greater cost. The second strand of the business was footwear, which my father had chosen to carry on because, as he shrewdly observed, "Most of 'em have two feet, and they always need two shoes to put on 'em". And both the cycle trade and the footwear gave rise to a moderately profitable repair business.

The third estate of our commercial empire was, of course, the post office. My mother had worked as an assistant for fifteen years in the post office over

CHAPTER 12. THE BUSINESS AS I REMEMBER IT

the way, and after her marriage she became the postmistress of Washford in her new home; and she held the position until the day of her death, forty-five years later.

Our shop was one huge room occupying the whole of the extension, but divided by a partition, with a floor laid in wooden blocks in herringbone pattern, and a ceiling of grooved and tongued deal. The shop front was mainly taken up by two huge plate-glass -windows set in frames part oak, part pine, and four inches thick, and the front door and porch were set in one corner.

The display window was generally occupied by one or two bicycles suspended from hooks, and a varied selection of shoes, slippers and cycle accessories. Along the right hand side of the shop ran the post office counter, a massive structure of red mahogany twelve feet long, purchased from the mess deck of a destroyer that was being broken up in Watchet harbour. The counter was surmounted by a brass grill and a kind of miniature signal-box or glass cabinet in which we kept a variety of official forms whose age-long incapacity for use rendered them inestimably precious in the sight of the Postmaster General. Underneath were five huge drawers, which might have served as coal barges but that they were crammed with post office supplies and forms; and underneath these were more shelves, all laden with post office envelopes in their scores, forms in their hundreds, and governmental trivia in their thousands and tens of thousands. At the far end of the counter stood the post office scales, solid, black, imposing, with a range of weights from an ounce to seven pounds; and there they stood until the late 1930s when the Post Office, recognising their dependability as unsuitable for a go-ahead public corporation, removed them.

Down the left side of the shop ran another stand of shelves on which were displayed electric lamps, greetings cards, flower and vegetable seeds, cycle parts, inner tubes and a selection of small goods of many and varying kinds. Behind this, and facing the door, was the telephone kiosk painted in a brown which seemed to have been evolved in the more secluded recesses of Bournville; through this kiosk we sent and received telegrams, sometimes ten or twelve a day. The telephone had the property of picking up the

Figure 12.1: The receipt header for the shop, highlighting the diverse range of services available at the post office.

broadcasts from the local B.B.C. station, and I remember that, before we owned a wireless set, we heard over this improvised radio the abdication speech of King Edward VIII.

On one of the lower shelves was a commodity which was much prized up to the war but has now disappeared from daily use: calcium carbide, which we kept in cylindrical one pound tins and sold for fourpence. Well into the 1940s carbide cycle lamps were very popular in our area; for the carbide gave a brighter, clearer light than electric batteries. The men who cycled to and from the paper mill in Watchet would call in regularly between half-past five and six to exchange their empty carbide tin for a new one.

And along all three walls of the shop, piled up from waist level to ceiling, was the principal stock-in-trade, footwear: light boots, heavy boots, ladies' boots from before the Great War, Wellington boots, boots adorned with brads, tips and cues, hobnail boots in every size from the twelves for a six-foot farmer down to the tiny hobnail fours for a two year old toddler - or maybe hobbler; shoes of every probable shape, and not a few rankly improbable; "I can always fit their feet", said Father, who had no great love for the vagaries of female fashion; "I can fit their feet, but I can't fit their heads.": slippers and plimsolls, bootlaces and insoles ("socks" they were called); and those perfect accoutrements for the ploughman behind his team, leathern leggings.

CHAPTER 12. THE BUSINESS AS I REMEMBER IT

All these treasures were found in the front shop. Beyond the partition, and reached through a green baize curtain, lay the sorting office; on one side a boxed staircase led to the first floor. Along two of the other walls were the rows of shelves for the sorting of the letters and a desk for Father's business papers; and on the third side stood the telephone exchange, a standard which, for many years, had barely fifty numbers on it; but those fifty were sufficient to bind my mother and father to the service of the Post Office day and night for nearly twenty years.

The sorting office was busy out of all proportion to the usual work of a village post office, for by some quirk of authority we had been chosen as the centre of distribution for a large area - of West Somerset. Out two motor vans, one a bull-nosed Morris Cowley, the other an Oxford, covered the Brendon Hills and the eastern half of Exmoor, delivering mail to the scattered villages of Dunster, Wheddon Cross, Exford, Withypool, Winsford and a score of isolated farms. Another postman delivered the village and two girls served behind the counter.

Competition for employment as a postman was strong in the 1930s, and entry was practically restricted to ex-servicemen, so there was a peculiar fitness in the names of one of our postmen, Jim Lee, Bill Bellamy and Tommy Atkins. For those who were sociably inclined, the work was interesting; they met dozens of people on their rounds, and never exactly the same people two days running.

Sometimes, in the holidays, I would be allowed to travel in the mail van, and I have often suspected that those journeys did more than any other single experience to create in me the romantic frame of mind under which I have always laboured and for which, paradoxically, I am profoundly thankful. In winter we would set out from the office in darkness and pass through Dunster and Timberscombe as the lights still glowed in the cottage windows. As we climbed the thousand feet up to the Rest and Be Thankful at Wheddon Cross, the stars were paling and the beech hedges and the cairn of Dunkery were struggling out of darkness into the grey of morning. Then we would pay our visits to those villages of which I had so often heard but which, without the mail van, might have been at the ends of the earth, so little did children such as I travel outside their immediate neighbourhood: Exford, Winsford, Withypool, Luckwell Bridge. On other mornings I would travel with the Brendon Hill van and we would follow up the stream which came rushing from the windy uplands of Chargot and Leigh. For the first two miles, to Roadwater, I knew the country well, for the village held the home of my family; but beyond Roadwater, all was unknown, and as the road wound through the sombre pine-woods, and emerged into the higher pastures beside the stream, each new name had for me a quality of magic: Pittiwells Lake, Langridge Mills, Drucombe, New Mills, Greenland, Kingsbridge, Luxborough, Chargot. The hills drew me to themselves. We laboured up the steep of Vellers Way or, I had been told, Felon's Way, and I vaguely wondered who had been the malefactor and what his crime. Sheep stealing, maybe?

Twelve hundred feet above sea level now, and we visited one remote farmstead after another: Burrow, Gupworthy, Armoor, Swansey, stopping to drink tea and eat home-made bread by a beech-log fire. Held back by shyness and timidity, I did not learn from these many encounters all that I might have done; for while I loved to play in the woods and meadows, I also loved books too deeply for my own good.

But no one, not even a boy of fourteen or so, could be for long in the company of Will Bellamy without learning much to his gain and nothing to do him harm. For Bill was a man of acute intelligence, who had been kept by latent ill-health, family circumstances and the care of a widowed mother from finding a field of activity in which that intelligence could have full play. He read widely and critically - I remember his indignation at the "scientific" pessimism of some of the later writings of H.G. Wells - and not only was he singularly well-informed on politics but he could also explain them clearly and fluently. He listened regularly to the weekly "Letter from America" by Alistair Cooke's predecessor, Raymond Gram Swing, and I can recall almost as vividly as if it were yesterday a walk along the Luxborough lanes when he commented upon some of the different usages of American and English speakers. He never made an effort to impress, and because of that his breadth of interest was all the more impressive, and I always remember him with affection and gratitude.

CHAPTER 12. THE BUSINESS AS I REMEMBER IT

Nevertheless, and though I was less conscious of them, the lessons of the hills and tile stream, the winding lanes and the tops of the waving pines, went home, and they matured over long years, so that when, thirty and forty years after my childhood visits, I came to renew acquaintance with farmers who had been young men in those distant days, their recollection of "the little boy who came round with the mail" was all the passport I had needed.

A postman's life was an arduous one, but it had its rewards, and one of them was humour; dry, nonchalant, impassive, as in the passage of arms of the Exford postmistress with an inspector from the head office in Minehead;

> **Inspector**: Oh, Mrs Westley (it was not quite her name, but as Mercutio said, 'twill serve), your office is very well kept, but I'm disturbed to see that you have no fire-fighting equipment.
> **Mrs W**: Woll, us hab'm had no fire 'it, have us?
> **Inspector**: No, but supposing the telephone switchboard were to catch fire, what would you do then?
> **Mrs W**: Du? I'll tell 'ee what I'd du, you! I'd let the darn thing burn.

I treasure, also, the remark of one of my mother's assistants, Ivy (and that is not her real name, either) made with a complacency verging on pride:

> **Ivy**: Me mother do say I got a faace like a bladder o' lard.

Then there were the tales of the linesmen, a race noted for the vigour of their invective and the colourful adjective of their everyday speech. I heard of the legendary Bert who, standing at the foot of a telegraph pole and paying out wire to his mate up aloft, received a lump of molten solder on the back of his neck and mildly expostulated, "You must be more careful, George".

No less forthright was the Roadwater postman, Jimmy Lyddon, who, when ordered by a local magnate to stick a ha'penny stamp on a newspaper, retorted, "You stick en on yourself! I bain't goin' to lick the king's backside for 'ee".

The postmen were, of course, vital human links in the modest mailorder business which operated very simply and effectively. A farmer "out awver" would say to the postman, "Jim, tell Mr Court I could do wi' a pair o' hobnails size ten, will 'ee?" Jim would relay the order, take up the boots next day and - with any luck - bring back the payment. Everyone was satisfied with the transaction and, unlike the traditional mail-order businesses, the cost of postage was nil.

It is hard, however, to credit the conditions which had to be accepted for the sake of employment in the Post Office in the inter-war years. My father and mother set up in business at the beginning of the post-war depression of 1921 and the "Geddes Axe", and not for eighteen years were they able to take a holiday. These were the leanest of lean years.

Time and again a mother or father would come in, take a pair of shoes for their child, and say in conclusion, "It'll be all right if I pay next Friday, won't it, Mr Court?" or "I can't pay 'ee just now, Mr Court, but I'll look in next week". Others would offer him in part exchange some article, such as a thermometer, for which neither they nor he had any use. Others, again, would state in honest, straightforward fashion, "I don't know when I can pay 'ee, Mr Court, but I promise faithfully I will, just so soon as ever I can". My father knew well enough that that "I promise faithfully" generally meant a bad debt and that the customers more likely to pay were those who promised nothing: but he would agree, with much greater embarrassment than theirs, and explain to my mother, with the convincing argument, "Well, I couldn't let the little kiddies go barefoot, now could I?"

In this way they lost five hundred pounds; then, when a modest prosperity seemed possible, came the war, and Father worked all day and late into the night to make old things new. Their long hours, especially in the early years, are imprinted on my memory; and I seem to have been conscious that such hours were not the common lot and I felt the imposition. This was a normal day:

CHAPTER 12. THE BUSINESS AS I REMEMBER IT

3.45 am: Mother or Father gets up to take in the mail from Taunton; then back to bed;

5.30 am: Mother gets up, makes tea for the postmen, and starts sorting their letters;

5.45 am: postmen arrive;

6.30 am: out with vans; Mother tidies up from supper, does a little knitting or, in summer, an hour in the garden, cooks breakfast, answers telephone, visits and tidies up for tiresome old lady over the way;

8.45 am: girls start to arrive, open shop;

11.15 am: dispatch morning mail;

12.30 pm: cooking;

1.00 to 2.00 pm: dinner hour;

2.00 pm: open shop again;

6.00 pm: shut shop, have tea;

8.00 pm: begin evening mail;

8.45 pm: clear letter box;

9.00 pm: clear box again;

9.20 pm: dispatch evening mail; then (sometimes) get a light supper and sit down by fireside, except when telephone rings, till bedtime.

Throughout day and night, intermittent ringing of telephone - on one night, twelve trips downstairs between midnight and 3.45. Not even free from it on Sundays, except once a fortnight when one of the girls, Clarice, comes in for two hours in the afternoon. But in the 1920s and 1930s even such conditions as these were accepted; "better hard work than no work" they thought; and the Victorian vein of stoicism and duty ran strong in many of their generation.

A VILLAGE INHERITANCE

There was, indeed, much activity outside as well as in, for behind the house there stood - and still stands - an unlovely but capacious corrugated iron shed with benches and an inspection pit, in which my Father and a workman, Will Bellamy, carried on the repair side of the business: cars - until they grew so complicated that the equipment would not have been worth installing - bicycles, and boot and shoe repairs.

One problem, though, arose which no one could have foreseen. When he moved down from Roadwater to Washford, my father had left the post office and footwear business in the charge of a widowed sister, and with the aid of the telephone this arrangement worked splendidly. The crates of boots would be brought home from the station on a pair of bright red, iron-tyred post office trucks, and he would take a load up to Roadwater in the sidecar of his James 600, with his son perched on the top. Then he bought a Calcott open tourer with collapsible hood for what seems the exorbitant sum of £450 (considering that its price as scrap a few years later was £2) and travelled in style until the Road Fund Tax was raised overnight to a prohibitive level. One afternoon his sister telephoned through to say that a customer wanted Mr Court and no one else would do. Taking just the time to wash and slip on a clean coat, Father hurried out to the ear, stopped - as he thought - his son filling the petrol tank from a watering can in an attempt to be helpful, cranked up, and drove out. The Calcott chugged merrily along the valley until she reached the gates of the abbey on the outskirts of the village, and then the water began to work through the gravity feed, and Father accomplished the remaining two miles of the journey at a rate of one mile per hour. There were occasions on which he was more pleased.

From time to time, especially during the war, he would build a bicycle out of spare parts, and he taught me how to build a wheel, though of that I remember, and probably wrongly, only the arrangement of spokes in intervals of seven and thirteen. Of the mystery of shoe repairing I recall much more and although a boy's impatience made me, I am sorry to say, reluctant to learn, I believe I could re-sole a shoe:

CHAPTER 12. THE BUSINESS AS I REMEMBER IT

1. Cut out a pattern of the sole in cardboard;
2. Cut out the new sole as economically as possible from a bend of leather; soak new sole in water for thirty minutes;
3. Meanwhile, cut off old .sole back to instep;
4. (start work on other shoe);
5. Take out new sole, taper end under instep, lay face downward on lapstone, and hammer out to curve of foot;
6. Put shoe on the last; tack on sole;
7. Fasten with sprigs;
8. Trim edges with knife and rasp;
9. Dye edges;
10. Smooth and burnish with shaping iron.

So much, and more than I can easily tell, I remember of the family business; but the post office had yet another side of particular importance to me. The Post Office, in those days, provided a very cheap service, but they subsidised it to the public by the minimum payment of their employees for maximum service. I do not know what the postmistress's salary was, except that it carried no pension entitlement and that even as late as 1967, with responsibility for hundreds of pounds, it came to less than £10 a week; less than the postmen were paid, and the postmistress was expected to provide the premises, the heating, the lighting, even the pens and ink for the public, all without a penny contribution from the Post Office. (This explains, of course, why all sub-post offices are run in conjunction with a business.)

My cousins, who ran the post office in Roadwater, also provided the public telephone service before a kiosk was installed. They would obtain the number, which for a trunk call might take ten minutes, hand over the receiver to the caller, wait for the end of the call, ring back the operator, find the charge, collect the money, enter the call and the charge in the book, and balance it at the end of the week - for maybe thirty or forty calls; and for this the Post Office paid them weekly the sum of One Shilling. That was, of course, when the Post Office had found the service profitable and had given them a rise. To start with they were paid ninepence.

> up to half a mile: three-halfpence
> up to a mile: threepence
> up to two miles: sixpence
> over two miles: A shilling

The Post Office worked the same system for telegrams. They were cheap to send - twelve words for a shilling and a penny for each, additional word - and reliable and quick in delivery; a sender would be entitled to expect a reply from any part of the kingdom except the more remote settlements of the Highlands, Wales and Dartmoor within two or three hours, and the village postmaster had the responsibility of finding a messenger or going himself, and the scale on which he was paid, over routes cautiously measured by an official with an hodometer, were in the true tradition;

But the head office, maybe resentful that such easy wealth should come our way, would hold on to a telegram an hour, and if others for Washford arrived in the meantime, would send them out together, so that two or three in the same direction could be delivered for the price of one. (Any responsibility for delay, naturally, fell on the sub-office.) As my father said, after a four mile journey through deep snow to a farm a thousand feet up, where they did not even invite him in for a warm, "You didn't get very rich on telegrams". Still, for a schoolboy the penny-halfpennies and threepences were a welcome addition to pocket money, and one young King of the Road on his shock-absorber-fitted drop-handlebar super-lightweight, aluminium-framed, New Hudson might easily, in the course of a summer day, accumulate two shillings, half-a-crown or even more. But I have other memories as well, of those wartime journeys I made as a boy of sixteen and seventeen, and I remember the dumb apprehension of the women who came to the doors of the cottages to take the telegram from my hand, and their brave quietness as they laid away their happiness and their love.

We no longer carry on the family business in the old way, but in one very pleasant respect it lingers on. I have mentioned the two girls who served behind the counter, but they were two of many. For forty years my mother, the postmistress, took girls from the village and trained them in postal work.

CHAPTER 12. THE BUSINESS AS I REMEMBER IT

Some stayed with her until they were married, others went on to a head office, a few - in later days - found parts of the work, such as detaching stamps in a straight line, so complicated that they soon left work too. But most of the girls have remained in the district, with their children, and a few - how time hurries on! - with their grandchildren; sometimes we meet, and it is pleasing that they recall their days in our post office. And here, though without giving the praise they merit to those who served so well, or leaving out the two who were pestiferous nuisances from start to finish, I am glad to chronicle the names of:

> Clarice, Vera, Gwen, Muriel, Maggie, Violet, Eileen, Margaret, Rita, Barbara, Ruth, Viola, Kathie, Gillian, Judy, Joan, Marion, Reta, Berry, Kay; and last of the line, and in a place by herself, the devoted and faithful Miss Bates.

And that, I believe, concludes the glad, eventful history of a post office in a West Somerset village.

13 The Bakehouse

Glyn Court

On the parcel of ground bought by my father there stood seven buildings, one of which was a bakehouse, a two-storied structure of sandstone, with a large window downstairs and a loft door above, both faced with brick quoins. For many years - possibly for half a century - the bakery business had been carried on over the road in conjunction with the post office by James Bellamy.

It was here that my mother came to work at the age of sixteen as a clerk and telegraphist. She remembered Mr Bellamy was a kindly, mild-mannered old gentleman with pince-nez. He was a widower with one daughter who, sadly, had inherited little of his mildness; her tongue gave him little peace, and often he would come in to dinner and go out again leaving it untasted. He was a lonely man, for not only had he no happiness and little society at home, but he had also joined a small and, at that time, particularist religious body, the Christadelphiaans, and henceforth had no contact with the village chapel; (the village had no Anglican church): and as he and his daughter were the only Christadelphians in the district, loneliness was inevitable.

His bakery was an annexe to the post office, and his oven one of the old type which was heated by burning faggots and bundles of twigs inside; then the dough was baked by the heat of the ashes, which were raked out before the next baking.

Mr Bellamy covered an extensive round with his pony and trap, travelling to outlying farms with a regular order to supplement the home-baked bread. He kept his own bakehouse scrupulously clean, and was fascinated and shocked by the lower standards he found in some farms. In one in particular he was greeted by "None to-day, Mr Bellamy, I'm baking myself. - Here, you young rip, gi' me that!", and his horrified gaze fell first on the grey, speckled dough, then on the hands kneading it, then on a child playing with a lump of the mixture among the ashes in the hearth, and lastly on the hand which swooped down to snatch the dough and thrust it, ashes and all, in with the next batch for the family.

In the orchard over the way he had started to build a house to which he meant to retire, but he died while still at work and his daughter sold the shell of the house to my father. The village had lost its bakery, so father, although he was still living in Roadwater, set up a new one, installed a modern coke-fired oven and rented it to a young baker from Williton, Henry Chilcott, together with a cottage for his wife and month-old son, Colin.

It may sound improbable, but right up to the 1950s every village of middling size in this district could support a bakery, and in days when the general taste had not been vitiated by packaged pap, the extent of a baker's trade depended on the quality of his goods, and of course his rounds over-lapped with his competitors'. Mr Chilcott and his son - later, Colin alone -ran the business unaided for forty years, and the excellence of their bread and the richness of their dough cakes and buns were proved by the length of the round they covered, to farms four or five miles away in different directions. In the early days Mr Chilcott ran a delivery van, and his cheerful manner and smart appearance - together with polished leather leggings - made him a welcome caller. Then, as the road tax was viciously increased, he was forced to change to a B.S.A. motor cycle and sidecar, but no doubt it did the work as effectively, even if in less comfort. I suspect, though, that in the 1930s the expense of running even the B.S.A. became too great for a small business, and a delivery bicycle was brought into service, and Colin would take his cheerful way round the village, up the river valley to Stamborough and Leighland four miles away, or over the hills to Fair Cross, Yarde and Stream, taking with him everywhere a song and a cheerful word for everyone. Sometimes, although ten years older than I, he would put up with my company on these rides, and on walks in the country, and would stop and show me the age-old crafts of boyhood, producing an ear-splitting whistle with a blade of grass and making a popgun out of an elder twig and a length of spring from an old lady's discarded corset!

CHAPTER 13. THE BAKEHOUSE

The bakery was, I suppose, typical of hundreds, it measured about fourteen foot square, and on the left as you went in you saw the great oven, like the belly of a whale when the heavy door was raised by a massive lever. Under this was the proving oven, in which the dough was placed to rise.

Against the further wall stood the huge wooden "trow", in which Mr Chilcott would knead a hundredweight and more of dough at a time. The baking tins were stored on a rack, but greased and laid out on the floor each morning to receive the dough. From the ceiling hung two long hooks which carried the ten-foot "peels" for drawing the bread from the oven. In one corner a flight of steps, without a handrail, led up to the loft, into which the flour was loaded through an outside door by a pulley and chain; but it had to be brought down again, painfully, by hand. Every day of the week, except Sundays, Mr Chilcott or Colin would be up at half-past five to open up the oven, stoked the night before, and to start work, and one of the pleasant memories of my boyhood - more pleasant for me, no doubt, than for those who worked at it - is of the musical clink-clink of baking-tins being deposited on the bakehouse floor.

When, indeed, I think of the bakehouse I think of music, for music ran strongly in the family, Mr Chilcott had, until coming to Washford, played the flute in a chapel band in Williton, but that activity, like so much else that was good, was crushed out of existence in 1914, and after that he took up his instrument only rarely. Colin, however, had taken to music as soon as he could speak for himself. At five years of age he was learning the piano, at eight he was learning the organ. Soon he was helping the organist on Sundays besides, and he went on making music in this way, and many others, until life left him.

The organ could not be the only outlet for the music in him, he needed more, and in the 1930s he and his father formed a small strict-tempo dance band: Colin played the piano, two other lads played the saxophone and the violin and his father kept time on the drum. Unlike more recent groups they did not set out to deafen the dancers, and perhaps for that reason the "Night Revellers" in their uniform of blue tunic with yellow edging, were all the more welcome, and they built up a list of regular engagements till 1943 put an end to their activities. In the 1950s ill-health brought on by the innumerable particles of flour compelled Colin to give up the bakery and take other work; so another village industry closed; but his music went on. He married a lady who was a singer, and they made their home, still next door to the old bakery, a place of music and constant cheer.

14 The Women of the Family

Clare Court

Now that we have reached this stage in our narration, readers will have observed that most of the characters who figure so prominently in this book are men, but I hasten to assure them that this is not intended to prove anything in particular. In an age when the liberation of women has become a subject which regularly hits the headlines, it seems only fair to pay some tribute to the female members of the family who for generations, worked away behind the scenes performing all the monotonous chores which enabled the menfolk to make full use of their own talent. There is little doubt that their personalities and intelligence had a very strong influence in the work of the family as a whole. There were of course sisters, cousins and aunts too numerous to mention individually, but I feel it worth recording something of the lives of the two women whom I actually met and came to know the best - William's sister Selina, and his wife Ada, my mother-in-law. Their names crop up frequently in the story and their influence (on William) probably stronger than any of the others.

The first and most obvious fact on which I feel qualified to pontificate is that any woman who becomes a Court by birth or marriage, need not expect an easy life. Interesting maybe, rewarding, demanding, varied - yes, certainly, and if my own experience is anything to go by, continually fraught with the problems brought about by combining a public life with an insufficient income. Looking back over the family history for the last seventy years and probably longer, one sustaining factor is very obvious - that the women considered it was their mission in life to smooth the path for the men in whatever projects they were engaged. Grandfather William Court, for example, spent much of his life working for the Temperance

Cause and was a well-known figure in the area as he travelled from village to village on his white pony in order to speak at meetings. On Sundays, the pony bore him to preaching appointments, while at election time he was to be seen covering the same ground in the Liberal cause. As his wife was a semi-invalid, perhaps it was fortunate that he was so well provided with daughters - three altogether, who naturally enough took great pride in their father's activities and attended to all his wants.

When Grandfather died, the mantle of family responsibility descended to William, the second son (Lewis, the eldest having entered the ministry and left home). Two of William's sisters, Selina and Lily, had lost their husbands and were therefore constantly available. The third sister, Tilly, was unmarried and kept house for him until her death. It is hardly surprising to record that William was hopelessly spoilt by his sisters, particularly by Tilly. They had always been a close-knit family and William and Tilly understood each other particularly well. When poor Tilly died at the early age of forty, William was jolted out of his comfortable and well-regulated bachelor existence and it was probably this as much as anything which finally brought him to marry. So the patient Ada inherited the task of looking after William and always made it clear that she regarded this as a privilege. It is of course a firmly established country tradition to pamper the men of the house and I could point to several homes in our village where strict unwritten rules regarding the division of labour are still observed. While living in North Devon for ten years I came across many examples of this total dependence on the woman of the house, some of them very amusing to a bystander. One conversation which stays in the memory and was actually overheard between two young men:

> **First Young Man**: Didn' see 'ee up the dance Friday night.
> **Second Young Man**: No.
> **First Young Man**: Why didn' 'ee cum then?
> **Second Young Man**: Mother ad'n cleaned me shoes.

In the face of such telling argument, what remains to be said? "Women's work", however, an expression which must surely bring on apoplexy in ardent

CHAPTER 14. THE WOMEN OF THE FAMILY

Figure 14.1: Grandfather William Court and his pony, Dapper

supporters of the Women's Liberation Movement, was not necessarily a derogatory phrase. It was the allotted share of the toil of daily living, accepted by women as an essential part of the pattern of life. For example, at Roadwater there were two houses, a Post Office and a family business to run, not counting activities connected with the Chapel, such as the preaching and Temperance Meetings. William with his sister Tilly and his father, (Grandfather), lived at Oatway House, also looking after the other old man, Grandfather Grinslade. The women's task was to look after the men, and to run the Post Office. William spent his days in the workshop dealing with the boots and bicycles and rarely if ever came into the shop. Great importance was attached to the men's preaching and everything possible was done to ensure that they were able to do the necessary study and preparation for this work. The garden which stretched up from Oatway, was "men's work" of course, though William always used to grumble about this and avoided it when he could. All the men were very helpless when faced with the simplest domestic task. When Glyn was born and William was left alone in the house for a while, he lived on bread and cheese for several days having no idea how to prepare anything else. Tending the fire was woman's work - here again, considerable labour was involved as there was no proper storage space for fuel at Roadwater and logs and coal had to be brought some distance to the house. Ada rarely complained, but years later occasionally even she did raise her voice at William's reluctance to have anything to do with fetching coal and making up the fire. I recall a characteristic little episode which took place in about 1951.

My husband's parents were seated cosily by the fire while Glyn and I fitted in as well as we could around the rather large table that dominated the room. As frequently used to happen, Ada was dozing off in her chair; and the fire was getting a little low. She had already left some coal in the grate ready for this moment, but it never seemed to occur to William that he might be able to put it on himself. Instead, his voice was heard - "Fire wants mending, Adie"! Adie dutifully complied, but I was glad that she had the spirit to register a mild protest at being roused from her chair after a long day which had begun at five o-clock. She was, after all, in her middle sixties. But it takes a long time to change a countryman's habits and Ada was not the woman to instigate a confrontation.

Anything in the nature of preparing food, shopping, washing and wiping dishes - all this was a field which was completely unknown to the men of the family. Over a long period of time, as in all businesses, there were periods of relative prosperity and periods of depression. In the prosperous times there was plenty of help available and the necessity for a helping hand was not quite so pressing. Grandfather always had a married couple living in at Oatway - the husband assisted with the business of cutting out and making the boots, while the wife helped in the home, performing those tasks which we nowadays tend to minimise but which in those days were a major operation such as the week's washing. First of all the water had to be drawn, then carried to the copper in the washhouse, in the orchard. Kindling had to be prepared and dry wood brought to light under the copper. More tubs of water had to be filled for rinsing and scrubbing purposes. So without a woman to help, washing day was very hard labour. Besides, Grandmother was delicate and had to take to her bed at an early age. In more modern times, up to the end of the thirties, as I have written elsewhere, Glyn's parents always had at least two employees and often more working for them at Washford. There was always one man, and sometimes

CHAPTER 14. THE WOMEN OF THE FAMILY

two, working out in the workshop at the boots, shoes and later bicycles. In the post office there was a girl at the switchboard and another doing the counter work. Then, of course, there were frequent arrivals and departures of the postmen and van drivers, not to mention the village baker whose business was also conducted on the premises. There was always a helping hand available when it was needed, and the "girls" in the office frequently turned away from their duties to take a turn at looking after the child, a welcome distraction from routine. In later years, of course, help became much harder to obtain, and the supply of girls dwindled drastically. Their quality also dropped noticeably, as increasing opportunities for education creamed off the abler girls and sent them to grammar schools. Poor Ada was never able to understand this - changing time hit her very hard, and she gradually became burdened with more and more responsibility with less and less help and a smaller income. William worried about this a good deal and tried to ensure that she would have assistance after his death, but was too old and sick to be able to work out a satisfactory solution.

Thinking of the girls, one is led into trying to count up all those who passed into Ada's care over the years. They came in all sorts' and sizes, mainly local, often very able, and tended to stay for years. When times improved sufficiently for Glyn's parents to take a short holiday the girls even slept at the house, answering the phone at all hours and balancing up the accounts at the weekend. Alas! However, even the best girl will marry and it was always a sad day when having trained a willing assistant and come to rely on her services, she left and had to be replaced by a raw recruit. Here again changing times made things more difficult to those who were accustomed to the old order, and it would no longer be taken for granted that the girl would do up the accounts before leaving on Saturday evening. Not so many years before she would not have expected to leave until they balanced, and more than one disconsolate boyfriend waited in vain on a Saturday to take his young lady to the pictures.

Often in after years, the young ladies who had since matured into homely married women, would come back to see Mrs Court, and "the office" as it was always called, would ring with noisy laughter as the proud mother showed off her children and told all her news. After her departure, peace would descend once more, and Granny would shake her head and smile, and pass some mild comment. "She always was like that! The office was always noisy when she worked here!"

As far as housework was concerned, the women of the family of course always did their own, and even though she had a large house to look after, Ada would not have dreamt of asking another woman to clean it for money. In fact even when she was growing old and infirm she found it very difficult to delegate the cleaning to the willing daily lady and never stopped apologising for not doing it herself.

Alas poor Ada! She dearly loved polishing the oak floors and panelling that William had made and felt deprived when she could no longer do this work. The polishing was a sort of consummation of all the long years they had spent building the house together, giving spiritual contact with its departed creator. It is easy to sneer at these pleasant old-fashioned ways but when one looks at the insecurity of society today one can perhaps appreciate the advantages of the system in which the men's and women's roles were clearly defined. Only today in the Sunday newspaper I have read a very serious and well-meaning article about the insecurity of so many partners in modern marriages brought about mainly by the increased status; liberty and earning power of women, with the subsequent feelings of inadequacy which such independence induces among the males. Such problems were unknown to the generation of which I write, and although I for one would have no wish to return to those days, I still cannot repress a mild feeling of regret that while rejecting one role, women do not seem to have altogether succeeded in finding another which is satisfactory for the well-being of society as a whole.

When poverty lurks only just around the corner, there is little time for niceties and fanciful notions. Greatest and most dreaded ogre of all was the spectre of the Workhouse, Although times in the twenties and thirties were not quite as hard as they had been, there was still precious little money to waste, and no one could tell what lay in the future - so the safest and best way to insure oneself was to have a regular income, however small, from some modest investment. Cottages were cheap to buy, especially if

CHAPTER 14. THE WOMEN OF THE FAMILY

purchased complete with tenant, and with a little renovation would often be improved sufficiently to bring in a higher rent than the accepted few shillings a week. One could hardly criticise William for failing to anticipate the effects of inflation. Already in his lifetime, the cottages were becoming a burden and had long since ceased to pay their way. When after the 1939 war, four cottages of Grandfather's block at Watchet were demolished, the principal emotion was a heartfelt sense of relief.

My husband's mother, Ada Palser, was not a Somerset woman by birth but had been born hard by the shores of the Severn at Lydney in Gloucestershire. To the end of her life, although she rarely revisited her native town once she had left it, she was always a stout defender of the county; one of her favourite phrases, when the beauties of West Somerset were being described, was "Mind you, there's lovely country in Gloucestershire". And very true, as many readers will no doubt agree.

Her father was a railwayman on the Great Western and the family lived in a four-roomed stone cottage by the side of the railway line just outside the town. The family name, Palser, is the same as Palliser, a fence-maker, but in her grandfather's time they had been farmers and millers at Wootton-under-Edge. Her mother's job, apart from looking after the family of six children, had been to open the crossing gate for trains to pass about five or six times of day. The lane past the cottage led down to Lydney's small but characteristic harbour on the tidal Severn, now full of pleasure craft. We visited the spot a few years ago and spent a fascinating hour or two trying to relate the present reality with the past as it had so often been described to us. The cottage is no longer there but a happy chance, its appearance had been faithfully recorded by an enthusiastic amateur artist, who was only too pleased to make a copy of his picture for us. One tree in the orchard still survived, together with the remains of the pigsty. This little building was of some importance in the lives of the family as its occupants furnished additional protein for the family's diet, providing in addition to salt pork and brawn, meat for home-made faggots (the sage also grew in the garden) and pure lard to make lardy cakes with dough fetched from the baker. "We lived well" she often used to say - "My father earned twenty-eight shillings a week - that was good money in those days. We always had plenty to eat, and we could often pick up coal along the line. Oh yes, we were well off".

Another of her recollections was of sitting on the steps of Lydney Cross waiting for Lord Bledisloe to drive past with his bride after his marriage in the early 1890s.

When we revisited the crossing, the gate had been replaced, but only comparatively recently, by a more modern device - do-it-yourself model (captive wives no longer being readily available) has been installed. The lane from the harbour, past the cottage and into the town seemed remarkably unspoilt and cannot have changed very much since Ada's childhood. As for the cottage itself, however, a heap of grey stones was all that was left - it had been demolished in order to improve visibility on the railway line.

When Ada was fourteen years old, her father was offered a better position with the G.W.R. in Swindon, and so the whole family prepared to move. Ada should have been leaving school by now but her mother was reluctant to send her to start an apprenticeship for such a short period as a year and allowed her to continue her education a little longer. So there she stayed, at the Church School in Lydney, a valued friend and assistant to the "Governess" who taught her to work those elaborate and delicate crochet patterns in which she took so much delight.

On arrival in Swindon, Ada's employment could not be deferred any longer and it was here that she first entered the Post Office.

In her delightful book "Lark Rise to Candleford" Flora Thompson describes her own humble beginnings in a village Post Office in Buckinghamshire. Much of this life she describes must have been almost as Ada knew it - though already, by 1901, there would have been slight changes. Flora Thompson, with the delicate observation of a true artist, notes the gradual alterations which were taking place in the decade, the 1880s. As Ada was born in 1884 she was only a few years later than this, and although village horizons were widening, there must have been many similarities. Flora

CHAPTER 14. THE WOMEN OF THE FAMILY

Thompson describes how the hours of work in the Post Office were so loosely defined as to be almost permanent. Even Sundays was not sacred, as this was the day on which the Irish labourers used to come in to send their money home.

After starting work at Candleford, several months elapsed before Flora was even allowed to have a half day free in which to visit her mother. Commitment to work was expected to be total, though actual working conditions were probably relatively good in the Post Office. By the end of her life, Ada was so used to this that her whole life, waking and sleeping, coming and going, was completely ruled by the Post Office. Flora, as did Ada when she first came to Washford three years after starting her apprenticeship, received her board and lodging. Her spiritual, physical and moral welfare were under the close surveillance of a kindly mentor. Ada was similarly guarded, though her Miss Bellamy was noted for her sharp tongue. The work was far from unpleasant, involving as it did meeting all the folk of the surrounding district, writing letters or helping to compose telegrams for them. There was also a certain intellectual satisfaction in the deciphering of telegrams by Morse Code. Ada always enjoyed this and was well-known for reading the messages aloud as the buzzes came over the line. We still have the clock which was used to help in sending telegraph messages. It was not as efficient as a teleprinter perhaps, but infinitely more satisfying to use. Altogether life as a post office assistant was a very much happier lot than being tied to a factory bench in a Lancashire cotton mill, or permanently cooped up in the basement scullery of a large house. There was one gentleman's residence outside the village and the "gentry" used to feature quite regularly in Ada's reminiscences. She had a respect for true gentility and courtesy, but could not abide "jumped-up" parvenus.

During the period 1904-1920 Ada regularly attended the Methodist Chapel where she was a keen member of the choir and it was there that she met her future husband, William, also a Postmaster, at Roadwater. They postponed their marriage for years, as William was supporting a family of nephews and nieces, and, being well looked after by his unmarried sister, saw no particular urgency to change his situation. When he and Ada finally married in 1920, Ada was thirty-four and William forty-four. Many times he would joke in after years "I'll never get married so young again". But Ada regretted her late start. She would have liked to have had more children. Often, when struggling valiantly in her seventies with my energetic family of youngsters, she would laugh ruefully and say "I ought to have been younger".

Weddings are a time for sentiment and a time for gifts. Both of these were to be had in plenty and in particular a handsome marble clock from the people of the village. As for sentiment, not only was the list of subscribers to this gift recorded, but it has descended to us in its entirety. A glance at this list gives an interesting microcosm of village life at that time. At the head of the list stand Mr and Mrs Lysaght of Chapel Cleeve with a princely donation of two pounds each. This is an interesting sidelight on social change, as the Lysaghts had made their money in business and subsequently purchased the mansion of Cleeve where they remained for some thirty years, the house later becoming a hotel. Next came the Stoates - pillars of the prosperous farming community and faithful standard-bearers for Dissent since the 1790s. Next in size of donation come the gentry, the Leighs of Bardon. After that, nearly every farm and village family of the present day is represented. The good lady who collected all this money, largely in shillings and sixpences, is not known to us, but is none the less immortalised by her letter which is enclosed with the list of subscribers;

> *Dear Miss Palser. I hope you will understand this. I feels rather shakeing today, thank you ever so much miss for your letter I hope you can read this, if not, you must see the book, when you comes home, they are giving you a good present, and it will surprise you when you comes home I hear miss you are to be married next Tuesday, wish you the best of luck, and I hope miss you will have it nice and fine for the wedding. I have done all I could for you miss, and wish I could do more for you, will miss I suppose, if my man gets work he his in Bridgwater I am to be married soon, that is true miss, and miss Palser, miss Bellamy told me when you comes home, you was going to let me have a box, and miss if you will sell it to me. I should be please, as I can't afford to buy a new one, do you think miss*

you could let me have it the last week in this month as I shall be going away for a holiday. I would do anything for you. if you will be kind enought father as been out of work 4 weeks now makes me miserable. bad job for me. now miss if you cant unstand I will send you the book, your truly with Love M.Lewis.

And from a lady who evidently relished a touch of mystery:

Hearing when I was home last that you was collecting for a present for Miss Palser on account of her forthcoming marriage + leaving Washford P.O. (I have visited the P.O. for years) you will find my donation for £1.1.0 - one Guinea enclosed please use to that affect.

from a well Wisher.

A guinea indeed! More than the gentry! Who can she have been?

My mother-in-law was in her sixties when I first came to know her and one of the first things that struck me when I first came to Washford was how hard and long she worked every day of the week. Although the post office no longer held the important place that it once had in the area, it was still necessary to rise at an hour which seemed to me impossibly early in order to take in the morning mail. Her alarm clock, as I recall, was always set at ten past five. My father-in-law's health was failing, so in addition to their responsibility for all the post office work and caring for a sick husband, she had to deal increasingly with the shoe business as well. She never complained about this, and I was continually amazed at her capacity for endurance. She had inherited from her Gloucestershire forebears that stoicism tempered with simple humour which enabled them to bear the harshness of their existence. As she would have expressed it, "tidn't no good to complain, dear, is it?"

Though not at all demonstrative by nature Ada was a person of strong feeling and capable of deep affection and loyalty - especially to the family. Her particular weakness was for young children, and like many women of her generation she took great pleasure in spoiling her grandchildren. Not that she would have admitted it of course and each new gift of toys was accompanied by an apologetic "We never had it"! The children of course took full advantage of this kindly figure with the silvery hair who rarely if ever scolded and could usually be relied upon for moral support when maternal favour was in short supply.

Ada loved to recall her own childhood. "Mother was a good mother", she would say, "we were always well-dressed, and well fed, but we were afraid to go near her. The only time she praised us was when she was talking about us to other people - then there were no children like hers! But we never had the love".

Starved of maternal affection in her youth she may have been, yet she amply made up for the lack in later life by lavishing her own on her nearest and dearest.

Growing up as she did in a working class home with few comforts and luxuries, she was accustomed to a more spartan style of living than her son and daughter-in-law. She rarely complained of the cold, and never in her life used a hot water bottle. Her appetite was also very moderate and she would often forget to eat for a day or so. Not that she begrudged spending money on food, for there was always an ample supply. "I keep a good table", she would say with justifiable pride. In fact I would frequently be alarmed at the quantities of food which I saw being put away in the larder, knowing full well that we could not possibly eat it all. Her tastes in food, based on old country ways of preserving with salt and vinegar, was different from mine, and it was at Washford that I first tasted pickled eggs and nasturtium seeds. Milk was always flowing in abundance, bread literally burst out of the bin. One of her little weaknesses was an inability to resist salesmen at the door, so that frequently she would buy a cake or loaf that she did not really want. She rarely bothered to see what she already had in the larder, so that like the shop new was put on top of old with rather alarming results. When we came to visit her we used to do our best to eat up what was fit for human consumption, this reducing the accumulation to manageable proportions - but to my horror I would find the next day that

CHAPTER 14. THE WOMEN OF THE FAMILY

she would have bought three or four more large cakes, thinking that we would not have enough. And so it went on until after her death I came to turn out the larder properly. There was a sizeable bin, about the size of a small dustbin, full right to the top with packets of cake. We used what we could but the birds had the bulk.

I often wondered why she used to buy so much cake. It was almost as if the substance had a peculiar fascination for her, I surmise, perhaps erroneously, that it was for her a symbol of prosperity and affluence dating from childhood memories when cake was a rare and much prized speciality reserved only for treats and Sundays.

Ada was clever with her hands, a great lover of gardening and particularly talented with the knitting needle and crochet hook. In her younger days she spent most of her evenings working at crochet, and many and various are the pieces of work that she produced - table mats, edgings for tablecloths, in patterns of varied complexity. There were so many of these in the house that it seemed impossible to use them all, but I try to give each one a turn and very attractive they look when well starched and preseed. The quality of the cotton must have been excellent as they have withstood many a laundering with little sign of wear for nigh on seventy years.

One of these cloths has an interesting story and dates from her young days at Washford. Having become accustomed to seeing Ada constantly bent over her work crocheting during the evenings, James Bellamy rather light heartedly dared her to create a whole Biblical picture by this method - in short, to translate into slip stitch, chain, doubles and trebles the tale of Daniel in the Lion's Den. The challenge was no doubt made in the same spirit in which an older man will dare a young woman to wield his spade or shoulder his heavy load, but Ada was not the woman to take such a challenge lightly. The idea appealed to her, and she stoutly maintained that she would tackle Daniel and his lions. Incredulous as only a man can be who knows little of such feminine matters, James Bellamy persisted in doubting her ability to fulfil the task and proceeded to set the seal on his incredulity by offering her a half sovereign if she really could achieve it. Ada set to work at once, and found the challenge a stimulating and absorbing one - so much so that she spent the whole of one winter's evenings not to mention a considerable number of balls of crochet cotton executing her design. At last she completed the cloth and worked a fringe to finish all off in the correct manner. But the half sovereign failed to materialise. James Bellamy had either forgotten his offer, or as seems more likely, changed his mind about parting with the money. After Ada's death, I found the cloth which had been put away for years and lost, though not the memories which went with it for I had often heard the tale. The tapestry (for it almost deserves the title though worked entirely in white cotton) is about the size of a small tablecloth. It depicts a heavily robed Daniel with prominent Jewish nose, recoiling from the brilliance of the angel's rays in the top right hand corner. Daniel perhaps is not completely convincing but one cannot fail to succumb to the charm of the two great bounding lions - one heavily bearded like a Victorian patriarch pretending to be very fierce, the other not even trying but very much enjoying having his likeness taken, like a modern television comic looking full at the camera. I imagine that Ada had copied the design from a picture in a book of Bible stories or perhaps from a family Bible.

Another hobby which never failed to delight her was dressing a doll, but as she was late marrying and did not have a little girl of her own to dress one for, William's nieces were the lucky recipients of her handiwork. Two of the dolls that she must have dressed in about 1910 survive almost intact and I have described them in the chapter about the museum.

In case I am making Ada seem like a plaster saint I must hasten to add that she had her little weaknesses. A strong streak of peasant obstinacy was probably one. (Her son finds his share very useful particularly in the political field.)

She did not really enjoy, as who indeed does, having her home disorganised by the invasion of children though loving the children themselves. Her religion was not of the spiritual order but strongly practical. I do not think she ever quite forgave God for taking William away from her - at any rate she stopped attending services after his death. She could be very disapproving, to the extent of being uncharitable, of certain people whom she disliked.

CHAPTER 14. THE WOMEN OF THE FAMILY

Once dismissed to the doghouse, you were unlikely ever to be brought back into favour. One of her very forgivable little foibles was a love of bright sparkling gems and jewellery and she was rarely seen without one quite large ring, a splendid emerald set about with diamonds. Absent mindedness (and not due entirely to old age I am sure) frequently caused her to lose things, notably her spectacles, and no garden tool of hers would ever be found in its correct place. This trait also caused many a burnt dinner or ruined pudding - though she never missed the mail and only on very rare occasions was she not up to meet the postman at ten past six.

Before concluding this brief sketch of my husband's mother I must not forget to mention her love of music - particularly songs and choruses. As a girl, she had enjoyed the privilege of piano lessons. Her mother was very strict about practising and allowed no excuse, such as the icy coldness of the parlour, to prevent the daily half hour stint. Her teacher was a Miss Howells, sister of the composer and professor at the Royal College of Music, born in 1892, Herbert Howells. She remembered often seeing Herbert as a small child seated on the steps of the house as she passed along the street. Unfortunately she did not keep up her playing, but continuing her mother's tradition devoted her energy to ensuring that her own son practised every day. A curious and amusing little secret came out after her death. It transpired that when we were not at Washford, she would often sit at the piano and play some of the tunes she had learnt as a girl. She would also sing songs which she had learnt as a girl, sixty years before, complete with many verses. For some reason known only to herself, she did not want us to know that she played - though Glyn had sometimes found sheet music on the piano and had his suspicions. The children were quite hurt at this little deception which sprang, I am sure, from a harmless mixture of self-effacement and a tiny streak of obstinacy. She did enjoy a secret! Miss Bates, her assistant for the last few years, was often sorely tempted to tell us things we were not aware of, especially when Ada's health became worse, but so strong was my mother-in-law's personality that Miss Bates never dared to break the silence that had been enjoined upon her.

Ada's greatest friend and confidante in the immediate family and the only female member to venture far afield had been her sister-in-law, Selina.

During the last decade of the nineteenth century, when jobs for working class girls were virtually unobtainable in her own area, Selina had sought employment as a lady's maid in "gentlemen's houses". Her first post was in the service of Bishop Moule at Cambridge. He was the author of several books of popular theology and also won a certain fame in his day as a hymn writer. Selina always spoke with warmth of the happy time she had spent in service at his house for the good Bishop's Christianity extended beyond the pulpit into the household, even to a shy maid with a Somerset accent. Perhaps he recognised intelligence when he saw it. At any rate, he would have been very surprised to learn how often his name was mentioned in that remote valley in Somerset for at least fifty years afterwards. From time to time, when visiting the relations at Roadwater, we would be shown a photograph dating from this period - it portrays a pale, serious girl most improbably garbed in academic dress. It appears that Selina had been dared by her fellow servants in the Cambridge house to don cap and gown and record the event for posterity. Accordingly she slipped off to the photographer on her afternoon off in order to have her picture taken. Anxious to escape detection, she walked right across Cambridge and sought out a photographer on the other side of the town. Imagine her chagrin and embarrassment at the service the following Sunday evening when, on placing her collection in the box, her eyes met those of the chapel steward - none other than the same photographer in his Sunday best! As far as has been recorded Selina's scrape did not get her into trouble, but judging from the frequency with which she related the tale in after years, she had a lurking fear that the photographer's eye, like the judgment of Cain, would follow her to the tomb! Perhaps too she had a yearning for the academic life, as her education had been limited to a few years spent at the tiny Church School at Leighland. Be that as it may, the portrait does not convince despite a certain period charm, mainly because the aggressive pose and confident manner of the blue-stocking is lacking. There is something too about those large serious eyes, almost imploring "Don't be cross with me - it's only a little joke"!

CHAPTER 14. THE WOMEN OF THE FAMILY

This happy employment lasted for several years until the Bishop won promotion which bore him away to the North, Selina was asked to accompany him but felt unwilling to go so far away from home.

She had never really felt at home in Cambridge despite the excellence of her situation, as she always used to say that the countryside was too flat, and that the climate affected her health. However that may be, she survived to the age of ninety-one so the bracing winds of East Anglia cannot have done her much harm after all. Her next situation was with the Rashleigh family at Menabilly near Fovey, and her work consisted of looking after the two young ladies of the family, Miss Rachel and Miss Kathleen. Many were the tales she used to tell of those days -the private path to the beach, exciting comings and goings of the gentry and of watching balls from the top of the staircase. The setting will be well known to readers of Daphne du Maurier, for she used it in her novels and the name Menabilly is thinly disguised as Mandalay. When her sight failed, Selina used to love to listen to radio versions of the du Maurier novels, and no doubt was able to offer many comments on the accuracy of the local colour. Only part of the year was spent at Menabilly, as the family also had a town house in Cumberland Terrace and thither they would all go to spend the winter.

After over fifteen years in service, Selina returned home to marry her Christopher who was a butler at a gentleman's house at Kingston St Mary near Taunton. Alas the marriage was short-lived and after only five years Christopher died of an undiagnosed illness - appendicitis perhaps, the cure for which was still its early stages.

Thenceforth, life became a long and tedious struggle and it was only with the help of the family that she was able to survive. She returned to Roadwater and took over the running of the Post Office, where she remained until her death over fifty years later. Towards the end of her life she lost her sight but right up to the end she never lost her charm and sense of humour. An expert needlewoman, she continued to sew until her sight prevented her. In appearance she was always scrupulously neat and despite her tiny income, well-dressed. Even at the age of ninety, I remember her sitting out of her bed attired in a pink dressing gown with a matching bow in her hair! While remembering her with affection, I regret that we had not been nearer in age. I feel that we should have had much in common.

15

We Inherit the Property

Clare Court

I now take up our own story again, after seventeen years of married life, during which Glyn and I moved about to teaching posts in various parts of the country, finally coming to rest in North Devon. By this time we had four children, three daughters aged thirteen to seven and a son of twelve. We had stayed five years in Ilfracombe, mainly because it was within convenient reach of Washford so that we could keep a discreet eye on Glyn's mother without making her feel that we were interfering. Widowed two years after our marriage, she had struggled on in a spirit of fierce independence, endeavouring to run both shop and post office with very little outside help, until one day the postman, bringing the early morning mail, received no answer to his knock. We suddenly found ourselves the owners of the property, with the added responsibility of a busy Post Office to maintain and organise. We were both occupied in full-time teaching, the children having reached the age where one salary was quite inadequate to feed, clothe and generally provide for them, so we were not free to come to Washford except at weekends. Added to this was the problem of conducting operations from a distance of forty miles, problems of sharing the car, not to mention the strain and expense of so much driving.

We had of course spent a good deal of time at Washford over the years, and had had plenty of opportunity to see what needed doing. However, we had always respected Ada's right to run her own home and business in the way that she had wished and had not attempted to interfere, though readers will hardly be surprised to hear that I had often been sorely tempted! Ada enjoyed meeting people and chatting to them in the post office and this was a part of her life which she did not wish to change or share. She had, after all, spent her whole working life in Post Office service and had been Postmistress in the village for over forty years. Consequently there were very few folk in the area whom she did not know or to whom at some time she had not rendered some service. But Alas! People grow old and infirm, and although mentally still very alert, by the time of her death at the age of 81 she only managed to conquer her physical problems by a sheer effort of will. Walking had become a major problem, yet she had to be on her feet for much of the day. Needless to say, we had been very much alive to the necessity of persuading her to give up the responsibility of the Post Office. Various schemes had been suggested and at times we quite thought that we had succeeded in persuading her to rest after her life-time of service to others, but after thinking things over she always decided to carry on. This would have been well enough had it not been the anxiety over the large sums of money which of necessity were kept on premises. For the last two or three years of her life we worried a great deal on her account, but so careful was she to hide her difficulties from us that it was not until after her death that much more alarming information came to light. She had, for example, had several falls which we had never heard about. Fortunately neighbours, friends, postmen and others who came regularly to the house were all keeping an eye on her - how annoyed she would have been if she had known, but how grateful we were for their watchful attention for when Ada finally collapsed it was not long before helpers were on the scene. She died peacefully having had the satisfaction of working right up to the last day of her life, and speaking to those she loved before going to her well-earned rest. She had been in the service of the Post Office for sixty-six years.

It will not be hard to imagine that there was a considerable emotional shock to overcome at this time and it was probably a good thing for everyone that there was so much to do. The children were terribly brave and sensible and only the youngest one gave way unashamedly to her grief. In view of Ada's increasing age and infirmity and the fact that she had been struggling on her own for fifteen years, it was hardly surprising that the shop had not been spring cleaned or turned out for some years. In fact, as work progressed, we began to wonder if it had ever been turned out since it was built in 1921! We only had a few days of the Whitsun holiday in which to make the first

CHAPTER 15. WE INHERIT THE PROPERTY

Figure 15.1: A view of Hill Head House in the early 1970s

frontal attack, as we were both teaching and all the children were at school. I think it is perfectly true to say that this was the most exhausting Whitsun holiday that I have ever spent in my life. As if the turning out process were not enough, I had added domestic problems of cooking for a family of six on a worn-out cooker. As I remember it, an old cast-iron Jackson, only half of the top hotplate and one side of the oven used to function. There was also a paraffin oven, and several oil stoves dotted about the kitchen. (A recurring nightmare had been that Ada would have an accident with them and set her clothes on fire, but a merciful angel must have been keeping an eye on her.) The cooker was soon replaced and I simply insisted on a fridge - I knew the kitchen well enough and did not need long to work that out.

There is a certain satisfaction to be derived from having a "good turn out", and everyone, including the children, entered into the operation with gusto. We also had two kind ladies to help us, Miss Bates who had been assisting in the Post Office, and Cousin Kathie, who devotedly performed many thankless tasks for us in our absence. One of the disadvantages, which soon became apparent, was that it was impossible to close the shop while we were working as customers were continually coming and going, collecting pensions, or buying one 2 1/2d stamp - a never-failing source of astonishment to me but apparently a popular village pastime. I was amazed when one customer, a woman, came up to the Post Office three separate times in one day in order to buy a stamp. Later on, when I came to know the business better from my side of the counter, I ceased to be amazed at anything, but this was yet to come. At that time we were very eager to put a respectable face on things, but as work progressed we soon discovered that the slightest attempt to move anything from some of the shelves brought down choking clouds of dust - not exactly conducive to good customer relations!

We tackled the top shelves first as they looked fairly straightforward, being filled with piles of fairly large boxes rather than many small articles. It turned out that the boxes contained literally dozens of pairs of hobnailed boots - a standard form of footwear among farm labourers and formerly a good steady selling line. From the state of the boxes and from the handwritten prices in my father-in-law's writing it was obvious that they had been there for at least thirty years. I was puzzled by the algebraic symbols which appeared on the boxes and were repeated in pencilled writing under the insteps of the boots. Such combinations as *lty*, *xy*, *opi* recurred with mystifying frequency but the explanation was quite simple. The letters were code for the cost price of the footwear, and the code, which apparently everyone in the family knew as well as their own names, was based on the extraordinary word DOLPHINET - D was 1, 0 - 2, L - 3 and so forth. 10, 11 and 12 were represented by x y z, hence the preponderance of these popular mathematical letters as 10/11 was a usual price for the older pairs. Another combination which I came to know well was *lty* - 39/11. Kathie informs me that she became so familiar with the code in her years of running the Roadwater business that she could add up columns of the code letters as readily as figures. As the boots were so heavy to move, and both William and Ada were getting older, it seemed that as the years went by they had more or less forgotten what was in the boxes and under pressure from travellers ordered fresh stock which was put up on the top of the old.

As the customers had gradually been drifting away over the years, particularly after William's death, sales became less frequent and the boots

CHAPTER 15. WE INHERIT THE PROPERTY

piled up higher and higher towards the ceiling. Removing them all was a major task - I challenge any normal healthy housewife to carry more than four pairs of heavy nailed boots at once, even fewer if they are size tens and elevens! To the uninitiated (as I was) it should be explained that there are several sorts of nail boots, light, medium and heavy and there are numerous variations of toe-cap and tongue. The problem was what to do with them all? Fortunately we had several outbuildings and after a certain amount of trial and error we eventually got the boots out of the shop and arranged them all in a building which we always refer to as the "Toc H". The children were of absolutely invaluable assistance in removing the boots from the boxes and carting wheelbarrow loads of perishing cardboard and rubbish up into the garden to be burnt. Altogether we counted about seventy-five pairs - and this in a small village shop! Throughout this operation it became obvious that we would have to have a sale of some sort. Though previously we had had virtually no experience of the business - indeed had never been allowed to help - it turned out that I had quite a business flair where this sort of thing was concerned. A month or two more elapsed before we were sufficiently well organised to have a proper sale, but once the idea was established in our minds it was a great help in working out how and where to store the outdated stock.

Meanwhile Kathie and Miss Bates were doing their bit behind the Post Office counter, and soon they too were raising dust, throwing away old envelopes, or pulling out old telegram forms and envelopes to add to the rubbish heap. More and more boxes of old shoes were being discovered - children's boots and shoes going back to the early years of the century, ladies' shoes of the 1920s, obsolete football boots, goloshes, even dancing pumps and leather gaiters. At this time the Automobile Association men still used to ride around on motor cycle combinations and they were the only customers who still used gaiters. The patrolmen used to come from miles around to buy them from us, and staunchly maintained that they were the best possible gear for keeping their legs and ankles warm and dry.

One brave soul started to explore the space under the large shop window. Apart from large quantities of cobwebs, and a generous supply of thirty year old cardboard boxes, it gave forth numerous bicycle accessories including a pair of handlebars, a couple of mudguards and a splendid carbide lamp. The children were highly delighted to find some toddlers straps made of solid leather with nice little metal bells on them - although long past the age of wearing such things my seven-year-old refused to take them off for days.

Of course, there were quite large quantities of stock which were fit for nothing and had to be thrown away. Torch batteries for example, out-of-date films, several venerable toothbrushes, and a strange substance called "Amovon" Foot Paste. I wondered why there seemed to be so many tins of this commodity on every shelf, looking strangely out of place with its grotesque little illustration of a 1920s type sporting man wearing a huge cap. Apparently, during the bad years of the 1930s an unscrupulous "traveller" desperate for trade, had deliberately falsified a reluctant order for one dozen boxes of this medicament to twelve dozen. Too busy or too unwilling perhaps to protest, William had retained the goods and there it was after thirty years.

The supply of shoe laces was also fruitful - some of them very broad and floppy, had been in fashion in the 1930s and by 1967, funnily enough, were once more being worn. To my shame I confess I threw the laces out for the dustman, but later discovered that my prudent preserver, alias Glyn, had saved them. This was a recurring performance, but I am pleased to say that I have now learnt more civilised ways and hoard in the best Court tradition.

What else did we achieve in that first mad rush of enthusiasm? A higher standard of cleanliness certainly, for as work progressed the Parkinson's law of spring cleaning started to come into effect, in other words as fast as we succeeded in scrubbing and cleaning one part, we realised how dirty was the part next to it. Fortunately, or unfortunately according to how you view the matter, Whit Monday was an official closing day so that we were able to make a thoroughly good job of exhausting ourselves. We even managed to splash some paint on the ceiling and walls. The more we progressed, the more it became obvious that we would have to write off a large amount of the stock and sell it for whatever it would fetch. So on the following day,

CHAPTER 15. WE INHERIT THE PROPERTY

with the children helping, we made a start by putting out quite a few of the old shoes at give-away prices, The children entered wholeheartedly in the sale idea and hid themselves behind the shop curtain in order to watch the proceedings. Tuesday is a busy day in the Post Office as the Family Allowances are given out, and there is always bound to be a steady flow of mothers and babies coming into the shop. As the previous day had been a Bank Holiday there were also a few pensioners as well. There was great excitement and loud stage whispers could be heard:

"Sh! There's someone coming in!" (Giggle, giggle, fidget, heavy breathing)
"She's looking at the shoes. She's buying them – quick come and look"

etc. and so forth. Unfortunately this keenness had worn off by about ten o-clock in the morning! The word soon got around the village and people began to pop in and disappear again very quickly in order to tell their relations the good news about our bargains.

For a few weeks the children continued to enter into this new game with tremendous enthusiasm, becoming very excited, every time we succeeded in selling something. For a while, we kept a few sweets, and nothing would satisfy them but to have a small stall of their own in the shop. The youngest child carried this enthusiasm a little too far, as she felt so disappointed if no one bought anything that without telling anyone, she locked the door of the shop. When the customers, mostly friendly village ladies, found they could not get out they were held to ransom and forced to buy something. At this point parents intervened and hastily unlocked the door before losing their customers for good!

On many other occasions the children came in very useful, particularly in the later stages when we could not afford paid help, as they would guard the shop and call us if anyone came in. My eldest daughter must have done most of her O-level revision with the door into the shop partly open, and often interrupted her studies to sell a greetings card or a pair of bootlaces Though not likely to produce a certificate at the end, I feel it was education of a different sort. In fact the children often used to do small jobs about the shop which took a great deal of time and patience, and even when quite young, my eldest daughter had become accustomed to helping Ada to sort out the birthday and greetings cards. She became very possessive about them and if it had not been for her assistance we should never have managed to keep the cards tidy. Another job which the children never minded doing was sorting out the miniature cars. These used to live in a special stand under a pilfer proof cover. Unfortunately not only was it pilfer proof, it was also owner proof and occasionally the whole set of cars, numbered from one to seventy-five, would fall out while I was struggling with the cover on to the floor. Replacing them all took hours and it seemed rather a lot of work in order to make the modest sixpence profit on each car. As with all small items of trade one needs a fast sale and quick turnover to make it worthwhile selling them.

The children could often be induced to do little helpful jobs if I paid them a small wage, and the rate fixed for Joy, who was ten at the time, was sixpence an hour. After one enthusiastic week's work during the school holidays she managed to earn one pound - perhaps it was as well that no youth employment officer was on the scene to work out how many hours of work she had put in per day.

Over the next few months there was a great deal of rushing to and fro between Ilfracombe and Washford, and we wore out a good many tyres as we continually crossed and recrossed the lonely hills of Exmoor. Friday night was rather a headache, as Glyn had inherited willy-nilly his mother's responsibility for the Post Office and therefore, every week on Friday night the accounts had to be balanced up. The G.P.O. is a singularly bad employer in this respect. Our cousin, also a village postmistress, was completely flooded out in 1961 (to name but one occasion) by the nameless stream. Although there were three feet of sludgy water in her living room and Corn Flakes and postal orders floating around it it, she was not allowed to close the office. Instead of being allowed to get on uninterruptedly with the task of cleaning and drying her ruined home, she was obliged to hire the Village Hall (at her own expense of course) and conduct operations there. As a special concession in view of the floods, she was allowed to close in

CHAPTER 15. WE INHERIT THE PROPERTY

the afternoons. This happened on several occasions and certain articles of family furniture have permanent red shadows in their crevices - relics of floods in Grandfather's day. One hopes that the works undertaken by the Water Board will spare the inhabitants of Roadwater such misery in future.

Fortunately Glyn had had plenty of experience in counting rows of stamps, checking postal deposits and withdrawals, postal orders, pensions and so forth as it was the only department of the family business for which his mother considered that his University education had fitted him. Towards the end of her life I never ceased to be amazed that a woman of her age could add up long columns of figures with such effortless ease, but as my talents lie in other directions I was always only too pleased to leave this tedious task to them, and therefore I was not much help on Fridays. After Ada's death it meant that Glyn had to rush out of school on Friday afternoon at four o-clock and drive straight to Washford, where the accounts frequently would not balance. It then took quite a lot of the night and half of Saturday to get them right. Quite often the whole family went for the weekend but as anyone who has had two houses on their hands for any length of time will know, it is not exactly a picnic moving at regular intervals from one to the other with four children in tow, let alone having to count the stamps as soon as you arrive. We were in any case already leading a very full and busy life in Ilfracombe with frequent weekend engagements. The children were at school and naturally had all their friends and interests there, and Glyn was constantly working for his church and the Liberals, all of which was quite enough without inheriting a post office as well. Most of our social life was tied up with Liberal fairs, dances and suppers with Jeremy Thorpe, not to mention the regular bouts of canvassing and committee meetings, and we were reluctant to abandon all this happy activity. This conflict continued right up to the last day that we lived in North Devon. As the months went by it became increasingly obvious that we had loaded ourselves with an intolerable burden. Two houses to maintain with only a little money coming in to keep them going, two cars and the children - we could not possibly afford to continue without taking some decision. But by this time it was too late to do the sensible thing and sell the property. The voice of reason was very insistent that to sell was the only reasonable course of action. Unfortunately there were two major obstacles to this - neither based on logic or good sense, firstly, Glyn had promised his Mother that he would keep the house that his Father had built (he wanted to anyway) and secondly, we had by this time become hopelessly optimistic about all sorts of exciting projects for the shop which if fulfilled were going to change our destiny. Children with a new toy would be an apt, if hackneyed, metaphor. Dreaming of a new wave of prosperity our fantasies knew no bounds, and we eagerly embraced and swallowed success stories of village stores expanding into small empires. At one point, I remember, we mapped out the orchard as a park for our fleet of delivery vans. There was literally no limit to the variety of stock which we thought we might sell, and certainly no bounds to our enthusiasm at that time, how thankful I am that the orchard project never came to anything! The sight of the grass overshadowed with apple-blossom is worth far more than a quarter of an acre of tarmacadam, while the early morning song of blackbirds and thrushes too is infinitely precious. I can even learn to love the cooing of the rapacious pigeons in the copse at the top of the garden when I think that had our wild imaginings been realised we should have been completely hemmed in by the sound of the internal combustion engine. A narrow escape indeed.

16 Brief Flirtation with Commerce

Glyn Court

The summer holidays came on, and we spent the whole of the time at Washford, It was during this period that we discovered for the first time the delights of buying stock for the shop, and hardly a week went by without our driving off to Bristol or Exeter to visit the wholesaler. Shoe repositories had changed very little in fifty years, and we had a very interesting time poking around in the dusty corners of Quicks and Ware's in Exeter, or Lindrea in Bristol. On these visits one was impressed by the old world charm and courtesy that seems to be a tradition of the boot and shoe trade. Some of the assistants seemed almost as old as the stock, and they were obviously no more enthusiastic about modernising their premises than Glyn's parents - "enthusiastic" is hardly the word, the thought of changing anything would never have entered their heads. The office at Quicks was a dark brown enclosure wherein dwelt hard-working clerks sitting at high mahogany desks.

On receiving the first account we were pleasantly surprised to note that it was written out in longhand in flowing, cursive script. Ware's business is conducted in an old tanyard in the village of Woodbury near Exeter - a convenient stopping-point for me when going to visit my parents. From time to time they told us the adjacent stream overflows and ruins all their stock - a story with an all too familiar ring to our ears. Their accounts are headed with a Biblical reference from Proverbs. On looking up this reference, we found the words: A false balance is an abomination to the Lord but a just weight is his delight. We thought this a pleasing touch in the hard world of commerce. Alas! Times are changing rapidly and most of the trading is now done in modern estates where I greatly doubt that one would have the great fortune to discover, as I did at Quicks, heaps of ancient hobnailed boots, just like ours, pushed into a corner.

Another excursion was to Associated Wholesale Stationers in Exeter where Bert, an amiable character in a grey pullover and with a strong Devonshire accent dispensed stationery, bail-point pens, jig-saw puzzles, maps of the South West and novelties. A rather endearing feature of these display rooms is an almost total disregard for the seasons, and a very pronounced disregard for what we have come to understand by "advertising". At Associated Wholesale Stationers, for example, it was always Christmas, Christmas decorations and "lines" being an important part of their trade.

In order to sell the decorations of course they must be displayed, a tiresome business which necessitates climbing up on to steps and sticking pins into the ceiling. Hardly surprising then that once the season was over the decorations stayed up, becoming progressively more tatty and dusty as the year wore on. Presumably the new season brought new lines, but from my experience, albeit limited, of small wholesalers I should say that they often take nearly as long to clear one item from their shelves as small retailers. Somehow, it does take away the glamour and novelty of Christmas to see last year's decorations still up in August - the normal trading month when preparations for the attack on the Christmas market seriously begin. The most popular visit that we made that summer was to the Christmas Trade Fair at Bristol. This was altogether a much more sophisticated business with a huge variety of fancy goods, crockery, handbags, novelties, ornaments and toys from every imaginable country. We took the two eldest children with us and we fell prey to a particularly charming representative on a Chinese stand. We bought a large amount of goods, ranging from hand-painted fans, ivory bracelets and cotton birds, to bowls and spoons for a ridiculously small sum of money - I think we spent £25. Toys of course attracted the children, and before we knew where we were we were acquiring teddy bears, plastic fire engines, badminton sets, buckets and spades, sailor hats and the like. Here again we were astounded at the quantity we could purchase for £25 or so.

CHAPTER 16. BRIEF FLIRTATION WITH COMMERCE

This sort of buying was not to prove our undoing as there is always a sale for cheap, attractive goods of this sort, but we came seriously unstuck on the footwear. The shop was now beginning to look much brighter and more attractive, and we had been painting the walls a little at a time, covering shelves with Fablon and generally making the whole place look much lighter and more attractive. Our customers were delighted at the change, and lulled by their favourable comments into a false idea of success, we invested fairly heavily in a new stock of shoes. To anyone considering selling footwear, we could probably give some very helpful advice - mainly of a very negative nature. We had to trust our own instinct plus advice from salesman on what to buy. You immediately run up against all sorts of problems. First, just think of all the different sorts of footwear. Take men's to start with: you have brown shoes, black shoes, good quality, cheap ones, lace-ups, brogues, slip-on casuals, heavy duty work shoes, reinforced boots, cricket boots, canvas casuals, sandals, slippers - the list is endless. Say you select a well-known brand of lace-up brown shoes in a popular price. What sizes? Say six to eleven. You are almost bound to be left with the sixes and need two or three pairs of eights. Are you keeping the half sizes? No? Then on the first day a customer will ask for a half size. Do you fancy wellingtons? A simple task, I hear you say, just order one or two small ones and lots of popular sizes. Ah, but everyone wears wellingtons. And they come in light, medium and heavy, roughly speaking, with subdivisions. Very well then, you will keep a complete stock of wellingtons from infants' fours up to men's elevens, including a few coloured short pairs for ladies. So let us add them up - fours to thirteens, not forgetting that you need two to three pairs of some popular children's sized to make sure that you do not miss sale, say twenty-five pairs, and then from ones to large elevens, another twenty-five pairs of so, allowing for a modest choice between the cheapest and better quality. That is at least £50 worth of wellingtons -and in a bad week you may not sell any, so all your lovely money is tied up in rubber and plastic.

One could go on indefinitely thinking of types of shoe one might try to sell - plimsolls, white and black (here again many different qualities and styles), children's sandals (the thirteens always sell out and often cannot be replaced), ladies', gents' and children's slippers (a much easier thing to sell) and greatest problem of all, ladies' shoes. Suffice it to say that a small shopkeeper would be well advised to keep well away from any line with a hint of fashion to it - we unfortunately thought we knew better. Our shoes were excellent value from a popular wholesaler whose name you will never see advertised in the press or on television, and we were able to sell them for about thirty shillings a pair at a time when most stores were charging about £3 for well-known makes. However, we had not reckoned for the sophistication of the present day villager and with the reluctance of our customers to actually part with cash for the goods. Coming from a middle-class background myself I had had it well drummed into me that one always paid for goods, did not contract credit agreements and so forth, Glyn too was rather vague about such matters, although we had often heard his parents grumbling in a general way without taking much notice. Consequently we were totally unprepared for the carefully calculated exploitation of our apparent new-found wealth.

There were various gambits and ploys to all of which we fell innocent victims. One was to establish a relationship with us by buying goods over a period and paying for them, and then one day the customer had "forgotten her purse" or "come out in a hurry" but could she have a pair of shoes, wellingtons, or whatever it was. We of course say yes, the goods disappear and so does the customer. In the case of those who had to come into the Post Office in order to collect pensions we soon devised a system where we kept back five shillings per week of the Family Allowance until the debt was paid. Needless to say we did not dare charge interest for this service - we were only too glad to get the money.

William and Ada often used to tell many tales of the depression days when the stock was literally rotting on the shelves, and the whole area lay suffocated under a blanket of poverty. Customers would come in hopefully offering to exchange goods for a pair of shoes - William was notoriously kind hearted and in this way unwittingly acquired all manner of rubbish. One of these items, a large thermometer, lay around for years. Its owner apparently had said that he would redeem it when times improved. But mostly they simply took the goods, squeezing out a tear or two for the occasion, and depended on time to erase memory of the debt. As he used to say, "They'd

CHAPTER 16. BRIEF FLIRTATION WITH COMMERCE

come in with the children, point to their bare feet and say 'Can't 'e let me have a pair of boots for 'en, Mr Court?' How could I refuse?" Altogether William used to reckon, that he lost £500 in bad debts during this time - it was probably even more than that as many of the debts were never written down.

Quite recently my husband ran into a farmer who remembered a fairly typical incident which illustrates William's rather vague approach to business matters. William had fitted out the farmer's family with boots and shoes and in due course the customer naturally expected to pay for the goods which he had received. He found it, however, extremely difficult to persuade the courteous and absentminded William to present him with the bill. The debt dragged on for a month or two and Mr J., honest fellow, worried at the delay, reminded him several times of his desire to pay. The conversation proceeded something like this:

> **Honest John**: I'll be up Saturday to pay for they boots!
> **On Saturday, William**: Let me see now, 'twas one pair, wadn' it. That'll be nineteen and six, mister.
> **Honest John**: One pair be darned! Twas dree, sna. (it was three, don't you know). I owe 'e dree pun, you! (I owe you three pounds).

Another gambit which we learnt to distrust was to send the children up to the shop, hoping that we would entrust them with the desired articles. "Mum says, have you got a pair of slippers size four?" We soon learnt to harden our hearts, and just sent one slipper out.

By about half way through August, we had sold quite a few pairs of the old footwear at knockdown prices, but there were still so many pairs lying around outside that we decided to have one big sale to try to get rid of them all. So we turned out the "Toc H" to make room for the goods. This in itself sounds quite simple, but it necessitated a major clear out and another bout of exhausting physical labour. The building, a rather pleasant stone structure with a slate roof, stands just to the back of the house. It must have been built about a hundred years ago, and for a long period was a stable for the Post Office horse as the Post Office had always been in this part of the village. You will probably wonder at the name - Toc H - but the explanation is quite simple. During the 1930s when the stable was no longer in use, William devoted quite a lot of his time and energy to converting the loft into a committee room for the Toc H. The room downstairs became yet another place to put things for which they had no particular use. William replaced the old loft ladder with a nice little staircase and knocked out the bricked-up spaces and made new 'windows upstairs and downstairs. Always a lover of the picturesque, he used up some of his stained glass (provenance uncertain but probably bought in sales) to beautify the door which replaced the old stable entrance. Later on, when the idea of the museum suddenly sprang on me, this building was the obvious place to put it.

For the time being however the most urgent task was to clear out the two rooms and make then sufficiently presentable for the public to see. Both upstairs and down were crammed with rubbish of various sorts. Most of the things in the upper room were household goods which belonged to an aunt who had stored them there about twenty years earlier. She was still alive but we just hoped she had forgotten about it when we carted most of the rubbish out to the bonfire. There were rotten mats and masses of brown pictures, crumbling lino and we counted pieces of five beds - box springs, feather mattresses and heavy wooden and metal sides. These were more of a headache and as they were too large to be carried down the stairs, had to be thrown out of the window - the children enjoyed that part as much as their parents! Very little of interest turned up apart from a rather nice patch-work quilt. The room is light and pleasant and, once it had been emptied of its contents, amply repaid our efforts. When the happy day arrives, if we can stop the rain getting in through the old slate roof, it will be even better. Downstairs the work was heavier going, however. Oil drums were our chief enemy here and it was a problem to know what to do with them all. Later on I made an illicit trip to the dump, an ancient slate quarry of bottomless depth. The Bedford van was packed with an assortment of these rusty drums, and I hurled them one by one over a chain link fence which had been specifically erected to prevent such malpractices. They made a most satisfying noise when they reached the bottom a full ten

CHAPTER 16. BRIEF FLIRTATION WITH COMMERCE

seconds later. I also seem to remember bundles of pieces of marble from old washstands, too small to be of any use. They followed the oil drums. In one corner stood a very interesting French harmonium. We have never discovered where this came from, though the girls had a great deal of fun playing it. Grates and boxes, including the original ones in which the petrol pumps had been delivered forty years earlier, lay around in mouldering heaps everywhere. I thought we were never going to stop sweeping away cobwebs and dirt. When we had finally cleared the room up as well as we could, we had time to notice the floor, which is beautifully cobbled and tiled, but absolutely ruined by so many years of leaking oil and dirt. We laid down all the old mats which we had found on the floor and over seven or eight years, the worst of the oil has gradually worn away.

After a week of this frenzied cleaning, we had sorted things out sufficiently to hold the sale. Bearing in mind that we had no paid assistance and had never been involved in anything remotely resembling a sale before, we made quite a fair success of it. Of course, we had to advertise the venture, spending five whole pounds on a block in the "Free Press" and the rest was done by word of mouth and home-made signs. We had no proper equipment for making notices- I turned out quantities of old cardboard boxes and shoe advertisements, in short, any piece of cardboard which could by fair means or foul pass muster as a signboard and painted "Shoe Sale" all over them. There was no paint fit to use and we had forgotten to buy any so I used black leather dye which I had found in the shop and some ancient varnish from a rusty tin, slapped on with a fossilized brush whose bristles had long since matted into a solid block. We made as many signs as we could and fixed them on to whatever was handy including the telegraph pole at the bottom of the garden, using rusty nails or pieces of Post Office string. Considering the abysmal amateurishness of our efforts, and the general confusion which reigned while we were trying to make the preparations, the results were astounding. The holiday season was at its height, and a showery day was certain to bring in plenty of curious visitors. The rows of hob-nailed boots, having been duly polished by the cleaning lady (a mammoth task which took the whole of a day) proved tremendously popular with the local men, and as they were only marked at thirty shillings a pair, sold at a great rate.

Boys' and mens' shoes sold as fast as we could put them out, some for as little as five or ten shillings a pair. The Grannies of the village "sent up" and got themselves fitted out with good quality solid leather open-top bunion shoes for a pound or so. Downstairs in the Toc H, we put all the "hopeless" shoes. These consisted of literally dozens of pairs of black leather walking boots such as were worn by children in the early years of the century. We doubted whether they had been much worn as late as 1921 when William built the shop, and I can only assume that he had brought with him all the remaining stock from Grandfather's business at Roadwater. There were elastic-sided boots, and football boots with high tops - they just would not sell even at 2/6 a pair. Do you remember those rather dashing two-coloured men's canvas shoes of the 1930s? The sort Bertie Wooster sometimes wears with plus-fours? We had some for one shilling. Afterwards of course we wished that we kept more of these shoes but unfortunately we had not yet conceived the idea of using all this material to start a museum, as explained in Chapter 19.

One interesting observation that came out of our discoveries was how much smaller feet must have been fifty or sixty years ago than they are now. There were quite a few ladies' shoes' of the period leading up to the first world war, and they were in tiny sizes, ones and twos. Even a child would not be able to get them on nowadays, as they are so narrow in fitting.

A very pleasant side effect of the sale was the number of people who came in with reminiscences of the "old days" and stories of how they had had their first boots or bicycles from Mr Court or his father. Unfortunately the coming of the motor car destroyed the close relationship between shop and village which existed even up to the beginning of World War II, and many people did not realise that our family business still existed, let alone that it was struggling to renew its life. Since William's death in 1953 there had for obvious reasons been a gradual falling-off in the number of men calling at the shop. The old-fashioned way of life had somehow allowed time for a leisurely chat over every purchase. It was, after all, a serious business to buy a pair of boot which would last you for several years or even a lifetime. In Grandfather's day, when the profit margin on his work was so tiny and customers few and impoverished, it could be a life and death affair to spoil

CHAPTER 16. BRIEF FLIRTATION WITH COMMERCE

a pair of boots or aggravate a customer by poor workmanship. Something of this tradition lingered on into the forties and fifties. A typical encounter would go like this:

> **Customer** (usually a man in his late fifties or sixties) to girl behind counter giving her a scornful look as if to say "I id'n going to be served by the likes of you": *Mr Court about?*
> **Girl**: *I'll go and see.* (Longish pause while William is informed of the presence of Mr So and So, collects his wits and proceeds in leisurely fashion into the shop, puffing rather.)
> **William**: *Well, Mister, how is it then.* (Like most countrymen he had two languages and would speak pure dialect when occasion warranted.)
> **Customer**: *All right.*

Then would follow a lengthy discussion on whatever was the burning issue of the moment, trouble over a footpath, a new shelter for the village "rec" and allied matters. After some minutes of this:

> **Customer**: *Well, Mister, 'ave 'ee got a pair of boots to fit me then?*
> **William**: *Let me see, 'tis a eight, idn' it, Mister?*

Then would follow the dignified ceremony of finding a suitable pair, laying down the small C.&R. mat always used for trying on (this had been in use for thirty years and was never replaced) and usually the customer would be satisfied, even praising all the previous boots which it had been his privilege to obtain from the establishment. This last perhaps would not be completely disinterested, as the transaction would invariably end with William giving discount on the purchase thereby reducing even further his already modest profit.

In the sad years of widowhood Ada used to lament the changing times, and on these occasions she would often talk about the old days, finishing up with the very true observation "Twas Dad's personality sold the stuff".

Self-pity however was not the main purpose of her reminiscences, she just loved to remember all the happy days and have a little chuckle over all the ups and downs of their life.

17 Times Best Forgotten

Clare Court

That first summer we spent the whole of the school holidays wrestling with all the problems at Washford, and by the time they came to an end everyone, including the children, was feeling very exhausted and longing to get back to our own home. As if the shop and house were not enough to deal with, we had also inherited the enormous garden with lawns and flower beds and ornamental stonework, not to mention the orchard and vegetable patch. Somehow Glyn managed to keep the grass cut but everything else had to wait and a large part of the garden had more or less reverted to wilderness with neck-high brambles where the raspberries had once been. The birds had a wonderful time but the sight of so much neglect was becoming rather depressing and more than once I wondered how we could ever possibly restore the garden to something of its former order. Not only that, but it was far from a picnic running our daily life in a house which had been occupied by an old lady living alone for fourteen years. I have already mentioned the fearsome cooker, but another major problem was how to do the washing. Until quite recently Ada had used the old copper in the washhouse. The iron fire bars under the actual copper had long since worn away and it was difficult to keep the fire burning at all as the whole fire, coal, sticks and all, tended to fall right through at intervals, Occasionally, just for the fun of it, I had lit the fire and had a good boil up, and I must admit that there is a certain satisfaction in setting alight a roaring blaze beneath the copper and hearing the bubbles start to work! Rinsing was done in a large galvanised bath outside the door and wringing by hand. Ada had never possessed a wringer and was very proud of the fact that she could wring out more water than any of the other women in her family. After the washing was finished, all the water you no longer needed was tipped down the path, and eventually found its way into a drain - one of the many mysterious clay pipes that shoot under the garden in all directions leading to obscure bramble-clad outfalls in forgotten corners of fields.

The washhouse would have been quite an important meeting place in bygone years as it served three cottages. I often think how much we have lost by doing our washing all alone in our kitchens. In parts of Italy and France and Africa still one can see the women enjoying a lively gossip as they beat out their clothes on the banks of rivers or in those murky washing places in the back streets of towns. Perhaps the Laundrette is a good thing if it gets people out of their houses and into a place where they can still chat together and render small neighbourly services such as helping one another to fold the sheets.

There is one more amusing story about the washhouse. There was a tap quite near the door which William had fixed for general convenience and watering the garden, but one day arrived a man from the Council Offices to have a little look round, the object of the visit being to assess the property for rates. Before his arrival William disappeared "around the back" with a spanner and shortly afterwards announced that he had removed the tap, as he was afraid the official might notice it and. put his rates up. Naturally I expected him to replace the tap as soon as the representative had departed, but no! He never got around to it and so for years every Monday Ada uncomplainingly carried buckets of water from the kitchen to the washhouse, a distance of twenty yards or so. She finally had the tap replaced about twelve years after it had been removed. I thought it was a very laborious way of doing the washing. Not only was washing difficult, but the house had never been wired properly for electricity. There were lights, but the wiring had perished and there were weird arrangements of monstrous ugliness, with three or four wires all leading out of one small plug. We had never managed to persuade Ada to regard electricity with respect and the miracle was that nothing blew up. There had not been any power in the house at all until recently, when Ada had three points installed in the main living rooms so renewing the wiring was the first job that had to be done, which meant that in addition to coping with all our other problems, we had to endure the inconvenience of floorboards being taken up all over the house for several weeks. It was unfortunate but the house had been built a few

CHAPTER 17. TIMES BEST FORGOTTEN

years before electricity came to the village. The original lighting, the latest thing at the time, had been by acetylene gas from a large tank in the garden. The pipe still leads into the house but we do not get rid of it as it makes a useful rack for hanging up the shovel and dustpan. The ornamental gas brackets lingered on, although there is only one left now. There again, it had a use, as a towel hook in the bathroom. Apparently the acetylene used to run out at awkward moments and plunge the sorting office into total darkness just when the mail was being sorted. The arrival of electricity in the village was greeted as a great boon - though the cost was a continual annoyance to William and Ada. The difficulty has always been that the size of the house makes it very expensive to run. The main rooms are quite large and the shop and sorting office were also built to generous proportions. Consequently lighting and heating have always been rather a headache. I think that, having always lived in small dark cottages, William longed for more space to live and breathe, and larger windows to welcome the sun and air into the house. Having built the house facing the brisk northerly breezes from the Bristol Channel, not only did they discover the practical problems of maintaining the large spaces they had created, but I think they felt rather lost in them. They always lived in the smallest, sunniest room, and tended to fill the rest of the house up with very large, heavy furniture. As the windows were large, Ada was convinced that everyone passing the windows would see in and that she would lose what little privacy she had, so consequently all the casements were heavily draped with rather dark curtains which were never fully drawn back. This used to annoy William who constantly complained that he had built the house with large windows in order to get plenty of light!

Bearing all this in mind no one would be surprised to learn that I was glad to abandon the rather gloomy house for a space and return to normality. It was now four months since we had inherited the property and it was becoming obvious that we must face up to the problem of what we were going to do with it all. One thing was certain, it would be quite impossible to continue much longer running two homes on a schoolmaster's salary. The income from the shop might develop in time, but up to the present we had spent far more than we had received despite valiant do-it-yourself efforts. I was already beginning to think that the charm of do-it-yourself was limited. It was all very well up to a point, but rather beyond a joke when one was perpetually so rushed and exhausted that there was no longer time to enjoy an excursion to the hills or take the children to the beach. We did not even have time for a holiday apart from a few snatched days and were beginning to feel the strain.

To cut a long story short, a suitable teaching post in the area eventually materialised and after a year of confusion we were finally able to move ourselves, our children and all our possessions into the house. This was by no means the end of our problems but it did mean that we were now totally committed to Washford, its pleasures and its pains, its treasures and its trials. For a long time the house and I did not get on very well together - I was after all the intruder who wanted to change everything and the house disliked change. Even the garden seemed to resent my sudden appearance on the scene. After seven years however we have reached an understanding and now view each other with mutual respect.

18 Problems

Clare Court

At this point it seems to be the moment to give a brief account for the sake of anyone who might be interested, of what it is like actually running a shop. There must be many other people without previous trading experience who have taken over village Post Offices and stores, though perhaps not built over the ashes of their ancestors. They no doubt would be able to add much to what I am about to disclose - not that there is anything particularly sensational to reveal, merely a sizeable collection of small things, some pleasant and some less so. It will probably seem laughable to many readers but at the beginning of our new venture we actually bought a "Teach Yourself" book of shopkeeping - it probably contained good advice but all the conclusions I have since formed have been based on practical and not academic knowledge. Most of the information of which I am about to disburden myself was gleaned between 1968 and 1971. At the time it seemed much longer than three years.

There is no denying that one of the most satisfying and important aspects of shopkeeping is the feeling that all the hard work and effort one puts into it is for oneself and one's own family, rather than for an employer or an impersonal organisation. It is this independence which sustains many small shopkeepers who exist on tiny profits in the face of rising overheads and cut-throat competition. Another advantage which is not to be despised is the convenience of being able to buy goods at cost price. The profit on footwear is reckoned to be thirty per cent out of which taxes and overheads, such as postage, have to be paid. When we first began trading, thirty per cent seemed to us to be a very good profit but it was not long before we discovered the snags - the many pairs of shoes for example which never find a buyer and are left on the shelves; coloured slippers which quickly lose their newness and fade when displayed in the window; the occasional faulty pair of shoes which has to be returned to the wholesaler by post usually unless one is lucky enough to catch the traveller and obtain credit. We very soon came to learn that the nominal thirty per cent in reality represents a very much smaller profit than it would seem at first sight; quite apart from the wear and tear on one's own constitution. We never claimed anything out of the business as payment for the many hours of work that we put in to it, and after enduring a year or two of back breaking labour for very small financial returns, we began to feel increasingly reluctant to continue such a thankless task.

One must not forget, though, the satisfaction of completing the task of rearrangement, of making a pleasing display of all the brightly coloured slippers, toys and fancy goods in the window. Even in a small village like ours it was surprising how much interest was shown in our activity every time it became apparent that we were taking all the goods out of the window and altering the arrangement, it was impossible to work late at night without the whole of Lower Washford knowing about it as the light from the large window shone forth like a beacon, and we could be sure that at least one customer next day would make a special little journey up the road by Walnut Tree to see what we had been doing.

I have mentioned how we enjoyed visiting wholesalers and trade fairs, but this of course was a modern innovation made possible by the motor car and unknown to parents or grandparents. Trade had always been conducted in a very leisurely and courteous fashion with travellers, whose visits came around about three or four times a year. In theory at least if not in practice one is expecting the traveller when he calls, for he usually announces his intended visit by post card a few days before his appearance and there is an unwritten rule that he will collect any outstanding payments with his fresh order. Over the years of trading many travellers had become like old friends to William and Ada and Aunt Selina, and their visits were welcome until the last few difficult years, when both parties knew that to make an old lady add more stock to what was already mouldering away in corners of the shop was about the last thing any sympathetic person would wish to do. Some of the travellers of course were more likeable than others, and we were suitably grateful for the one or two who really tried hard to help us find the right stock for our particular shop and did not exploit our innocence.

Journeying from shop to shop in isolated rural areas must be quite a difficult way of making a living as often our modest stationery order would not come to more than five or six pounds gross, and even this would have taken perhaps over an hour of the traveller's time. Yes - although I frequently groaned inwardly at the arrival of the traveller, who through no fault of his own tended to drop in at the wrong moment, now that they no longer call, I miss them!

I have already spoken of the close personal relationship which had always existed between shopkeeper and customer. Postmistresses of course are notorious for knowing everyone's business but it must be said for Ada that she very rarely discussed the private business of her customers with us. A very different relationship existed between ourselves and the later generation of villagers. I was not local which put me at a disadvantage straight away and the twin barriers of education and a twenty year absence from the village were well-nigh impossible to bridge. We struggled manfully, but both sides knew that we did not speak the same language. Not only did we not know the villagers names, who had married whom and how many children they had, but we found it difficult to summon up much interest in such matters.

One of the disadvantages of shopkeeping too, which we had hopelessly underestimated, was the amount of effort which is required to keep the shop itself clean and reasonably tidy. The glass counter had to be polished, the window had to be turned out from time to time and rearranged, and shoes which had been tried on had to be put back in their correct boxes and replaced on the shelves. All this takes time and energy, but it was completely uneconomic to employ anyone to perform these simple tasks for me. So on many and many a weary evening we laboured away, making price tickets, propping up toys or gifts which wanted to fall down, and wrestling with tiresome little peg board fittings.

Cleaning the window of the shop was an operation which was fraught with not inconsiderable hazard, the first of which was its size and height, and second, its close proximity to the road. It had been purpose built in order that William should be able to hang up the bicycles he had for sale for generous display space would not have disgraced a town store. There was a stone ledge running around the outside near the base of the window and by dint of clinging on to the supporting struts it was just possible (for I am fairly tall) to reach the top of the window and clean it. After a while I became fairly adept at jumping up and down off the ledge though I never looked forward to doing so as the villagers used to pass facetious remarks when they saw me working. As cleaning the window was rather a dirty job I did not wear my best clothes for it, and usually protected my hair with a cotton sunhat. Imagine my annoyance one day when just jumping down from my perch, girded with my armoury of dusters and brushes, not forgetting the hat, my eyes met those of a senior school colleague just driving past in his car! I had always kept my two lives completely separate, but truth will out sonner or later, and it took a long time for my wounded pride to recover.

And dusting, too, endlessly dusting. Whose idea was it, I used to ask myself, to buy all those Chinese fans and cute little rabbits? How do you get dead flies out of the front of the window, a spot they seem to particularly favour, without knocking over all the jigsaw puzzles, babies shoes and West Country guides that are so carefully arranged between you and them?

Greetings cards are a very steady seller, but why do short sighted senior citizens come in to buy one without their glasses, so that you have to drop everything to read out the verses to them - and then after lengthy consideration, the verses fail to appeal and you do not succeed in selling it. A laborious way indeed of not earning the penny profit. Greetings cards are a real eye-opener where character study is concerned. By the type of card chosen one could (someone probably has) write a small paper on that person's background, education, tastes and social class. Flowers, particularly pink or red roses, are easy winners where cards are concerned. Closely following them in descending order are pictures of puppies, kittens, children, bluebell woods and horses. Humorous cards do not go down well in villages, neither do cards in what we have come to label "good taste", plain colours and lacking an invocation to Grandmother, Granny, Grandma, Gran, Nanny or Nan. Yes, believe it or not, all six appellations are catered for and a card which is not labelled with the relationship of the loved one has little hope of selling. Another pitfall with greetings cards is the rate at which they become soiled and unsaleable, or lose their envelopes, which is one of the reasons for the high price the customers are so ready to complain about.

After we had been keeping the shop for a while, some of the customers started to ask for gardening items such as potting compost and slug pellets. William had always held the agency for Webbs seeds, a very respectable steady seller, though not very profitable in a small business such as ours. One season, out of interest, we worked out our profit on the sale of seeds and after deducting postage for returning the end of season surplus, the sum came to the grand total of 6s. 5d! Gardening is a very popular pastime in villages and there is constant demand for fertiliser, weedkiller and so forth. We found a very good wholesaler in Taunton and were able to get excellent quality goods delivered regularly to order, which was one advantage of living on the main road. This is a part of the business which we thoroughly enjoyed and had we continued trading for a longer period, would probably have worked up quite a good turnover. We kept a few tools as well as flower bulbs and potted begonias and hyacinths at Christmas time. They helped to give the shop a pleasant atmosphere and introduced a new and distinctive earthy aroma, which blended with the old-fashioned homely smell of leather and post office ink.

All the time that this was going on we were endeavouring with partial success to continue our normal lives, I at my teaching post and Glyn at his very demanding job, which entailed working on Saturday mornings. The Saturday business was a very sore point as it was the one day of the week when a few customers used to come in, and this meant that I was completely tied to the shop. Glyn would return home in time for a late lunch at nearly two o-clock and I (by then thoroughly out of humour after a boring morning indoors) used to leave him in charge and go to do my shopping. In reality I was prompted by a desire to get away from everything connected with the shop. Saturday had always been a happy family day on which we would go to town, have a little outing or do our gardening and I do not think I ever forgave the shop for ruining our weekend.

Perhaps it is just as well that life is a mixed affair and even when things were not going well there could be an occasional pleasant and enjoyable day. Take an example, one might start the morning by selling a pair of shoes, then perhaps a workman would come in for a pair of boots and by a happy chance the size and sort that he wanted was reposing on our shelves. Five pounds in the till - a small miracle! Then perhaps a customer would come in who remembered Glyn as a small boy and there could be much pleasant swapping of reminiscences. The summer season was particularly enjoyable in this way, as long lost friends would occasionally appear with their children, who would obligingly spend all their pocket money with us. Often, visitors from large towns would be amazed at the low prices of the goods in our shop which cheered us up no end, as the impression given by some of the local customers was that we were fleecing the coats from off their backs and living in luxury on the proceeds.

Every now and again though we would go through a period of hopeless disillusionment over the whole project, and at these times the very sight of the shop would induce a feeling of revulsion. All we wanted to do was to get as far away from it as possible, live a normal life again and have a much needed holiday. After two years, we gave up the Post Office so that we could at least close the shop if we wanted to. Trade dropped off so we took to being closed most of the day and opening at tea-time when the men were on their way home from work. We obviously lost some trade, but quite often, after getting rid of the Post Office, I would stay in the whole morning and not one single customer would appear. There was a bell on the door, but we often did not hear it, as the house is large and the walls are thick. However, most people knew if we were in, and would come to the back door if they wanted something. This dragged on for a while with an occasional burst of success, but after a year or so it became obvious that we would never get rid of all the shoes that we had bought. However, patience is a great virtue where retail trade is concerned. A very good example of this axiom is the story of the cheap ladies calf length boots which Glyn brought back from Bristol one day, early in our ownership before the novelty of trading had worn off. He bought three pairs of those boots and as they were only priced at 39/11 we succeeded in selling two of them

CHAPTER 18. PROBLEMS

fairly easily. The third pair, however, obstinately would not sell which was hardly surprising as they were of a vivid shade of magenta, and had such narrow cut legs, that even would-be purchasers found it quite impossible to get them on. After standing around for a year, these boots became a sort of evil genius, leering at us reproachfully every time we went into the shop. They fell over several times, and on more than one occasion were liberally splashed with floor-washing water. Refusing to stand up on their own they had to be continually propped with rolled newspapers. We tried them by the door, we tried them in the window, we tried them on the counter - nothing worked.

After three years, the village was as bored with them as we were. Eventually, when we were on the last lap of our discount sales and, resigned to living with the boots for ever, I wiped them yet again with a damp cloth, knocked out the dead spiders and remnants of cigarette ash which had found their way inside, and out them in the window with a card declaring that for £1 they were a bargain and - cri de coeur in hope of salvation - suggesting that they should be dyed black. The rest is easy to guess. I was in the garden one Saturday when one of the girls rushed out to me, breathless with excitement, "Mummy, there's a girl in the shop and she's TRYING ON THE PURPLE BOOTS". The atmosphere was heavy with expectation as I rushed back to the scene of action in my gardening clothes. My eyes were drawn, nay riveted, to the important area in the field of action - the girl's legs. Instantly I knew - here at last was the girl I had been waiting for. Thin as a lath, with legs like sticks, she was on her way to the chilly, rainswept seaside, intending to paddle but had forgotten her wellies. Not only were the boots what she needed - she had. obviously fallen in love with them, whereupon Mum obligingly produced the £1, to the satisfaction of all concerned.

For an hour or two after this the house echoed with the refrain, "We've sold the purple boots"!

Several little morals could be drawn from this story, one of which is that if you wait long enough and patiently enough, eventually you will find a customer for the most unlikely goods. I could tell similar tales of other goods which seemed impossible to sell - round toed men's shoes size 5 1/2 spring to mind, or old fashioned ladies shoes size 2. On a day when your mind is miles away a little old lady or gentleman will come in and be delighted to find the tiny size they require. Perhaps I romanticise but it is almost as if the goods had been waiting patiently all those years to be claimed by their rightful owner, so happy is the moment of discovery when it eventually comes.

At sale time we had continual struggles with our conscience when it came to trying to price the stock. Often when we took some of the leather boots and shoes from their boxes, not only were they in perfect condition, but prices marked on them seemed so ridiculously low that we felt tempted to alter them just a little. I particularly recall one pair of John White's gentleman's light leather boots in a box marked 49/11. They had been on the shelves a few years but as they were perfect we felt that they were worth several pounds in modern money. So just on this pair I (rather naughtily) fixed a label - 69/11 49/11. Not really dishonest, just encouraging the customers a little! All the other shoes I marked at the correct prices. A day or two later, the shop door opened and in came a pleasant, politely spoken man,

> **P.P.S.M.:** *Good morning, Madam. Are you the owner of the shop?*
> **Me** (not sure whether greater prudence lay in agreeing or disagreeing): *Well, my husband is, really.*
> **P.P.S.M.:** *Oh well, you'll do.* (No escape!) *I just happened to be passing and noticed you had your "Sale" Notices up.*
> **Me** (in true peasant fashion, not eager to commit myself): *Oh - yes.*
> **P.P.S.M.:** *I'm the Weights and Measures Officer so it seemed a good moment to just stop and have a little chat about the regulations governing reductions and so forth. I find owners of small businesses often don't realise that they can be breaking the law.*

CHAPTER 18. PROBLEMS

He proceeded to explain that it was not permitted to claim genuine reductions on goods unless they had been marked at the higher price for (I think) three months and looking around the shop for an example, in order to show me in the nicest possible way, the pitfalls that await a decent honest trader like myself.

> **P.P.S.M.**: *You see, Madam, say you had altered the price on a pair of shoes say from £3 to £4 and then crossed it out, that would be against the law.*
> **Me** (feeling rather uncomfortable): *Yes, I see your point - but what about the rise in the cost of everything? Some of these boots and shoes are worth a lot more than they're marked and we have to pay rates etc. Aren't we allowed to put the price up at all?*
> **P.P.S.M.**: *Oh yes, indeed, but you must prove that they had been marked up a month before you held your sale.* (Looking round once more for an example) *Now, take that pair of boots* (upon which he fastened on the very pair I have mentioned, the one guilty felon in all that innocent looking row). *Say you had just marked that up and then crossed out the price - that would be illegal.*

How I did not blush I shall never know, I was quite expecting him to demand to see the empty box the boots had occupied on which was plainly marked the cipher 49/11, but after continuing to tighten the screws a few seconds longer, he let me off the rack and proceeded to other matters.

For weeks afterwards I awaited his reappearance with bated breath but he never came back. I think he was genuinely unaware of my discomfiture but I never quite made out how he came to pick on that one pair of rather old-fashioned but worthy boots of all the dozens of pairs on display. I think my mind must have been concentrating on them to such an extent that his hand was guided in their direction. A narrow escape indeed - but it had the effect of making us much more careful afterwards.

Figure 18.1: The house, shortly after restoration from the fire and conversion of the shop

This dragged on for a while and then at this point fate stepped in and on the 9th May 1971 the unbelievable happened. On one of the ill-starred Saturdays, fire broke out in the back room of the shop. While the children and I were shopping in Minehead, we learnt of the fire from neighbours. Rushing home we found that the blaze was already extinguished. In the midst of the charred and evil-smelling mess our feelings were unanimous - shock, horror and incredulity, but more than anything, an overpowering sense of relief. We had tried hard but this was the unforeseen end of a long and painful chapter.

19 Making the Museum

Clare Court

When one looks back over the past eight years, or indeed over one's life as a whole, it is difficult to remember the exact moment at which certain events took place, and neither of us is quite sure of the exact time at which the idea of the museum first came to us. The germs of the idea must have been born in the first summer at Washford. We had been moving out, as I have already described, many items of furniture from the house - sideboards, cupboards, tables, chests of drawers - all these and many more, not forgetting of course the famous beds of solid oak. Whatever could be done with such an abundance and superfluity of furniture? A large load went to the saleroom, undistinguished items of no particular value for the most part, but many articles remained which could not be so summarily disposed of. For example there was the oak sideboard complete with "top", which had been made and carved by Uncle Lewis and elaborately decorated with a veritable cornucopia of wooden fruit surmounted by his own initials L.H.C. skilfully intertwined. What was to be done with it?

Uncle Lewis had died childless so there were no direct heirs to take an interest in something so intensely familial. The base part was functional, and could conceivably be used as a sideboard, but the whole design of the piece was indelibly stamped with the style of the 1920s period. Besides we already had a modern beech sideboard and I had no intention of replacing that with a dark oak model, however lovingly carved and however splendid an example of Uncle's art it might be. It was already a full time occupation dealing with the many articles which had been made (or more often begun and never completed) by Glyn's Father without including the handiwork of Uncle as well. If we continued at this rate we might as well throw the field open to the whole of the rest of the family including their relations - or so I argued!

"And how about Grandfather's table?"
"Which table do I mean, you say? Or which Grandfather?"
"Well, one of the Grandfathers. Does it matter much anyway?"
"Well you know the table I mean. It's been out in the shed for years."
"Oh yes. I remember. Kathie gave it to us, but we aren't to get rid of it - she wants to know where it is."
"Use it? No, of course, she never used it. She had lots of tables."
"What did she keep it for then?"
"Because it was Grandfather's, of course!"

In the face of such crushing arguments what could one do?

So we put these sideboards and tables out in the building which we call the Toc H. Most of the old shoes had been cleared away by this time, and the downstairs room with the cobbled floor received two heavy oak cupboards and Jim Slade's sofa. This particular item had always irritated me beyond measure, I grew up in a period when Victorian furniture had gone completely out of fashion and I could not for the life of me think why my parents-in-law kept this ugly horsehair couch in their house. The room in which it was stored (though "stored" is perhaps too grand a word, they had more likely just put it there one day, and left it) was the "middle" room of which I have already spoken. This was one of the rooms which had been allowed to get into a very poor state of repair, and indeed it had presented a sorry spectacle for many a long year. It had been painted once when the house was built, with greenish blue distemper, but so long ago that there were patches of discolouration all over the walls, and as if this were not enough the ceiling was badly cracked and more grey than white. Over the fireplace the rain had been leaking in for a decade or two and the plaster was flaking off. The sofa stood forlornly along one partition. Not only was tile horsehair upholstery sadly dilapidated, and one leg broken, but to complete the sorry sight, the cushions had been encased in an old mail bag to prevent the stuffing from falling out. As the sofa was never used for sedentary purposes, over the years Ada had gradually filled up the space on the seat with cardboard boxes containing odds and ends of various sorts.

CHAPTER 19. MAKING THE MUSEUM

I had often said that if the day came when we ever inherited the house, the first thing that I would do would be to get rid of the sofa! However, when the time did come one's feelings were very different from what one had imagined they might be, and somehow it no longer seemed quite so clever or satisfying merely to throw away a piece of broken old furniture. Besides, Glyn knew a little more about its owner than I did and did not like to see it consigned to the rubbish heap. So the sofa joined the sideboard, and a heavy oak Elizabethan style cupboard in the Toc H.

When the time came for us to be moving all of our own furniture into the house the problem of space was becoming more and more pressing - until suddenly one day I had an idea. Instead of just keeping so many articles which for various reasons, mainly sentimental, could not be got rid of, why not concentrate them all in one building, using the spare furniture to display the items? There was plenty of wall space to hang pictures, spare tables on which to arrange exhibits and glass fronted cupboards in which to put more valuable or fragile articles. The unwanted sideboards and chests also had drawers in which to stow things which would not be exhibited but which have a certain interest. Once the idea had been born, we both embraced it with enthusiasm. I must admit that one of the principal motives which activated me at the beginning was the desire to set aside one definite place in which to store all the old things. I am naturally a fairly tidy person - not fanatically tidy, but I do like having things in order. From the very moment that we definitely started working with a museum in mind, everything started to fall into place. Of course a prodigous amount of energy had to be expended on the physical removal of the articles and assembling them all in the two rooms. For example, Grandfather's sewing machine had been standing for years in the wash-house at the rear of the premises. It is extremely heavy, the base being made of cast iron and the work table of some heavy hardwood. I found an old tin of bicycle enamel and smartened up the iron work a little, splashing some varnish on to the wood. We managed to manipulate the machine on to an old pushchair belonging to one of our children, and with a great deal of pushing and shoving succeeded in getting it around to the Toc H and up the not inconsiderable step. Occasionally we are asked if we would be willing to lend it for exhibition - unfortunately the answer is "No!"

- we are very sorry, but prospective viewers must come to the machine and not vice versa!

Having got some furniture into the rooms, we felt we had at least got a rough foundation on which to build. Upstairs was more of a problem, as the room is quite large but we did not feel equal to the task of heaving solid oak sideboards and the like up the stairs. To begin with we spread an old carpet and then arranged a few of our spare tables (about four altogether, not counting several that had been sent to the sale room!) This started to look promising, and Glyn then had the idea of using the old mahogany counter from the shop. Glyn's father had always prized this wood very much, as he had purchased it at Watchet harbour when a ship called the "Fox" was being broken up, I always imagine it as having formed a table or work top for a steward or in the officers' mess, and it certainly used to look very nice in the shop when well polished. This turned out to be quite a successful idea as the counter top, being in two pieces, stretched around two sides of the room. Admittedly the legs were not quite on a par aesthetically with the top, consisting as they did of old washstand bases and similar humble supports. Once this was up, we were able to put the glass fronted cupboards and bookcases on the top - these were reserved for more precious and fragile exhibits. In odd corners, we placed various odd chairs to fill up the spaces.

We were painfully aware while doing this that the room badly needed decorating, and we somehow found the energy to splash some emulsion paint on the worst parts of the walls. The windows were in a bad way and it did not exactly help matters when, in an enthusiastic access of cleaning feruour, I cast one open and the whole frame fell out completely, smashing to pieces on the ground. This was a minor disaster but Glyn somehow managed to screw the pieces together rather amateurishly and more or less nailed the window back into place.

Once the donkey work was over we were able to start actually bringing things in and arranging them. This was far and away the most enjoyable part, though even this involves a great deal of walking about. It is surprising how many miles one covers simply going back and forth into the house to

CHAPTER 19. MAKING THE MUSEUM

fetch scissors, drawing pins, cards, felt tip pens, hammers, dusters, polish, window cleaner, Brasso and all the dozens of accessories necessary to make the exhibits look fairly presentable.

All this would be very well on its own, but we were encumbered with the shop and quite often had to run down to it to see to a customer, quite apart from keeping the home running smoothly and children fed and reasonably clean. We knew that unless we had a deadline to work to, we would never be ready in time so we fixed an opening date and the last two days were really hectic. When reading the Duke of Bedford's book "A Silver Spoon" I could not help smiling at the similarity of our experience with his! He describes how he and his family worked themselves into the ground preparing for their first opening, even washing and cleaning priceless tea sets and solid gold dinner services by hand. When the visitors came and were asked what they had liked best, one said "That lovely set of brass"!

Glyn took on the job of arranging all the photographs, an extremely difficult task as there were so many of them. They had mostly been collected by Uncle Lewis, and he had usually written on the back of them who, what or where, which proved very helpful. It is of course quite impossible to display them all, but is a never-ending source of interest to visitors, especially those who remember the valley as it was years ago. Sometimes we are visited by people whose parents or grandparents were born in the district, and occasionally we have been able to show them a photograph of one of their relations, or the cottage in which they lived. (The main problem with displaying photographs, apart from their tending curl up and pop out of the mounts, is the effect of daylight on them. Unfortunately we were too busy to think about such things when we first arranged our museum and sunlight did cause some of them to fade. So we fixed up old curtains and try to keep out the daylight when the museum is closed, and this has worked very well on the whole.)

The girls and I tackled the task of arranging the Edwardian dolls. For years they had been lying under Ada's bed in an old suitcase, and she had occasionally shown them to the children. They have rather a pleasing family connection as the two best ones belonged to a cousin who still lives in the village, and they were dressed for her as a little girl by Ada when she was a young woman, Ada always used to say that she could happily spend all her spare time making dolls clothes as she loved doing it so much. As a young woman she delighted in any work that required very small stitches, tiny buttons and minute tucks. This was a legacy her last year at school when hours spent sewing was considered a suitable occupation for a working class girl. Unfortunately Ada did not quite fall in with the pattern that was probably expected of her - plain sewing did not appeal to her at all and as far as I can remember she never made any garments at all for herself. But the dolls were very well equipped and the hats she had plaited out of raffia. Not only did we have their spare underclothes, but a whole box full of little petticoats, chemises, spencers, and the like which must have belonged to her departed sisters and relations. Most of these clothes were very soiled, and as they appeared to be made of strong cotton I tentatively soaked and boiled them in a well-known brand of detergent. After this operation they shone forth in pristine whiteness. The more delicate articles I washed carefully in soap flakes and these too responded very well. After this little venture I wrote to the manufacturers of the detergent informing them of the results of my tests but they were not impressed and I did not even receive a free packet of soap powder for my pains. So much for big business!

One of the dolls had a broken leg, china of course - but this was easily repaired. Rather touchingly, although she must have been broken for at least fifty years, the owner having long since grown up, the pieces had been carefully preserved in an old shoe box and fitted together perfectly. We had never done anything like this before but the results seemed fairly satisfactory. We finally arranged them in an old glass cupboard, sitting down on velvet couches, (in reality my children's building bricks covered with a piece of old velvet curtain) and they appear to be having a little tea party with a doll's tea set. The finishing touch was given when our cousin came in and saw them, for she was able to tell us their names, Lily and Dorothy.

The boots and shoes presented quite a problem. We felt they would be interesting and they also came in useful for filling up odd spaces. However, they had been lying around for so many years that they needed sorting out and cleaning, and this alone was a major task. Displaying them too had its problems - boots and shoes stand up quite well, but taller models have to be padded with paper to make them stand up. I labelled them hopefully with approximate dates which are very inaccurate - it seems difficult to place some of them to within a year or two as most books on the subject only go up to the beginning of the twentieth century, which is when most of ours begin. Occasionally an old lady or gentleman will come in and recognise a style that they themselves wore when younger and this is very helpful in trying to fix an approximate date. Gradually no doubt we shall succeed in filling in the missing background information to some of our exhibits, but as we do not set out to give an accurate historical catalogue but rather to set the atmosphere of a period, we do not think it is a life and death matter to have a few inaccuracies in our assessment of dates and so forth. Apart from anything else, it gives visitors great pleasure to be able to give us information, and this surely should he one of the functions of a museum - to stimulate discussion and communication. We have often noticed that if there is one thing that many people enjoy doing, it is correcting you if you are wrong.

As the time grew shorter towards the advertised opening of the museum the pace quickened to a frantic gallop. Many local people were now aware of what we were doing, as we had gone to the expense of having bills printed. (These cost five pounds - we did not repeat this rather extravagant gesture.) Then the local press sent along a reporter and we suddenly felt the excitement mounting, and an earnest determination to achieve the best possible result with the limited means at our disposal. When the reporter came to see us we were still hopelessly unprepared - everything was lying around in confusion and any resemblance to a museum (or "exhibition" as we were calling it) was purely nominal. Nevertheless he was impressed and wrote a very helpful and appreciative article in our local journal.

On the last evening we stayed up most of the night getting things arranged and making tickets. It is unbelievable how long it takes to write out all the labels - but it is an essential part of the work. In my haste I dropped a shoe box full of Edwardian dolls and broke one of the heads. Shame on me! However, I think this was the only casualty.

Figure 19.1: A view of the Museum collections. A collection of artwork, shoes and machinery can be seen.

CHAPTER 19. MAKING THE MUSEUM

Figure 19.2: Newspaper coverage of the opening of the museum

The first day started very well - people came in rather hesitantly at first, but by the end of the week we had shown about a hundred people around. Some of the visitors had read about our venture in the local newspaper, or seen the home made notices which we had fixed up. Others had known the family for years and came out of a mixture of sentiment and curiosity. About half way through the week, we were visited by Independent Television and had the thrill of seeing ourselves turning the handle of the sewing machine and displaying the dolls.

One of the snags about our little collection (really "museum" is such a grand word, but somehow we have got into the habit of this designating it) is that, owing to the very strong family ties and connections of most of the exhibits we feel rather hesitant about asking for help from volunteers. The museum is unique in that all, or nearly all, the exhibits were collected by one family - not wealthy landowners, commissioning works of art to beautify their houses, but ordinary working folk. Often, the reasons for keeping the articles were sentimental but many things were saved by Glyn's Father out of a love of the quaint and curious and because he could not bear to see them thrown away. A charcoal smoothing iron falls into this category. We have been given a few articles which were used at various villages in the parish, and could probably acquire a great deal more if we had the time and energy and money to devote to collecting it, but we feel that the museum would not be quite the same. Its unique character and flavour, untidy and dusty though it frequently is, is given by the characters and occupations of the members of the family. Take for example the family business - bootmaking allied to a Post Office. That in itself is an unusual combination, and one which I do not think I have ever seen anywhere else. Methodism, (in the particular brand which moved the spirits of our ancestors, the Bible Christian Connexion), the West Somerset Mineral Railway, the coming of the bicycle and the motor car, all these had their influence and have left their mark on the museum.

For this reason, the very uniqueness, albeit a trifle inbred, of our collection, renders it difficult for us to seek official aid. We love showing people round, but it is very time consuming and so are not able to open the museum very often. So until we can do the job really well, we soldier on alone, keeping

CHAPTER 19. MAKING THE MUSEUM

Figure 19.3: Parts of the museum were occasionally used for external exhibitions. Somerset County Council chairman, Mr. William Knowles, opens "Somerset Life a Century Ago" which was presented to help celebrate Minehead Festival

the daylight and rain out as well as we can, and lighting a paraffin stove in the winter months. The important thing is to preserve it all. Restoration, air conditioning and so forth can come when our fairy godfather visits us some time in the future. Until the happy day when, retired from teaching and politics, we sit at home and wait for people to come and visit us, we try to open the museum for a week during the school summer holidays. It is very hard work, cleaning, tidying and sticking up all the photographs which have fallen off, and a week of this is usually quite enough. In between whiles we are happy to show people around if they give us a little warning. We have been privileged to meet some very delightful folk when throwing our doors open to the public. The very first day of the opening in 1968 a young Canadian couple came in. Their name was Burnett, an old established Washford name, and it was good to feel that our little corner of Somerset had a link with distant North America. We have had visitors from many different countries, and the majority of them have devoured every word of information we have given them. Often, the visitors tell us very interesting facts which increase our own knowledge. One most rewarding factor is the pleasure that it gives people to see again some object which reminds them perhaps of their childhood or their apprenticeship or perhaps the home of their own grandparents. For example, one gentleman came in who had served his apprenticeship as a bootmaker in a factory in Leicester. He immediately spotted the shoe finishing machine - not one of ours, actually, but given to us by an elderly bootmaker in Watchet. Within seconds he had readjusted the bands which drive the various cogs and wheels, and had soon polished all our shoes for us. We all enjoyed this very much. Then there was a young married couple who came in and listened politely and as we thought, coldly, to our little peroration. I thought the wife was bored but it turned out that her hobby was wood carving! We have numerous examples of the woodcarvers art in various stages of completion, and also a set of wood carving tools. These were lying about in a corner, as I had not attached much importance to them since removing them from the old washstand where they had lain for years. To our amazement the young woman in question informed us that the tools were valuable - upon which we promoted them to a glass cupboard! A couple of years later I was showing a middle-aged man round who turned out to be an expert on old tools.

Within seconds he had whipped out his pocket magnifier and was examining the marks on the handles of the implements. They showed crossed rifles, the old sign of the War Office, discontinued in the 1890s. He suggested that Glyn's Father had probably bought the tools second hand, as they would have been surplus to Army requirements when wooden gun carriages gradually became obsolete. We remembered then that Ada had often told us how William had saved up his money in order to buy each tool, with the same dedication as a golfer collecting a set of clubs. Wages were low in the 1890s and possessions treasured, and this explained why Ada had always kept those hard earned tools so carefully after William's death.

Occasionally we get visitors who also keep a shop, or are boot repairers, and they too recognise the fittings and appurtenances of the bootmaker's trade. The old shoes are always popular. Gentlemen love to reminisce over the dancing pumps and recall how they used to take them to dances in a brown paper bag in their pockets. As a footnote to this item it is interesting to note that the Village Hall at Roadwater still sports a much-treasured notice "Dancers are requested to remove their Boots".

The crystal set is not particularly old - it is one that Glyn had when he was a lad, but it also evokes many memories among the old and not-so-old. We have repeatedly found that the things which people most enjoy looking at are articles which have passed out of use in their own lifetime - often very simple items. Take, for example, those round leather studs which used to be nailed to the soles of football boots. And the wartime collection, though small - a chance assembly of ration books, coupons, with a gas mask or two, is always tremendously popular. (The gas masks were out in the washhouse, still in their original boxes. Children love them!)

One of the cupboards is filled with all the small pieces of bric a brac, many of which are of no particular value, but interesting. For example, there is a piece of broken tile from Cleeve Abbey. My children found it in the stream when paddling around a year or two ago - the Water Board had just been engaged in flood prevention work, and no doubt the piece of tile had been washed out of the newly excavated river bank. Lying about the garden, as I have mentioned elsewhere, are numerous carved and dressed stones which obviously must have been pillaged from the Abbey many years ago. Apart from these chance remains we make no attempt to vie with the Ministry of Works in their presentation of the Abbey's history, after all, they are the professionals and have far greater resources at their disposal than we have. Our two worlds are very different and we have not many points of contact, but perhaps when the happy day arrives when the main road is removed from our midst, there will arrive a new era in which people on holiday can stroll pleasantly from one museum to the other. We do, after all, within the space of a few hundred yards, present two totally different aspects of life as it has been known in our valley. Perhaps there was even a member of our family in those distant days who visited the Abbey to repair the Monks' footwear, or carve pews for the church. Who knows? Although at the time of writing there is no record in Parish registers of a Court earlier than 1750, it is as likely as not that the family was already established in the area. Country folk, after all, did not move around very much, and even in these days, as a casual glance at the telephone directory will tell, just how localised some family names are.

20   Treasure Trove

Glyn Court

My wife has written of our putting together the "museum" and recounted the associations of some of the articles it contains, and I should like to continue the story, for scarcely a single exhibit is without a history to bring before the mind the characters who flourished and the social life that prevailed in this valley a century ago. Musing upon the lives of those men and women and the privations they endured, and the harvest that has come to their sometimes uncaring descendants, I am constrained to use of them words used nearly two thousand years ago: "As poor, yet making many rich".

But now to the homely treasures.

20.1   The Chest

The chest had, from the look of it, been through storm and flood; its metal clasps rusted here and there, its leather cover frayed; but still stout and sturdy, a Long John Silver of a sea-chest. A pattern of brass studs stood proud of the lid in the monogram of its original owner, H. C., Henry Court, my great grandfather.

Great-grandfather Henry, however, was not the old sea-dog some might like to claim for an ancestor. For a man born almost within sight and sound of the sea he had remarkably little salt spray in his veins, and that little, in his descendants, has been diluted almost to vanishing point. Still, he had spirit and even in his youth he showed determination not to be cribbed within the confines of a rural round and appressive poverty. He was born in 1802 and in the hard years after Waterloo, probably in his late teens, he set out for London to seek his fortune. He failed to find it, and this set the pattern for his descendants, but he did - which was more important to him - learn the trade of a cordwainer. After ten years away he came home with his travelling trunk, married and set up in business in the little village of Roadwater. But while in London he had also been in service in a gentleman's house (of the Trevelyan Family) and had there evinced an unusual love of study and reading. His employer made him a parting gift of several volumes of translations of Virgil and Homer, which I still have.

He witnessed the opening of London Bridge, but so long had he been away from home that on his return his mother did not at first recognise him.

His business throve as well as the hard times allowed and he employed several men. His was the only house in the village which received a weekly newspaper and the shoemaker's shop became, in true tradition, the village centre for social life and national intelligence. But additional income, when it offered, could not be refused, and when, in the early 1850s, the West Somerset Mineral Railway came to Roadwater, Henry was appointed their agent and the Company built him a house. He had a dog cart - literally - and the dog would take it down to ungerford to bring back the daily or weekly newspaper. Here he lived with his growing family for seven or eight years until his death at the age of fifty-nine.

20.2 The Sewing Machine

Our sewing machine, discovered in a corner of the washhouse, was also unique not only in its massiveness, but also by its origin, for it genuinely was home-made, and the work of a very remarkable man.

George Grinslade - known to his descendants as "Granfer George" - was born in Watchet a few months after Waterloo, the son of a sea-captain, and his childhood was passed in the shadow of the poverty of those terrible years. Ill-treatment by a step-mother, he was apprenticed to a shoemaker at the age of seven, and his early sufferings and privations marked him physically for life, though without impairing his spirits. On the contrary, they reinforced his strong will. In his middle twenties he was taken to Taunton hospital with some debilitating illness, discharged as incurable and told he had at most six months to live. George thereupon bought a herbary, gathered simples, brewed potions and lived another seventy years.

Living in an age of discoveries and engineering triumphs, he was interested, so said one of his grandsons, in "anything that had the power of 'go'". In 1851 he visited the Great Exhibition and was enthralled by what he saw; but what took his fancy as of most practical use was an early sewing machine. He thought, "I could just do with one of they for bootmaking", but the price was far beyond his modest purse, so he studied the design of the machine, observed the action, and, over the next eighteen months, with some slight help from the blacksmith over the drive wheel, made a sewing machine of his own. Indeed, he improved the original; the device for raising the foot had been only an india rubber band, but George devised a simple, efficient and easily adjustable lift by means of a cam and eccentric. And having built the machine, he used it in his work for thirty years; and when, after sixty years' inaction, I turned the wheel, a few drops of oil sent the shuttle flying to and fro as merrily as ever.

Mechanical ingenuity was only one facet of Granfer George's character, which was compounded of tenacity, industry and the inexhaustible curiosity of a lively mind. He had moreover an active interest in many movements for social progress and, with a few friends, founded a Friendly Society in Watchet. Quite early he became a Methodist, and had to undergo his share of the persecution which fell to that body in the distant days when it still possessed deeply held and firmly expressed convictions. In the course of the revival of 1859, when scores of people in Watchet were converted and joined the church, a messenger burst into prayer meeting to tell George that some of the roughs had set his corn rick on fire. "Leave 'em be, lad", said George, in effect, "I'm busy wi' bigger things than corn ricks, now".

Not that his convictions hampered his sense of fun, and Granfer George, in his time, together with many another young blade, had heard the chimes at midnight. His workshop adjoined the Star Inn, and for a time, being a sociable lad, with ready wit, he led the conviviality next door, until the brighter star set him on a new course. George and his friends made their own entertainment in robust old-time style.

The wedding feast, for instance. It was only a thatched cottage, but there was good cheer, and the family and friends of the bride and groom had crowded in, trenchermen were trenching, if that is what they do, with gusto, and a Niagara of ale and cider was cascading down brawny Somerset throats. No one had eyes for the workaday world outside the cottage, nor for the grinning lad who cautiously drew the door to and made it fast on the outside. No one noticed the two figures who crept round to the back, where the ground sloped steeply upward so that the cottage eaves came almost down to ground level. No one heard George's laborious climb up over the thatch to the chimney-stack; no one heard the thud of heavy objects thrown up from below. But suddenly in the festivities, clouds of smoke billowed out from the fireplace as George firmly planted his clods of earth on the chimney pot.

The coughing guests ran for the door, found it barred, thrust open the small windows, and choked and gasped for air until a jar of cider "douted" the fire.

Such buffoonery, of course, George outgrew, and his humour grew more kindly and considerate and the photographs taken of him in later life show an expression of cheerful serenity that all his sufferings could never quench. He retired from business in his seventies and went to live with his daughter and son-in-law in Roadwater. There he became a favourite with the village children, not least his great-grandchildren, and made with his own hands the few toys they had, and for years the boys cantered through the streets on a piebald steed with wooden wheels. Alas! Only his carved head now remains.

He loved the company of the very young, and would speak to them of the wonders of the world and, as a treat, display the coloured plates in his "Goldsmith's Animated Nature". Even the young in the animal world drew him, and I must recount a tale which I treasure as a link between two centuries. In 1969 or 1970 we were visited by an old gentleman greatly respected in the district not only for his character, his immaculate appearance and his knowledge of country life but also for his remarkable craftsmanship in wood. Mr Davis of Monksilver was born before 1880, and he told us that in the last year of the nineteenth century, he was quietly thatching a roof on a farm up from Roadwater when he heard a voice. He looked down and saw Mr Grinslade, as he called him, walking-stick in hand, leaning over a five-barred gate and holding converse - I think no other word will do - with a group of heifers in the field; and the audible, human part of the conversation went "Well now, me little dears, an' how old be you? About two, I expect. An' do 'ee know how old I be? I be eighty-five. What do 'ee think o' that, now?"

Of course he had his foibles. His son-in-law welcomed visitors of an evening and Granfer would tolerate them; but when the John How pendulum clock laboriously struck ten, granfer, although stone deaf, would look up from his reading and boldly announce, "Ten o'clock! Time everybody was in their own homes!" or "Mrs Browning, your husband will be wondering where you'm to."

His deafness once caused him some embarrassment. By way of preliminary, however, I must explain that in the 1870s, a certain landed family had entertained the Prince of Wales when he visited Exmoor for the stag hunting. The hospitality was lavish - the Prince would have certainly voiced his extreme displeasure if it had not been - and rumour said that the family had spent £30,000 which they could not afford. Thirty years later the squire was paying a visit to Grandfather William to discuss some matter of common interest, the Liberal Party or the abstinence cause, no doubt, and he was introduced to the old man, who registered no particular emotion. After a while the squire's attention was caught by a painting of his mansion which Grandfather's son Lewis had done when home on holiday, and he was examining it when an aged but vigorous voice interposed from the chimney corner, "That's Crampton Manor, Squire Turrell's place, Sir. They had King Teddy down there when he was Prince of Wales, and the old lady spent thousands and thousands of pounds and ruined 'em". Grandfather's embarrassment was extreme, but the squire saved the situation with a chuckle and presently took his leave. Granfer, when he understood the situation, was contrite: "Why ever didn' 'ee tell me who 'twas you? I woul'n ha' said it for worlds".

20.3 The Lapstone

On a bench in the iron workshop behind our house lay a heavy black stone, some eight or nine inches across and worn smooth by the tides of the Bristol Channel. Its shape was peculiar: an oval face, as smooth as wax except in the centre, where an area the size of a penny piece had been fretted away; and two other faces forming a depressed wedge:

But for its colour it might have been one of the numberless stones forming the walls of our garden, but it had its history, which went back a century or so, to the time of my grandfather, William Court.

William, born on May Day 1847, was the youngest of the eight children, but the second son, of Henry. He was barely twelve when his father died, but he had to shoulder the financial burden of the family, as his elder brother, fourteen years his senior, had run away after a violent quarrel which must be recounted later. William found employment as a fitter with the mining company on Brendon Hill, and soon showed qualities of leadership in the life of the village. He had been converted in a remarkable revival which swept through the district in 1859, and at sixteen he became a local preacher on trial in the Bible Christian Society in Roadwater. A little later, the Company sent him to their works in Ebbw Vale, but Grandmother Court pined for our green hills and wooded valleys, and after eighteen months they came home. William set to work to restore his father's business and buy back the family furniture, and took the lease of a William and Mary dower house, attracted to it by a kitchen spacious enough to accommodate the sixty or seventy members of a village society of which he had become the leader.

The expansion of the iron ore mines on Brendon Hill brought an unwonted prosperity into the neighbourhood, and within four years William's business was firmly enough established for him to marry. His bride, Christian Grinslade, came from the little seaport of Watchet, which Coleridge depicted

CHAPTER 20. TREASURE TROVE

in the "Ancient Mariner", and she was the daughter of a man in the same trade as his son-in-law but of quite remarkable creative talents.

It was on one of his visits to Watchet that William acquired the stone for his work, searching along the rock-strewn sea-shore for two hours until he found one of exactly the shape he wanted. This is how the lapstone was used - and still may be, though I suspect it may now at last be obsolete, though I used it -reluctantly I confess - as a boy in my father's workshop. The cobbler, with a paper pattern, cuts out a new sole from a bend of leather, pares off the instep and steeps the sole in a bucket of water for half an hour. Then he takes the stone, rests it on his lap with the flat surface uppermost, lays the sole on it face down, and hammers it until it has taken on the curve of the old shoe. This lapstone remained in fairly constant use up to the 1950s and acquired a patina compounded of beeswax, shoemaker's dye and, I suspect, linseed oil which gave it the richness of leather itself. It served Grandfather faithfully throughout the few brief years of mining prosperity and the long decades of rural decline; and the business went steadily along, though the depopulation, the drift to the towns and overseas, and the poverty of the farm labourers, prevented any development comparable with the efforts he expended and the hours he worked. By the 1890s the large town manufacturers were producing shoes at prices which the local craftsmen could not possibly compete with, but William turned this to his advantage, bought a cottage and reading room over the way from his home, turned it into a shop, laid in a stock of these ready-made shoes and continued both trades with increased profitability. Even so, profit for a week probably seldom exceeded two or three pounds, but this was sufficient for him to devote the rest of his time to the deep interests of his life.

These interests, I would almost call them passions, were so intertwined and interdependent that I cannot fitly give pride of place to any one, though I am: sure Grandfather would have assigned it to the last I mean to describe. As we discovered the lapstone represented his livelihood, so we found the symbols of the great purposes of his life; the gavel, the portrait and the plan.

The gavel was a simple, unimposing one of rosewood with an ebony handle; you felt that it had figured at meetings for form's sake and that no vigorous use of it had been needed because the tenour of the meetings had more often than not been harmonious. However that may be, finding the gavel brought us to the society which Grandfather had been deeply concerned with.

His childhood, even before the death of his father, had been scarred by tragedy: one sister had died as a child, another had borne an illegitimate child, and his elder brother, in a drunken rage, had struck his father down, left home for South Wales and, like Wordsworth's Luke, in the city given himself to dissolute courses. His brother's treatment of his father profoundly distressed young William; he determined to devote himself to attacking and, so far as he might, eradicating the causes of all such tragedies. Reading of the work of the Good Templars temperance organisation, he established a lodge in the village, and in a very few weeks sixty others had joined, attracted, doubtless, by the cause itself, others by the social life, others, it may be, by the element of ceremony. William, as was natural, earned great unpopularity with a certain element of village society; indeed, he would have considered he had failed if he had not earned unpopularity, for he was out to smite the enemy hip and thigh, giving no quarter and asking none. His own church, though nationally among the pioneers of the movement, was locally opposed to such modernistic notions and William came near to expulsion. However, he won through and in due time his work received a visible reward. As I have mentioned, he had leased a dower-house in the centre of the village because the kitchen was the one room large enough for meetings of the Lodge; but as members increased, they needed an even larger place to meet. He approached the lord of the manor in the adjoining parish of Nettlecombe, Sir Walter Trevelyan, who was an enthusiastic advocate of abstinence from alcohol and a patron and president of the United Kingdom Alliance. Sir Walter listened sympathetically, promised to help, and very soon built a spacious, well-proportioned hall on the edge of his property, within the village, for the use of the Roadwater Good Templars, requiring them only to give hospitality to other good causes when called upon. The Temperance Hall was opened with great excitement on a sunny July day

CHAPTER 20. TREASURE TROVE

in 1877 and William was presented with an illuminated address and an engraved and inlaid writing cabinet in recognition of his services. The hall served well and remained in pretty constant use not only for temperance gatherings but also for rallies, Sunday School anniversaries, Good Friday teas, and village concerts, for seventy years, and, though in sad disrepair, it still stands.

The portrait mentioned earlier was, if not unique, at least a highly unusual Victorian souvenir with a likeness stamped on a wafer-thin tongue of wood. I have no idea how or where it came into his possession but it represented the third cornerstone of his life, for it showed the People's William and bore the inscription "Printed on wood from a tree felled by Mr Gladstone at Hawarden". Grandfather did not, so far as I know, inherit the Liberal faith, but it was the inevitable political expression for a man of his convictions, and I imagine he came to it in the heady days of Mr Gladstone's first administration. Certainly, for the rest of his life, the times of triumph and the more numerous later days of disappointment, he boldly defended the faith, at considerable cost to his livelihood and standing. Political activity in the constituencies was more sporadic than nowadays, but at Parliamentary elections William with his ready speech, clear wit and command of language was the chairman for all Liberal meetings. Moreover, he was an assiduous canvasser, though admittedly he was ploughing stony soil among the predominantly Tory and Anglican farmers, and he often chuckled over a misadventure that befell him in a farmhouse on the hills near Withycombe. He had ridden over on his grey pony to try his eloquence on the farmer, but soon found that he could not budge him an inch. As he was about to leave, the farmer's two sons clattered in, grinning broadly and suddenly guffawing. William forebore to ask them the joke, and when he reached home and lit the stable lantern to rub down the pony the joke became clears the true-blue farmer's sons had anointed the grey pony with a blue-bag from head to foot.

The sign of his fourth cornerstone was a piece of flimsy paper about ten inches square, and ruled in a gridiron pattern, (or rather, some dozens of such papers); for this was the circuit "plan" still found today in every Methodist home and showing, quarter by quarter, the names of the preachers appointed to conduct services in each of sixteen chapels scattered over the Brendon Hills, Watchet, and Luckwell Bridge. For William's Christian faith was the rock on which he built everything else, and Sunday after Sunday and many week nights as well, he would travel on his grey ponies all over this wide circuit, placing his eloquence at the service of his beloved Bible Christian Church, the smallest of the Methodist Connexions and the one in which the sense of family was most strong. William began preaching at the age of sixteen in a cottage in Bilbrook, was adjudged promising, pursued his studies and preached continually for sixty-four years, until very shortly before his death in 1929, travelling more than thirty thousand miles, and representing his circuit for decades in the wider field of the West of England.

His greatest moment came when he was quite a young man. He was appointed to preach in the mining village of Gupworthy, eight miles away, 1,100 feet up, and in exposed country.

In the morning, the rain came teeming down and, knowing that the afternoon congregation would be small, he felt inclined to wait for the weather to clear. But he seemed to hear a voice saying "Go" and he and his father-in-law set off. The congregation was small indeed and the atmosphere cheerless, and he wondered whether he had heard aright. Toward teatime, however, the weather cleared, the sun broke through and a glorious evening began. A crowd of young miners came unexpectedly to the meeting room and as the service progressed William felt himself taken by a power outside himself. He spoke of the need for a man to make a visible decision and twenty-eight young men there and then took him at his word. In a matter of days the membership of this mining church rose from fourteen to forty-five, and it remained there until the closure of the mines and the dispersal of the community a few years later.

When William died, full of years, and having known his share of sorrows, tributes were paid to him by men and organisations throughout the West of England. But he would, I believe, have valued most highly the words written to his son by the squire whom he himself honoured: "I know of no man in this district who has accomplished more good than your father".

21 Men and Their Monuments

Glyn Court

Most of our wood carvings, it must be admitted, have no strange, eventful history, but they do represent an art which has not altogether lost its following, and they also serve me to introduce the character of my Uncle Lewis, who, like his brother William, practised wood carving with enthusiasm and considerable success; moreover, he loved the old life of our valley and committed to writing innumerable memories which else would have been lost beyond recall.

Lewis Henry, the eldest child of William, was born in Roadwater in 1870, at the same hour of the same day as his grandfather George, fifty-five years before, and he received the education that the parish had to offer: two year's at a dame school near the Valiant Soldier, two at the Church of England school in Leighland, and two more, when High Church influences were making grandfather uneasy, at the Wesleyan Day School in Washford. By then the closure of the mines, the flagging condition of agriculture, and grandfather's support of the Good Templar movement had so gravely injured his business that, with heavy heart, he had to take Lewis away from school at the age of twelve and a half, and the boy worked at the bench until there came an opening in the post office, and life began to broaden out. As a postman he was earning fourteen shillings a week - three or four shillings more than a labourer with a family to support   and his delivery round took him on foot over much of the Brendon Hills, covering fifteen or sixteen miles a day. At the furthest point of his travels he would have a wait of three and a half hours in an old railway hut, and he passed this time to advantage by buying a few books, including a Latin grammar, and studying them assiduously to improve his knowledge of literature and the world.

From his early years he had been unusually sensitive to the beauty of Nature, and when, at the age of ten, he with a number of other boys experienced conversion in a revival meeting, in a moment every feature of the landscape became, for him, transfigured; as for Wordsworth, each object, the stream, the hedgerows, the apple blossom, became "apparelled in celestial light". At sixteen he became a preacher and was eventually recommended, very much against his will, for the Bible Christian ministry. He went off to Portsmouth to preach his trial sermon, hoping and hoping that he would be rejected. To no avail: he was accepted, and began a remarkable career.

He was first sent to the Isles of Scilly, where the attention of the warmhearted Islanders softened the inevitable pangs of homesickness; (sixty years later his hosts were still sending him flowers). The seclusion and the absence of distractions made ideal conditions for his new studies, and the sea and the boundless sky, the majesty of the storms, the rich sunsets, the luminous air, made a profound impression on him. As he sat one evening on a cliff looking out toward Bishop's Rock, he heard of the death of Tennyson, whose poetry he had learnt to love in company with his dearest friend, the young organist of Roadwater. Now, the splendours of sunset and the moaning of the waves at the foot of the cliff stirred deeps in him that he had never known, and the mysteries of life, death and eternity swept in upon him with overwhelming force. That evening opened up to him a new world of thought and emotion that was to enrich his whole life. He discovered a gift for verse, and employed it for fifty years. He had a poet's faculty of seeing the eternal and unchanging in the ephemeral and everyday, and he had inherited his father's facility in the use of words. Scenes of daily life and, perhaps most of all, memories of Somerset awakened emotions which needed to find immediate expression. He did not strive after a painful and insincere originality, and it is not surprising that his devotion to poets of the past should sometimes have caused him to indulge too freely in the stylised poetic vocabulary of a former day. But his poetry was always genuinely himself, and it was read with affection by thousands who shared something of his experience of religion, beauty and art.

His first duty and his first pleasure was, need I say, the calling to which he had devoted himself, the exacting work of a Methodist minister, and he fulfilled it tirelessly and memorably.

After his superannuation he turned for creative relaxation to wood-carving and made oaken sideboards, overmantles, cupboards, bookshelves, but all his other work continued, preaching, visiting, writing, raising funds - he would walk ten or twelve mile a Sunday into his eighties. But inextricably linked with his devotion to his calling there had always been his love for the scenes of his childhood, for the memory of the men and women who had lived among them and given them life, and for the Bible Christian Church to which he owed his life's happiness. For all these he felt a gratitude which could only be expressed by re-creating the golden past; in pursuit of this he assembled, over half a century, an unequalled collection of letters, documents, photographs and souvenirs of his Church and wrote article after article on the characters, customs, homes and trades of our valley in the days of his youth: and I for one own the debt as incalculable.

21.1 The Sofa

To look at it, you would think it a very dowager of a sofa, and one of the old school, making few concessions either to elegance or to bodily comfort, A straight back, hard head-rest and horsehair seat might have delighted St Anthony, but even the resilient Victorians, you feel, might have drawn the line at such lack of comfort. But of course standards of comfort and luxury change, and privileges become prerogatives, and new generations make new demands; and the owner of this sofa in the late nineteenth century was not a fanatical ascetic but one of the gentlest souls who ever drew breath.

Like so many others in this history, Jim Slade was born in Roadwater, in the short period of prosperity coinciding with the working of the iron ore mines on Brendon Hill. His father Thomas, a blacksmith, had a modest share in this prosperity, for he was a hard worker and skilful, but the real business of his life was conducted outside the forge. He was wholly untainted by personal ambition, and his great care, after his family, was the village chapel, where he led the orchestra with his bass viol, and to whose progress he greatly contributed in later days. James inherited little of his father's strength, but a double portion of his musical skill, with his tender musician's fingers, and at eight years of age he was regularly playing the harmonium for Sunday services.

The course of his life was set plain, and his conversion while still a boy was almost a natural outcome, and one from which he never retracted. He became bound in friendship which became deep and lifelong with Lewis Court, and the two young men would share their thoughts and their hopes as they sat on summer's evenings on the wooded hillside behind the chapel and read Tennyson and Browning together. Lewis left home for the ministry, but Jim's delicate nervous constitution barred him from such a hard life of wandering. He stayed in the village and became the friend of Lewis's younger brother, Will.

He never lacked employment. His work as a music teacher occupied his days and brought him an income sufficient for his few needs, and his reputation grew; people regarded him with respect for his talent and affection for himself. To his friends he recounted a meeting on Taunton station with a Doctor of Music from Dunster, from whom he had had lessons many years before:

> "I don't know whether you remember me, Doctor. My name is Slade."
> "Remember you? Of course I do. After all this time I don't suppose it will do you any harm to be told that you were the aptest pupil I ever had."

His "free" time was taken up with training the chapel choir and from time to time organising concerts in the Temperance Hall, and his Sundays with playing the organ and teaching in the school. Then came the Great War, and the contented, self-contained village life drew to a close. The rigours of those years told hardly on him, especially as he felt constrained to undertake duties for which he was physically and temperamentally ill-suited, as a postman on weekdays and a local preacher on Sundays. His health gave way and he suffered a nervous breakdown, and though he recovered and experienced the delight of playing the singularly sweet-toned organ installed in the new chapel, his frail constitution had reached its limit. He only lived to be fifty-three and, after an early disappointment, he had never married, but his passing, and the memory of his music, caused his dearest friends a feeling of loss to which they were never wholly reconciled and an emptiness which no new friendships could ever fill.

21.2 The Engravings

The readers who have borne with me thus far will, I hope, agree that it is not parochialism that prompts the claim that this little plot of earth has produced a harvest of men of character out of all proportion to its acreage. We have good cause to be proud of the labourers and landed men who fashioned our landscape, of the builders who built our cottage homes, of the teachers who gave instruction, and of the preachers who taught wisdom. Nine out of ten of our forefathers passed their lives in backbreaking toil and left no memorial but a season's furrow; it was the one in ten who gave the work of which I have just written and who, through the byways of heredity, brought out here a writer, there an engineer, here a musician, there an architect, here a scholar, there a preacher. Yet it is a remarkable fact, for which I can offer no satisfactory explanation, that no artist of high rank has gone out from among us. Lack of opportunity cannot be an adequate explanation. It was a wise Dr Johnson who wrote, "Slow rises worth, by poverty depress'd"; but if the talent is there in sufficient strength and sufficient number, some of it will find eventually a way through. Sad to say, despite the unequalled man-made beauty of our landscape or perhaps because of it, we have not produced a landscape artist.

On the other hand, we have not been wholly neglected, and artists of international repute have visited us and even made their homes among us. The beauty of our rounded, heather-clad hills and wooded combes has given delight to the most unexpected characters, from mediaeval monks to modern machine-minders, and it is no wonder that creative artists have revelled in the harmony of colour. Turner paid us a visit on his tour of the West Country and south coast in 1821, and left a record of Watchet harbour and West Cliff, and of Blue Anchor, the Dunster marshes and the distant heights of Exmoor - and if the second picture, in Turner's inimitable way, shows a landscape re-arranged to the artist's taste, we feel there would be little point at this date in complaining to his somewhat impatient shade.

It was not until the 1870s that the railways made communication with the outside world - for what it is worth - generally practicable, but eventually a group of painters - one must use the word "group" even though they were not formally connected - came to accept the beauty of Somerset for itself without need of rearrangement, and settled among us. They were all of considerable renown and accomplishment, and two, possibly three, of them possessed qualities of originality and characterisation which make their subsequent neglect hard to account for except in terms of aesthetic fashion.

The first of them was J. W. North, a water colourist with a most acute sense of colour, who settled at Baggearn Huish House in 1885 and became very much involved in the life of the neighbourhood. He was a vigorous, dedicated Liberal of the Radical wing, and found himself more than once involved with petty tyrants over questions of public rights. His pictures have been dispersed among various art galleries, but one in Birmingham shows a riverside scene from our valley.

The second painter was Robert Walker, a disciple of Courbet but with a more sympathetic attitude to his subjects - unless it were that the subjects were more humane. Walker came under the influence of North in his landscapes, and his "Plough" and "The Old Gate" were painted in the neighbourhood.

Little is known to me of Robert Macbeth, except that he came to live in Bilbrook, on the road from Washford to Minehead. Like North, he was a water colourist and greatly influenced by him. But the fourth painter was known to all the art world of the late nineteenth century and his reputation was international.

CHAPTER 21. MEN AND THEIR MONUMENTS

Sir Hubert von Herkomer, the son of a Bavarian wood carver came to England in 1857. He was an outstanding example of the old industrious but warm-hearted German of pre-Empire days, and moreover he was an undoubted genius whose creativity took many convincing forms. He not only established a reputation as a portraitist of great insight and a genre painter of profound social sympathy, but also produced original work as an architect, interior decorator, operatic composer, orchestrator and melodist and toward the close of his life, producer and director of his own films. He excelled in all he attempted, not least in his family life. In his late forties, however, he detected a slight falling off in his awareness of colour nuances, and in 1892 decided to move from his home in Bushey to Somerset. His expressed reason is interesting: he wished to benefit from the company of J. w. North, whom he described as "a great colourist and a good friend" - and North's disciple Robert Walker had been Herkomer's early idol and examplar. But even more interesting are his mixed reactions to what he found:

"The house was un-get-at-able, and the loneliness at first appalling!" Country life was more primitive than he had bargained for, and he was suffering abdominal pains which made work a severe trial of his fortitude; "but" he cried:

> "what a country for the artist! The rich red soil, the undulating country, the apple trees tumbling about in their eccentric untouched shapes ... the dilapidated farmhouses; all a treasure ground for painter and poet. In spring, the first budding of leafage, like jewels set in the deep purple tonality given by the massing of tree branches not yet inleaf, the offset of the strong green masses of ivy growths that have taken overwhelming possession of the stems to which they are attached, give a witchery to this corner of England unsurpassed,
> I should say, in any part of the world,"
> We should only demur at "I should say".

21.3 The Boneshaker

How anyone can have contrived to propel our "penny farthing" along the rutted Somerset lanes of the 1880s passes my understanding, but propel it they did, probably by placing both wheels in the same rut, leaping aboard, and pedalling for dear life.

The acknowledged master pedaller was John Bond, and there is quite a story attached to his name.

He was born in December 1850, the eldest son of Willliam Bond, a herbalist. Round about his eleventh or twelfth year, I suppose, he was apprenticed to one of the Roadwater blacksmiths and towards the end of his apprenticeship - possibly for his master-piece - he decided to make a penny farthing. These machines had been made commercially for some time past and manufacturers were evolving lighter and more elegant models. But in general they were for gentlemen of leisure or the new well-paid urban middle class, not for the penurious countryman. John Bond's machine was the product of our simpler rural society; the essential bicycle, able to endure hardness, and offering no concessions to the weak.

The front wheel is of moderate height and the hub, the wooden spokes and the felloes are the work of a craftsman - probably the village wheelwright, Thomas Popham - but they are enclosed by an iron tyre half an inch thick, shrunk on to the wheel. The front forks are of hammered iron, and their shaft passes through the straight handlebar and is secured by a heavy bolt. The frame is a tubular S-bar with a projecting horn for the saddle and a simple upping-step. The twelve-inch rear wheel is more sophisticated, bound with a shaped rim which once carried a tyre, but the whole machine is of a massive simplicity. Even the saddle was an iron sheet, though no doubt it originally had a leathern cover.

John Bond took up his father's trade and travelled far and wide in Somerset and Devon suitably dressed in top hat and frock coat, and administering his herbal medicines to men and beast - the same medicines - with equal success. His penny farthing, of course, he only used locally, but his boys kept the wheels turning merrily and it remained much more than a nine-day wonder. John's nephew told me:

I can mind father telling me about a time they were up "Mount Lane" (a steep hill in Roadwater with a hairpin bend);

> "There were three of them up - Father on the seat, another boy on the step and another one sat on the handlebar playing a concertina. They came down the hill fine and picked up speed; but it was a rough old lane in those days and at the bottom

Figure 21.1: The Boneshaker, the penny farthing used by John Bond, on display within the Museum. The bike can still be found to this day within Roadwater Village Hall.

A VILLAGE INHERITANCE

the front wheel hit on a great stone. 'Twas a good job there was a hedge, because they all three of 'em got off a lot faster than they got on."

After twenty or thirty years of use the penny farthing was superseded by one of the new factory-made safety bicycles which, perhaps more than any other single factor, changed village life and destroyed the old self-contained society. The machine was left in an outhouse, until my father retrieved it as a memento of happier days. Years later, finding that he no longer had room, he deposited it on loan to Taunton Museum; and thence, forty years on, the penny farthing, by a natural movement, again found itself in the parish where it had been made.

21.4 The Post Office Clock

This clock may well be unique, unless a few remain in post office museums. The hours are marked by the letters A to K instead of 1 to 12, and the minutes between the hour markings by STUV. The clock was used in the old Washford Post Office in Victorian and Edwardian days, when telegrams were sent by Morse code, with the aid of a buzzer which gave two distinct tones, high pitched for a dot, low for a dash. The system of dots and dashes for numbers had not yet been devised, and times in the text of a telegram were given by these letters. Thus a telegram might read Arriving Washford 10.33 - and would be sent as Arriving WCR JFU. From TU (Taunton) to WCR (Washford).

My mother who came to the post office as a girl in 1902, rapidly became the most proficient telegraphist in the district.

21.5 The Motor Cycle

Like many another relic, the motor cycle stood unattended in a shed for forty years. Yet it was a splendid machine, a 600 c.c. chain-drive James which first saw the light of day in 1914. My father bought it, complete with a plywood sidecar, about that time (or maybe after the war) for £65, which was no small sum.

The original instruction book is still with us. The powerful machine needed to be treated with respect, and Father liked to tell us that the first time he tried to ride the James, she threw him off. Still, there was space to learn for the roads were unencumbered; and right up to his dying day he found it hard to accept that other motorists might, from time to time, be using the same stretch of road as ourselves. Providence, of course, worked hard on his behalf, and only once did he come close to an accident, when the James took the bit between her teeth in Carhampton, charged up behind an old woman of the village who was fetching water from the pump, and sent her buckets flying all over the road. My father knew better than to wait for explanation, nor did he linger in Carhampton on his way home.

He and my mother went on their honeymoon in the James, and they recalled that the hundred miles from Washford to the Wesleyan Chapel in Swindon, where they were married, had taken only a gallon and a pint of petrol. He went on using the combination till about 1928, transporting his stock to and from Roadwater, in the sidecar, with his son perched on the top and gazing for the lights of home on thehillside as they came down the valley. Then he bought a motor car, an open Calcott I tourer, for £450, and within a couple of years the road tax went from ten shillings to as many pounds, and the Calcott languished in the garage, gathering dust, until he sold her in the early 1930s to a scrap dealer - to my boylike regret, even then - for £2.

21.6 The Band Books

Three much-used oblong quarto music manuscript books, two of them in homemade bindings of pigskin, but all filled from cover to cover with compositions for wind band, all the parts neatly written out in brown ink, and bearing such an unexpected assortment of titles as "Queen Victoria's March", "The Somerset Waltz", "With my pipe in one hand and my jug in the other" and "Awake, arise, with angels sing", and inside the front covers "This book belongs to George Matthews, Pitt Mill, 1838": these are a simple record of much activity.

Millers, in the old rural society, were not always the most popular of men, particularly on the manorial estate; they were suspected of every kind of sharp practice from the exercise of monopoly to the adulteration of the flour they ground. But no such suspicions attached to George Matthews. He plied an honest trade and devoted his leisure hours to the music of the church, in the hamlet of Leighland on the hillside above his home, and the little church orchestra, as the Union Band, doubled the role of village band for the revels and other rare festivities which broke the harsh monotony of the farm labourers' round. Probably the band was heard to better effect in the open air than in the church, for the instruments as noted in the band books were, one might say, competitive in tone: two clarionets, an octave clarionet, a cornopean or two-valved cornet or a bugle, two B flat horns, a trombone and a "sarpent". In the matter of blending they would have left much to be desired, but George Matthews made the best of his resources, and at the close of the day he would often sit by the light of a candle and "prick in the notes" of an arrangement of a popular air or hymn tune or, more often still, compose carols, dances and marches which were within the compass of his players. Whether he had received any musical training I do not know; from the occasional inadequacy in his harmony I suspect that he had not, and the neatness of his notation marks him as an amateur! But that was of no consequence. He was an enthusiast, a creative musician, and also a disciplinarian who imposed his will on his bandsmen so that they performed better than they had thought possible.

George's method of rehearsal was individual. His mill stood by a stream in a deep valley of green fields and winding lanes. He would assemble his bandsmen in a field above the mill, run over a piece with them, issue his instructions and then withdrew to the opposite side of the valley and conduct from there. If all went well he would radiate contentment. But woe betide the musician who played a wrong note! George would come coursing down the hillside, across the bottom and up to the offending bandsman, and upbraid him with such energy that the rest of the performance was

CHAPTER 21. MEN AND THEIR MONUMENTS

flawless - unless, of course, the poor fellow was so shaken that false notes henceforth flowed in a stream.

At Christmastide they kept up the fine old customs of the waits, as Hardy so lovingly depicts them in "Under the Greenwood Tree", but these reached their peak under the leadership of George Matthews's musical successor, Thomas Slade. Thomas, born in the early 1840s, had known a childhood of dire poverty as one of the numerous family of a roadmender, but he had been apprenticed to one of the Roadwater blacksmiths, and his skill and industry won him independence. But man of business though he was, he was much more a man of music. Except in the company of his family and friends, he was reserved, even taciturn, and music, to him, meant more than words; if a dark mood fell on him, music would charm It away. One who knew him speaks of his musician's ears and delicate, tapering fingers, apparently so unsuited to the work of a blacksmith. In him there was a hunger for beauty of sound which would only be satisfied by a mellow concord of instruments. As a youth he conceived the desire to play the "bass viol", as the 'cello was called, so early one morning he took some of his savings, walked the twenty miles to Taunton, purchased the "bass viol", brought it home another twenty miles on his back, and did two hours' work in the forge before retiring to rest. He soon became a proficient player - not a virtuoso by any means, I suppose, but he held his line as choirmaster and leader of the orchestra of the village chapel with singular sweetness of tone. Local lore treasures the tale of one incident which took place in one village church:

Parson: The choir and orchestra will now render an anthem: Who is the King of Glory? Bass violist (sotto voce): Pass the rozzrum, Bill, us'll show en who's the king o' glory!

I wish I could attribute it to Thomas, but it does not seem quite in his character. Yet he had his festive side, and more even than the music of the Sunday services he loved the festival of Christmas. Both spiritually and musically it crowned his year, and the old carols which George Matthews had made popular were his delight as well, with their dignified phraseology, foursquare melodies and energetic fugal choruses: Angels from the realms of glory; Behold, what glorious news is come!; Mortals awake, rejoice and sing! He spared no effort to make the performance worthy of the occasion. The band and singers would meet for rehearsal in the week before Christmas, and late on Christmas Eve, when most of the village was asleep, they would gather with their instruments in the forge, threading their way by the glow of the embers past coulters and ploughshares and every kind of farming implement, and assemble in Thomas's parlour for hot peppermint cordial to fortify them for their journeyings. Then they would set off on their round of the outlying farms where they knew they would be welcomed. Excitement and laughter were in the tingling air, but as they drew near to the first farm, they all fell silent at Thomas's bidding. To his mind, music was the sister of silence; there must be no disturbance of the quiet of the night; the sleepers should be wakened not by a babble of inconsequential noises but by a concord of sweet sounds. The band would strike up the major chord which gave the singers the key, and presently a light would shine in an upstairs room, a window would open and a voice call out a greeting, then the front door would open and the waits would troop in to taste the refreshments laid out for them; then on to the next farm, and the next until at two o'clock, some of them steadier on their feet than others, they found themselves back on the bridge that formed the centre of the village, giving their retiring serenade to an appreciative, if somnolent, public. One further performance at the morning service closed their Christmas oratorio for that year; the carols would continue in Thomas's home, around his son's piano, over Christmastide, and the simple festivities and the visits of friends and relations would go on until Old Christmas Day, January 6th; but nothing could induce Thomas to sing or play one of the carols out of that season; he would have considered it an affront to the divinely appointed order of things. The carols, for being performed only in their due season, were all the more prized.

21.7 Marine Relics

It is with embarrassment that I confess to a lack of the true-born Englishman's love of the sea. In fact, for one born almost within sight and

CHAPTER 21. MEN AND THEIR MONUMENTS

sound of salt water, I am inordinately suspicious of the stuff. Fortunately some of my ancestors were cast in a sterner mould and led a seafaring life. Great-great-grandfather, Richard Grinslade, who flourished in the first quarter of the nineteenth century was a mariner of Watchet - not a captain, as far as I know; besides, he would have commanded a crew of two or three at most, for the boats which sailed from Watchet harbour were mostly small craft, fishing smacks and the like. They were very numerous, however, and at the height of the shipping trade some sixty craft were registered in Watchet.

Whether Richard owned one or not, there was no boat for his son George. Richard was thrice married. His first wife died after eighteen months; his second marriage, with a cheerful little soul, lasted as many years, and George was born to them on 31st October 1815. (I note, in writing these words, that it was a hundred and sixty years ago to the very day - or, as my mother would have said, "Your great grandfather would have been a hundred and sixty if he'd lived.") But Richard's third wife had no love for her stepson, and he was sent off while very young as apprentice to a shoemaker in Dunster. To telescope the events of half a century, George worked hard at his craft, attained a good financial position, invested in houses - for in those days the ownership of property was thought to confer rights and a good return of investment. In 1870 he ventured on a different type of investment and bought a half share in a boat, a forty ton ketch, the Union of Watchet.

His partner was, in his own way, as remarkable a man as George himself, a young sea captain, John Short by name, from one of the best-known Watchet families and married, I believe, to George's niece. Thirty years later he took his place in history when Cecil Sharp came to West Somerset in search of the vanishing folk songs. John Short, who possessed a fine baritone voice and a prodigious memory, gave him the words and music of over forty of the old songs - a greater number, I believe, than any other singer in any county. The Oxford Companion to Music contains a picture of him seated on the steps of Watchet West Pier.

The partnership went well for a couple of years. The "Union" was, like most of the Watchet craft, engaged mainly in the Bristol Channel trade, which gave the advantage that although the risk of shipwreck was as great as anywhere in the world, the voyages were short and the returns fairly rapid. She cost more to refit than they expected, but after that she plied steadily round the Bristol Channel and along the north coasts of Cornwall and Devon, transporting coal from Newport or Lydney to Port Tennant - in Cardiff - Neath or Hayle, and sand from Hayle to Bridgwater - in fact, from any port to any other port in this area. Her bills of lading show figures which nowadays are laughable.

The "Union" went on in this modest way for two years, and George Grinslade and Captain Short were coming to the point of seeing a profit on their venture, but the sea-gods decided otherwise. The "Union" was despatched to Burnham under the command of a relief skipper, who had not John Short's skill or seamanship. He ran her aground on Gore Sands, the shoal at the mouth of the River Parrett. She could not be refloated, she broke her back and became a total loss. She had been inadequately insured, if at all, and George, on the basis of "Once bitten, twice shy", never again launched out - whether literally or figuratively - upon the waves. I find it hard to criticise him for it.

21.8 The Watchet Tune Book

Where have all the craftsmen gone? – Gone to the factory every one.

It is a weary little cry, a despairing one, and moreover untrue; but the often heard lament for the absence of pride in good work proves that the craftsman, when he can be found, is still widely honoured and his skill respected. With the good craftsman, craftsmanship and artistry are one; with the great craftsmen, Inigo Jones, Benvenuto Cellini, artistry is art. The Greeks had the right idea in using the same word, techne, for both branches of creative work, and maybe our modern elevation of art casts an undeserved aspersion on the craftsman.

A technical artist of this double order was Thomas Hawkes, a land surveyor of Williton in the 1830s. In 1838 the Tithes Commutation Act was passed,

CHAPTER 21. MEN AND THEIR MONUMENTS

and local surveyors were commissioned to produce three maps for each parish, showing the ownership and use of every rod, pole or perch of land. Thomas Hawkes undertook several parishes, including his own, St Decuman's, and Old Cleeve, and the maps he delineated, or which were produced under his direction, were excellent, so precise, neat and clear that the very sight of them gives pleasure.

But Thomas Hawkes had other, wider interests than land surveying. He had, so some of his fellows might have said, his title to mansions in the skies. He was a Wesleyan Methodist and, like the founder of his church, loved music and set great store by the musical content of a religious service. The Methodists, both in Wesley's day and after, in Great Britain and in America, had adopted many hundreds of hymns' for congregational singing which were extraordinarily varied in their sentiments, their metres and the tunes to which they were customarily sung, and they had injected new life into the singing; but the hymn book contained hymns in no fewer than thirty different metres, and suitable tunes were hard to come by: "the tunes not suited thereto were an incumbrance, and calculated to mislead", wrote Thomas Hawkes, and he decided that he would "select, adapt, and arrange in classes, a complete set of tunes for all the hymns in the Wesleyan Collection". This was no small undertaking for a single unaided collector, but Thomas Hawkes's solution was novel. He wrote in his preface, "The work contains upwards of five hundred and fifty tunes, of which about two hundred and fifty are from standard works of the best ancient authors, and about three hundred ....were composed by modern and living authors, many of them purposely for the hymns to which they are set".

The two hundred and fifty include many of the seventeenth and eighteenth century names still found in modern hymn books; Handel, Purcell, Croft, Stanley, Harrington, Boyce, Arnold: but the authors of the three hundred will be generally unknown, for Hawkes seems to have wanted to accomplish a double purpose: to provide new tunes by using the resources present in his church and others of the same persuasion and at the same time give some of the many composers of merely local fame the chance of becoming known to a wider public.

The compilation must have filled his leisure hours for several years around 1830, and either by writing or by visits he corresponded continually with a score of musicians. They, too, cannot have found him the easiest of taskmasters, for some of them were called on to provide thirty or forty tunes to answer his requirements.

It would cost many days' searching old registers or census returns to find the residence of most of these men, but a few are known to me and others can be surmised from the pattern of the names of their tunes.

The most prolific, with seventy-eight tunes, was William Besley, who lived just two miles away in Watchet, a member of a seafaring and ropemaking family in Watchet who, until the last of the line, also a musician, died in 1975, traced their descent from a family of Huguenot refugees named Beza. The names of many of his tunes are presumably a record of his voyages around the Western coasts: Watchet, Floating Chapel, Parracombe, Coomb Martin, Berry Chapel, Ilfracombe, Mariners' Church, Freraraington, Hartland, Mount Edgecombe.

Another forty-five tunes came from Joel Thorne, who farmed Wibble Farm, only a mile away from Thomas Hawkes. John Heath, from Minehead, I surmise, contributed thirty-two. Samuel Gill, from the Langport district, twenty-four. John Jones (C.H.) from over the Channel, forty, and other local men any number up to a dozen. Thomas Hawkes himself wrote an anthem, "I will arise", and entrusted the editing and revision of the whole work to George Gay, organist at Corsham and author of a published collection of hymn tunes.

Gay carried out his work thoroughly, and the tune book contains very few printing errors; moreover, the engraver and printer seem to have entered into the spirit of the enterprise, for the standard of the typography is of the highest and a handsome volume of four hundred pages, printed on paper specially made in the local mill, and bound in half-leather, issued from the press of Thomas Whitehorn in Watchet. Maybe the plates were engraved elsewhere, but it is still a telling commentary on the vigour of life and musical activity in a small town that a country printer, who had set up in business there only two years earlier, should have felt able to undertake such a publication; and it says even more for Thomas Havkes's generosity of spirit: he put over five hundred pounds into the enterprise, and did not look to recoup much of it, even if the volume sold at £1.5, for he had determined to give a copy to every Wesleyan missionary departing overseas.

In the event, "A Collection of Tunes; comprising The Most Approved Standard, together with a Great Variety of Original Compositions" did not succeed quite as well as he had hoped. No one in particular was to blame, but the book had certain failings': George Gay had set out the tunes in four-part or eight-part harmony, which was ideal for the instruments of a church orchestra, and he had introduced new and very practical G-clefs for alto and tenor; but by the 1830s the organ was everywhere superseding the orchestra, and not all organists could cope with four staves; moreover, the tunes, though numerous enough, did not provide enough variety; true, they did not labour under that burden of stolid sameness which makes the old Ancient and Modern such a monument to weariness; many of them were melodious, rhythmically interesting, ingenious and energetic, but too many of them were cast in the same mould - that of the contemporary "fuguing" tune. It is an excellent form, it imparts vigour and life to the singing, but it bears the danger that the frequent repetitions can prolong the hymn beyond the natural period of the sentiment, so that the singer who has given voice lustily to start with, in time finds himself faint and hardly pursuing. An excellent form, but one to be practised in due moderation.

Thomas Hawkes's book, then, did not achieve the success he had hoped for it; or rather, in his own terms, it did not benefit as many people as he had hoped; but it did fine credit to his feeling for music, his generosity and his visions. If it is not in mortals to command success, he did more, and deserved it.

21.9 The Pictures

My grandfather, like his grandson - but unlike his son and great-grandson -seems to have had no ability as a draughtsman; but the walls of Oatway Cottage were hung with pictures, a few of which I remember.

A VILLAGE INHERITANCE

By the stair door, silver lettering on a dark red card reminded the visitor if he needed reminding - that "Christ is the Head of this house, the unseen Guest at every meal, the silent Listener to every conversation".

This, even as a child, I could understand well enough, and also some of the pictures; that of Dunster Castle, for example, was quite straightforward, and so was the huge framed collection of photographs of local preachers presented to Grandfather on his own preaching diamond jubilee: they were bearded and fearsome, but not puzzling. But the parlour contained a coloured print over which I cudgelled my wits time and time again. The title was clear enough, for I could read as well as the next boy, but nothing in the picture seemed to fit. The subject was a feast of sorts, but who was the fellow in the cloth cap presiding? And if it was a meal, where were the tables? And why weren't these sumptuously dressed personages getting down to the vittles? And where was the main course that all the fuss was about? No, decidedly "Luther at the Diet of Worms" was a puzzle for a small boy.

My chief interest, however, attached to a coloured engraving in a gilt frame which hung over grandfather's armchair by the fire. I first noticed the portrait when quite young, but after grandfather's death, and it never occurred to me to ask who had painted him. I hardly appreciated, of course, that this would have been an unusual event, quite outside the range of village life; this was grandfather's house, that was his armchair, those were his books; they all spoke of him, but none so clearly or eloquently, for me, as the portrait, for it showed him as I remembered him, an old gentleman of dignified aspect, with white hair, high brow, straight nose, and a full but trim beard which prickled when he gave you a birthday kiss. True, he appeared in a more romantic guise than in everyday life, dressed not in a sober suit but in an open-necked shirt and light-grey trousers, and leaning his right arm on the neck of his white pony, I did not recognise the hillside on which they were standing, but supposed it was way up above Roadwater, perhaps Treborough, where I had not often been, or on Brendon Hill which he climbed as he travelled to one of his weekly preaching appointments. Had I been a more astute little boy, I might have wondered at two more striking discrepancies between the picture and the old gentleman I had known. I

CHAPTER 21. MEN AND THEIR MONUMENTS

should then have asked why grandfather was wearing, of all things, a sword at his waist, and why the shirt he had on was scarlet.

These details, however, went unremarked; the portrait merged into the accepted, unexamined background. And only in my early 'teens did a chance remark of one of the family reveal to me that we had been entertaining heroes unawares; that the old white pony was a grey horse of twenty battles and that Grandfather, with his sword on hip and his shirt of blazing red, was not a Somerset shoemaker but an Italian patriot and soldier. "Grandfather" was Giuseppe Garibaldi.

How the portrait came to be there was not explained, apart from "Garibaldi was always one of Grandfather's heroes", but in the course of time I deduced the reason. Grandfather was born in 1847 and was growing out of childhood into youth at the time that Garibaldi was venturing his life to free Italy from foreign rule ; and make her one nation. His thirteenth birthday in 1860, for instance, fell on the day when Garibaldi and his quixotic Thousand commenced that Sicilian venture which, for its very daring and refusal to count the odds, even after a century makes one want to stand up and cheer. When the great liberator came to England in 1864, he was given a welcome such as "no foreigner, hardly even any native hero", had received. When the Duke of Sutherland's four-horse carriage, containing the son of the skipper of Nice in his red shirt and grey blanket, struggled in the course of six hours through five miles of London streets, amid half a million of our people who had turned out to greet him, the wild procession made its way into the quiet square (in front of Stafford House), startling its Royal and Ducal sanctities with democratic clangour. Then, amid a noise of shouting like the noise of the sea in storm, Garibaldi stepped out of the carriage, as calm as in the day of battle, into a circle of fair ladies and great statesmen on the steps of Stafford House, while the Duke's carriage literally fell to pieces in the stable, strained to breaking-point by the weight of thousands of strong arms that had snatched at and clung to its sides as it passed through a London gone mad with joy ... To the common people it was an unexampled privilege to carry one of themselves in triumph through the London streets. No doubt my grandfather, though far distant from the scene, was swept up in this tide of popular emotion, and the mutual admiration of Garibaldi and his other hero, Mr Gladstone, must also have impressed him profoundly. It must be confessed that he also had a regrettable admiration for Napoleon, though excusably this was for his genius and his meteoric rise, rather than for his work of slaughter; but bearing this in mind, I believe that he venerated Garibaldi for a similar reason: because the great Italian embodied for him all the latent moral and spiritual powers of those multitudes unknown to fame but bearing, in the elect, "hearts pregnant with celestial fire"; and most of all he responded to the "simple nobility" which clothes Garibaldi's every gesture, every word, every thought and made of him, as G. M. Trevelyan so eloquently expressed it, "The incarnate symbol of ... the love of country and the love of freedom, kept pure by the one thing that can tame and yet not weaken them the tenderest humanity for all mankind".

22 Epilogue

Glyn Court

I approach the conclusion of this book almost as reluctantly as I approached the task of writing my share of it, and I hope the reader will to some extent share my feeling. Yet with each line I write, the sense of incompleteness grows upon me. My wife and I have, in point of fact, written two or even three books under one cover: hers, with its salutary tale of commercial upheaval and domestic stress, is detailed and complete, the tale of an episode that is closed; but mine, or the book written jointly, is merely an inchoate fragment of the chronicle that might be written on this one family; it gives no more than a hint of the rich social life of these hills and valleys in the days of Queen Victoria; while as for the legends that hang about our ways and dwelling places, we have found no place for them at all, knowing that once started we could never make an end.

From this comes the consideration that while admitting that not all families have had the good fortune of a tradition of conserving the past, every family has a body of memories, both common and particular, every family has its oral records and traditions, no matter how vague or dispersed; and we hope that this book will encourage readers here and there to undertake the gathering and collation of these scattered records, so that the past lives of their families, of their neighbourhood and of their homes may live again in the present and enrich the future with the wisdom - and the follies - of men and women not wholly unlike ourselves.

Washford, West Somerset
6th April 1976 (My Father's Centenary)

23 A New Chapter

Philippa Harper, née Court

After nearly 30 years outside the family, when it was occupied by Betty Small and her husband, my husband Bryan and I bought the house back in March 2014. It was a key turning point in our lives. The whole family had missed the place greatly during the whole time.

I always felt hugely lucky to grow up in such a wonderful spot as Washford. We all loved the beauty of the home, the shop, the Post Office, the outhouses, the garden, the orchard, and were lucky to grow up when there was such a strong sense of community around us, with lots of kindness, good humour, and wonderful neighbours particularly in the family of the Bakers across the road.

Since then we've spent four years of hard work doing up the house and garden, as far as we can in keeping with its old spirit, and with respect to the endless patience, hard work and vision of our inspirational grandparents who built the place, and my hard-working parents who kept it going. We want to continue to care for Washford as best as we can. As everything grows so well, it is lucky that we both enjoy grass cutting and weeding!

We hope that the family will continue enjoying and caring for this space for a long time to come. Our own boys, Jonny, Chris and Mikey, have got to know and care for it too. We are really looking forward to this summer, when our youngest son, Mikey and his fiancée Agi will have a party here to celebrate the blessing of their wedding, and we are thrilled as the story of the house moves forward to the next generation.

Long Live Washford!

Washford, West Somerset
Spring, 2018

Printed in Poland
by Amazon Fulfillment
Poland Sp. z o.o., Wrocław